Moral Education in America's Schools: The Continuing Challenge

Moral Education in America's Schools: The Continuing Challenge

by

Thomas C. Hunt
University of Dayton

and

Monalisa Mullins
University of Dayton

INFORMATION AGE
PUBLISHING

Greenwich, Connecticut • www.infoagepub.com

Library of Congress Cataloging-in-Publication Data

Hunt, Thomas C., 1930-
  Moral education in America's schools : the continuing challenge / by
Thomas C. Hunt and Monalisa Mullins.
     p. cm.
  Includes bibliographical references and index.
  ISBN 1-59311-197-5 (pbk.) — ISBN 1-59311-198-3 (hardcover) 1.
Moral education—United States—History. 2. Character—Study and
teaching—United States—History. I. Mullins, Monalisa. II. Title.
  LC311.H85 2005
  370.11'4'0973--dc22

                                                            2004030571

CONTENTS

DEDICATION AND ACKNOWLEDGMENTS

Thomas Hunt wishes to dedicate this book to his sister Sue, and her husband Norb, and to his brother John, and his wife, Barbara, for their love and support over the years. Monalisa Mullins dedicates this book to her parents, Reba and Leonard McCurry, who taught her, by their example, the true meaning of moral goodness.

The authors wish to acknowledge Dr. Thomas J. Lasley, II, Dean of the School of Education and Allied Professions (SOEAP) at the University of Dayton, for his unwavering support of scholarly endeavors. They also wish to thank Dr. Ellis Joseph, Dean Emeritus of the SOEAP, for writing the Foreword to this book.

PREFACE

It was the tragedy of the Columbine massacre on April 20, 1999 that gave rise to this book. As the result of the shootings there, and several other acts of violence that occurred in or around American public schools in its wake, there was a renewed focus on moral/character education in American schools. Commercial programs featuring moral/character education were developed; the United States Department of Education recognized "Schools of Character"; and curricular programs such as Thomas Lickona's 4th and 5th Rs received more attention.

As this book will show, moral education has been a priority in American schools from the outset. Writing in the bicentennial issue of the *History of Education Quarterly* in 1976, historian Michael B. Katz penned "it would constitute a minor educational revolution if the emphasis, or primary goal of public schooling shifted from the development of character to the cultivation of intellect."[1] Katz is far from alone with this observation. For instance, the historical evidence presented in B. Edward McClellan's excellent book, *Moral Education in America: Schools and the Shaping of Character from Colonial Times to the Present* (New York: Teachers College, 1999) and in David Purpel and Kevin Ryan (eds.), *Moral Education: It Comes With the Territory* (Berkeley, CA: McCutchan, 1976) substantiate Katz's assertion. That the concern over moral education in American society in general and in American public schools in particular has not diminished is clear from Lickona's most recent book, *Character Matters* (New York: Simon and Schuster, 2004), which presents strategies on "How to Help Our Children Develop Good Judgment, Integrity, and Other Essential Virtues."[2]

It is also evident in organizations such as "Character Education Partnership" (CEP) that just announced its 11th National Forum, this one entitled "Exploring Pathways to Civic Character." On its agenda is a "full-day session on CEP's *Eleven Principles of Effective Character Education: The who, what, where, when and why.*" Thomas Lickona is among its featured speakers.[3]

Confirmation in the form of Gallup Polls from two periods, the 1970s and 1980s, and in the 1990s-early 2000s, attests to the primacy of moral education in schools. From 1972 through 1984, for instance, the public identified "Lack of discipline" as the main problem confronting American public schools. Other behavior-related items, such as "use of drugs" consistently retained a high rating, almost always surpassing any curricular concerns.[4] The 1976 poll revealed that 67% of the respondents wanted the public schools to "take on a share" of responsibility for the "moral behavior" of students.[5] A year earlier, in 1975, 79% favored instruction in morals in the public schools with but 11% opposed.[6] In 1974, 77% of those polled supported school-sponsored prayer in the public schools.[7] In 1981, the respondents by a ratio of approximately four to one (70% to 17%) favored instruction in public schools that "would deal with values and ethical behavior."[8]

Gallup Polls in the last decade reveal similar sentiments. "Lack of discipline" has ranked either first or second as the major problem facing public schools in every year since 1995.[9] In 2002, when it ranked second to "School funding," 76% of the respondents said that "discipline was a very or somewhat serious problem."[10] "Drug abuse," which ranked first from 1986 through 1991 ("lack of discipline" was second in each of these years), was again first in 1996, and along with "fighting, violence, gangs," was ranked consistently more serious than items such as "getting good teachers" and "low pay for teachers" during this period.[11]

It is interesting to note that in 1987, under the influence of then-Secretary of Education William Bennett, character education was promoted as an activity to be carried out by the public schools. The 1987 poll revealed that 43% of the respondents favored the public schools teaching courses on "values and ethical character."[12]

This past winter I was fortunate to enlist the services of a colleague, Dr. Monalisa Mullins, to serve as coauthor. Professor Mullins contributed Chapter Thirteen and Chapters Fifteen through Seventeen. She earned the title of co-author, indeed.

This book is not a comprehensive history of moral/character education in American schools, which is almost entirely devoted to public schools. Rather, it is an episodic history that deals with selected periods, movements, and individuals throughout the course of American educational history from the time of colonial Massachusetts in the 17th century up to present times. Chapter One reveals that while moral education was not the sole purpose of schools in Puritan Massachusetts in the colonial era, it indeed was an uppermost concern of the time. Based on Puritan theology, schools were to instill the truths of the Calvinist faith and inculcate their version of Christian morality in the students.

By the time of the American Revolution, the basis of morality had somewhat shifted to the position that there was an inexorable link between republican government, democracy, popular education, and virtue and knowledge, as Chapter Two shows. The teaching of leaders like Thomas Jefferson, Benjamin Rush, and Noah Webster is featured along with supporting testimony from legislation such as the Northwest Ordinance that stated, "Religion, morality, and knowledge being necessary for good government and the happiness of mankind, schools and the means of education shall forever be encouraged."[13]

The Lancaster Method, as practiced in New York City in the early years of the 19th century is the focus of Chapter Three. Wealthy philanthropists, such as DeWitt Clinton, gave of their means to provide what they deemed was an appropriate moral education for the children of the poor who were not being schooled by one of the various charity schools that had been erected by the city religious societies.

Chapter Four concentrates on the famous common school movement of Horace Mann et al. Dominated by Unitarians at the outset, the common school crusade of Mann looked to the state to found and operate primary schools that were financially supported by public taxes and intended for every girl or boy, rich or poor, in the state. Allegedly nonsectarian, the common school fostered a morality built on devotional Bible-reading and what were termed the "common core truths" of Christianity. Pan-Protestant to the core, the common school was to create a moral climate in the school that would eradicate social problems such as poverty and crime.

The common schools were destined for failure, the movement backers claimed, unless they were under state control and taught by persons steeped in the traditions of the common school. Chapter Five points out that the ideal situation, as envisioned by the movement's advocates, could be realized only by the state-run normal schools, which would prepare teachers immersed in the moral virtues of the common school. Never in the majority until the 20th century, the antebellum normal school created by Mann and his allies constituted the vehicle through which the morals expressed by the common school movement could be transmitted to the young to bring about a peaceful, harmonious, prosperous Commonwealth.

Chapter Six directs its attention to the South, assessing moral education in the ante- and post-bellum eras. The South's leading state, Virginia, is used as a case study. Particular attention is given to the educational efforts of Charles Fenton Mercer and Henry Ruffner prior to the Civil War, and to Henry's son, William Henry, Virginia's first state superintendent of public instruction, after the conflict. Like Mann before him, the younger Ruffner defended the common school, though segregated by race, from critics who assailed the moral role of public education, contending that it was incapable by its very nature of morally educating.

Chapter Seven represents a shift from public education to the moral efforts of the 19th century Catholic parochial school. Founded in the main to protect the faith of an impoverished immigrant population from the onslaughts first, of the pan-Protestant school, and second, from the "American" secular school, Catholic parochial schools played an indispensable role in preserving the religious identity of young Catholics. Catholic ethical teaching formed the basis of those schools' moral education.

Overlapping Chapters Four through Seven is the study of the Bible as an agent of moral education that occurs in Chapter Eight. The purpose of the use of the Sacred Scriptures, King James Version, in the common schools was clear: to imbue the minds of the students with the moral influence that the texts were calculated to convey. The state of Wisconsin, which witnessed an ever-growing struggle over the position of the devotional reading of the Bible in public schools, is employed as a case study. The struggle, which culminated in the decision by the Supreme Court of Wisconsin in 1890 that adjudged that such Bible-reading constituted sectarian instruction (the first such decision of its kind in the nation) and was therefore unconstitutional, was a devastating blow to the adherents of "Bible America." These people, steeped in the traditions of mainstream Protestantism, forecast a dismal future for the morality of Wisconsin common school students and its society as a result.

Like Chapter Eight, Chapter Nine's time span covers the events described in Chapters Four through Seven. Devoted to the *McGuffey Readers*, the chapter traces their history of being next only to the Bible as an instrument of moral education in the public schools. Estimates of more than 122 million being produced over nearly a century attest to their widespread use. They strove to unify the nation around a common school system, at first through Calvinistic moral teachings and later by more of a deistic orientation.

The Civil War had a plethora of major consequences for American society. Chapters Ten and Eleven treat two of the War's educational effects. Chapter Ten deals with the development of the "American" public school, "de-Protestantized "to some extent, especially in certain parts of the country. Patriotism, and the secular virtues that came in its wake, became the dominant force in moral education in many quarters. Mea-

sures such as the Blaine Amendment were put forth to minimize parochial schools, deemed "unpatriotic" by American nativists. It was at this
juncture that the belief was born that the public school is not only a bulwark of democracy, it is also a *sine qua non* for the continued existence of
the American way of life. The public school was the indispensable agency
that made America great; it was the means by which the American form of
government was preserved. All who supported it in this fashion were
good and loyal citizens, those who did not were suspect.

The War had another major, but strikingly different, effect on the
former slaves in the South. Chapter Eleven examines the particular version of moral education that the white patricians of the South, in league
with leading industrialists from the North, tried to impose on the Freedmen in the South. These attempts were embodied first in the segregated
common schools of the former confederacy, and second, in what James
Anderson has aptly described as the "Hampton Model" (Anderson, *The
Education of Blacks in the South, 1860-1935*. Chapel Hill: University of
North Carolina Press, 1985, esp. pp. 33-78). Using Virginia as a case
study, Chapter Eleven shows that the moral education designed for the
Freedmen consisted of trying to make them docile, moral servants of the
dominant white class, to be achieved through working with their hands,
ready to "accept their place" in a society that reflected the white south-
erner's interpretation of Christianity.

Chapter Twelve is directed to the thrust of moral education in the
schools of the early 20th century. Beset by a burgeoning immigrant population, which hailed in the main from southern and Eastern Europe,
many who located in the teeming cities of the northeast United States, the
nation turned to its public schools to make "good Americans" out of the
children of the recent arrivals. (Again, parochial schools were distrusted
as havens of the old world and its ways, including the Catholic religion,
were often dismissed as "unpatriotic.") Characterized especially by use of
the English language, the moral efforts sometimes resulted in separating
immigrant children from their parents, who, by clinging to their old
world ways, were not really able to qualify as "good Americans." National
Education Association documents, such as the "Cardinal Principles"
Report of 1918 serve as an illustration of the public schools' attempts to
inculcate the "right" virtues in their students, replacing the Church and
the parents in this attempt.

Born in Vermont in 1859, John Dewey became perhaps the best known
educational philosopher in the annals of American education. An analytic
thinker and prolific writer, Dewey looked to the schools to educate intellectually, morally, and socially. Chapter Thirteen addresses Progressive
educator Dewey's theories of materialistic epistemology and experiential
education, albeit in a most brief way, in a manner that helps us under-

stand the justification for a moral education curriculum. Reflective thought, Dewey believed, could transform a clouded moral situation into a clear one. Intelligence, then, can be as effective in the realm of morality and values as it is in science. An eclectic, Dewey held that moral education must reflect the individual's sense of purpose of gaining full citizenship within the community, while still maintaining the individual rights associated with democracy.

The Educational Policies Commission (EPC) was formed in 1935 and functioned until its demise in 1968, when *ad hoc* policy committees were chosen to supplant the EPC. Dominated over the years by persons affiliated with educational administration, the EPC concentrated on the teaching of democratic values in the public schools, which were regarded as the most fitting instrument for a democratic society, in a period of conflict with the "isms" of fascism and then communism. Its best-known publication in the area of moral education was published in 1951. Entitled *Moral and Spiritual Values in the Public Schools,* it declared that "there must be no question whatever as to the willingness of the school to subordinate all other considerations to those which concern moral and spiritual standards."[14]

The cognitive moral development approach of Lawrence Kohlberg makes up Chapter Fifteen. Based in part on the developmental theories of Jean Piaget, Kohlberg shaped his theory of the stages of moral development that are hierarchically integrated. Using hypothetical moral dilemmas as a teaching tool, Kohlberg posited levels of moral conscience ranging from the Preconventional (Level 1) through Conventional (Level II) to Postconventional (Level III). He suggested that our moral conscience progresses from an initial concern for the consequences of actions to a concern for approval from others, and culminates in the final stage, in which our conscience makes moral judgments based on the principle of universality and the internalization of ideals such as respect for others as persons of intrinsic worth. Kohlberg's moral development approach has been criticized as lacking sensitivity to the issues of gender and cultural variance.

Values clarification, which came on strong in the educational world in the 1970s and remained a force throughout the 1980s, is the topic of Chapter Sixteen. The movement stressed the role of the teacher as facilitator or discussion leader rather than a transmitter of a value system, their own or society's. The process consisted of seven steps, the three chief being (1) choosing one's values, (2) prizing those values, and (3) acting in accordance with those values. Spearheaded by Louis Raths, Sidney Simon, and Howard Kirschenbaum who claimed their program espoused value neutrality and respect for the pluralism of values, values clarification was roundly criticized as being subjective and as fostering moral relativism.

The final chapter of this book, Seventeen, addresses the current Character Education movement. Spurred by what is believed by many to be declining moral values throughout American society, a number of efforts have been put forth that involved the schools as a major partner to combat these social ills. Foremost among these efforts has been the work of Thomas Lickona. Arguing for the teaching of core values, Lickona has published several key books on the topic of character education. Advocating what he terms the "fourth and fifth R's," i.e., respect and responsibility, Lickona has urged the teaching of good moral conduct and decision making as necessary to offset the negative impact of social influences, especially those of the mass media. Lickona suggests that the core values are those that promote human rights and affirm human dignity. There are a number of other programs of moral education presently operating in public schools. One of the most popular of these is CHARACTER COUNTS! All of these models attempt to teach core values that can be taught directly through various course curricula. School organizations are also employed in the character education movement, as is service learning. There is some opposition to the Character Education movement, much of it stemming from parental groups who see these programs as a usurpation of family prerogatives and as a manifestation of what has been called the religion of secular humanism.

This book is an episodic, not a comprehensive, history of moral education in America schools, especially its public ones. It is a tale that is fraught with friction and controversy, even legal challenge. Given the nature of the topic, and the passion with which it has been and is currently viewed, it will ever be thus.

Thomas C. Hunt
Dayton, Ohio

NOTES

1. Character Education Partnership, "Exploring Pathways to Civic Character," Washington, DC: 2004.
2. Thomas Lickona, *Character Matters*. New York: Simon and Schuster, 2004, cover.
3. Character Education Partnership, "Exploring Pathways to Civic Character," Washington, DC: 2004.
4. George H. Gallup, "Sixth Annual Gallup Poll of Public Attitudes Toward Education," *Phi Delta Kappan* 56 (September 1974); 21; Gallup, "Seventh Annual Poll of Public Attitudes Toward Education," *Phi Delta Kappan* 57

(December 1975): 228; Gallup, "Eighth Annual Gallup Poll of the Public's Attitudes Toward the Public Schools," *Phi Delta* Kappan 58 (October 1976): 188; Gallup, "Ninth Annual Gallup Poll of the Public's Attitudes Toward the Public Schools," *Phi Delta Kappan* 59 (September 1977): 34; Gallup, "Tenth Annual Gallup Poll of the Public's Attitudes Toward the Public Schools," *Phi Delta Kappan* 60 ((September 1978): 34; Gallup, "Eleventh Annual Gallup Poll of the Public's Attitudes Toward the Public Schools," *Phi Delta Kappan* 62 (September 1980): 34; Gallup, "Thirteenth Annual Gallup Poll of the Public's Attitudes Toward the Public Schools," *Phi Delta Kappan* 63 ((September 1981): 34; Gallup, "Fourteenth Annual Gallup Poll of the Public's Attitudes Toward the Public Schools," *Phi Delta Kappan* 64 (September 1982): 38; Gallup, "Fifteenth Annual Gallup Poll of the Public's Attitudes Toward the Public Schools," *Phi Delta Kappan* 65 (September 1983); 35; and Gallup, "Sixteenth Annual Gallup Poll of the Public's Attitudes Toward the Public Schools," *Phi Delta Kappan* 66 (September 1984): 36.

5. Gallup, "Eighth Poll," Ibid., (1976):197.

6. Gallup, "Seventh Poll," Ibid., (1975): 228.

7. Gallup, "Sixth Poll," Ibid., (1974): 21.

8. Gallup, "Thirteenth Poll," Ibid., (1981): 39.

9. Stanley M. Elam and Lowell C. Rose, "The 27th Annual Phi Delta Kappa/ Gallup Poll of the Public's Attitudes Toward the Public Schools," *Phi Delta Kappan* 77 (September 1995): 41; Elam, Rose, and Alec M. Gallup, "The 28th Annual Phi Delta Kappa/Gallup Poll of the Public's Attitudes Toward the Public Schools," *Phi Delta Kappan* 78 (September 1996): 49; Rose, Gallup, and Elam, " The 29th Annual Phi Delta Gallup Poll of the Public's Attitudes Toward the Public Schools," *Phi Delta Kappan* 79 (September 1997): 42; Rose and Gallup, "The 30th Annual Phi Delta Kappa/Gallup Poll of the Public's Attitudes Toward the Public Schools," 80 (September 1998): 51; Rose and Gallup, "The 31st Annual Phi Delta Kappa/Gallup Poll of the Public's Attitudes Toward the Public Schools," *Phi Delta Kappan* 81 (September 1999): 42; Rose and Gallup, "The 32nd Annual Phi Delta Kappa/Gallup Poll of the Public's Attitudes Toward the Public Schools," *Phi Delta Kappan* 82 (September 2000): 46; Rose and Gallup," The 33rd Annual Phi Delta Kappa/Gallup Poll of the Public's Attitudes Toward the Public Schools," *Phi Delta Kappan* 83 (September 2001): 42; Rose and Gallup, "The 34th Annual Phi Delta Kappa/Gallup Poll of the Public's Attitudes Toward the Public Schools," *Phi Delta Kappan* 84 (September 2002): 43; and Rose and Gallup, "The 35th Annual Phi Delta Kappa/Gallup Poll of the Public's Attitudes Toward the Public Schools," *Phi Delta Kappan* 85 (September 2003): 50.

10. Rose and Gallup, "34th Poll," Ibid., (2002): 43.

11. Alec M. Gallup, "The 18th Annual Gallup Poll of the Public's Attitudes Toward the Public Schools," *Phi Delta Kappan* 68 (September 1986): 43; Gallup and David L. Clark, "The 19th Annual Gallup Poll of the Public's Attitudes Toward the Public Schools," *Phi Delta Kappan* 69 (September 1987): 28; Gallup and Stanley M. Elam, "The 20th Annual Gallup Poll of the Public's Attitudes Toward the Public Schools," *Phi Delta Kappan* 70 (September 1988): 34; Elam and Gallup, "The 21st Annual Gallup Poll of the Public's Attitudes Toward the Public Schools," *Phi Delta Kappan* 71

(September 1989): 52; Elam, "The 22nd Annual Gallup Poll of the Public's Attitudes Toward the Public Schools," *Phi Delta Kappan* 72 (September 1990): 53; Elam, Rose, and Gallup, "The 23rd Annual Gallup Poll of the Public's Attitudes Toward the Public Schools," *Phi Delta Kappan* 73 (September 1991): 55; Elam, Rose, and Gallup, "The 24th Annual Gallup/Phi Delta Kappa Poll of the Public's Attitudes Toward the Public Schools," *Phi Delta Kappan* 74 (September 1992): 43; and Elam, Rose, and Gallup, "The 28th Annual Phi Delta Kappa/Gallup Poll of the Public's Attitudes Toward the Public Schools," *Phi Delta Kappan* 78 (September 1996): 42.

12. Gallup and Elam, "20th Poll," Ibid., (1987): 24.

13. Quoted in Edward A. Krug, ed., *Salient Dates in American Education, 1635-1964*. New York: Harper and Row, 1966, 30.

14. Educational Policies Commission, *Moral and Spiritual Values in the Public Schools*. Washington, DC: National Education Association, 1951, 54.

CHAPTER 1

COLONIAL BEGINNINGS

INTRODUCTION

Bernard Bailyn, among others, has clearly shown that public education of the twentieth century was not the result of a straight line emanating from the schools of colonial Massachusetts (Bailyn, 1960). Jernegan observes, however, that these schools were "first in importance" in this era, in their "number, character, distribution, and quality." Education was also the responsibility of civil government, as then constituted (Jernegan, 1931, pp. 64-65). As such, they are selected to be the first schools to be scrutinized for their commitment to moral/character education.

William Bradford, as noted in the *History of Plymouth Plantation, 1620-1647*, reports that the early Massachusetts residents left Holland because of the "licentiousness of youth in that country," which posed a "danger to their souls, to the great grief of their parents and dishonor of God."[1] John Winthrop, the first Governor of the Massachusetts Bay Colony, put forth the following reason in his justification of their trans-Atlantic migration:

> 5. The fountains of learning and religion are so corrupted that most children, even the best wits and fairest hopes, are perverted, corrupted, and utterly overthrown by the multitude of evil examples and the licentious government of those seminaries.[2]

Moral Education in America's Schools: The Continuing Challenge, 1–8
Copyright © 2005 by Information Age Publishing

Cremin comments that the Puritans thought it would be different in the New World, where they sought to:

> establish a wilderness Zion, a community of 'visible saints' committed to Christian brotherhood and conduct. And within such a society education would assume utmost importance, not merely as an instrument for systematically transmitting an intellectual heritage, but as an agency for deliberately pursuing a cultural ideal. (Cremin, 1970, pp. 15-16)

A half-century after Winthrop's lamentation, Samuel Willard appealed to the moral concern of the colony's original inhabitants when he penned that it was "their love to your souls" that led them to come to the New World, and "it will be horrible ingratitude in you to slight it."[3] It was this moral concern, Bremmer (1970) comments, that contributed in a major way to the founding of schools and to the Laws of 1642 and 1647 which dealt with educational matters (pp. 72-73). Morgan (1966) supports this thesis when he remarks that the "covenant of grace" which drove the Puritans referred not only to the individual but also to their society. People needed to be able to read to learn the divinely-given lessons contained in the Scriptures. The Puritans insisted upon education, "in order to insure the religious welfare of their children" (pp. 6-6,11, 88). Bailyn (1960) agrees, stating that "seventeenth century records abound with efforts to rescue the children from an incipient savagery" (p. 28). Put another way, Morgan (1960) avers that salvation was "impossible" without education, indeed, the "ultimate purpose" of education was salvation; hence the "main business of education was to prepare children for conversion by teaching them the doctrines and moral precepts of Christianity by which salvation could be attained" (pp. 89-92).

MANIFESTATIONS OF MORALITY IN PURITAN SOCIETY AND SCHOOLING

Bremer (1976) contends that the Puritans believed that knowledge was important for reasons of religion:

> God revealed himself in nature, history, and the Scriptures, and it was man's responsibility to study and learn the lessons thus provided him. Education was also important if men were to know and obey the law. (p. 180)

As early as 1642 the Massachusetts General Court required the select men of every town "to take account from time to time of all parents and masters, and of their children, especially of their ability to read and understand the principles of religion and the capital laws of their country" (p. 181). The

Court called attention to the danger of boys and girls associating with one another, and required that they "be not suffered to converse together, so as may occasion any wanton, dishonest, or immodest behavior."[4]

Krug observes, though, that the Law of 1642 said nothing about schools. Five years later, in 1647, the General Court enacted what has become known as the "Old Deluder Satan" law, which held that it was "one chief project" of the "Old Deluder Satan" to "keep men from knowledge of the Scriptures." It then legislated that in order "that learning may not be buried in the graves of our fathers in the church and commonwealth, the Lord assisting our endeavors," towns with fifty householders were required to establish a school which would teach reading and writing, to be supported at least in part by the community; towns with one hundred householders were ordered to set up a grammar school, again at some community expense (Krug, 1966, pp. 9-10). Learning, it was thought, was necessary to "distinguish true from false religion" (Nord, 1995, p. 64).

Moral behavior was expected both at home and in society as well, aberrations of such to be dealt with severely. For instance, in Connecticut in 1642 any child or servant who engaged in "any stubborn or rebellious carriage" could be punished with "hard labor and severe punishment.[5] Four years later the ruling body of Massachusetts legislated that an incorrigible child of "sufficient understanding," who cursed or smote "their natural father or mother," could be put to death, unless the parents have been "unchristianly negligent in the education of such children, or provoked them by extreme and cruel correction."[6] The Massachusetts School law of 1648 embodied similar concern, calling on the select men of towns to keep a "vigilant eye" on parents and masters who were "too indulgent and negligent of their duty" in seeing to the proper upbringing of their wards in teaching the "principles of Religion" and "knowledge of the Capital lawes."[7]

Efforts, including laws, on behalf of religion and consequent good moral behavior of the young continued in New England as the seventeenth century progressed. Despite these efforts, the Connecticut School Law of 1690 bore witness to their failure, observing that despite the previous efforts for the "education of children and servants, there are many persons unable to read the English tongue, and thereby incapable to read the holy word of God, or the good laws of the colony."[8]

DUTIES OF SCHOOLMASTERS

As would be expected, teachers in the Massachusetts Bay Colony were expected to inculcate the truths of religion and instill the principles of morally upright behavior in their youthful charges. A report from the regulations of Dorcester, Massachusetts in 1645 holds schoolmasters to "diligently instruct ... likewise in point of good manners and dutiful behavior towards all, especially their superiors ... meeting them in the street or otherwise."[9] It was the schoolmaster's responsibility to:

> every second day in the week he shall call his scholars together between twelve and one of the clock to examine them what they have learned on the Sabbath day preaching, at which time he shall take notice of any misdemeanor or disorder that his scholars shall have committed on the Sabbath, to the end that at some convenient time due admonition and correction may be administered by him according as the nature and quality of the offense shall require; at which said examination any of the elders or other inhabitants that please may be present to behold his religious care herein and to give their countenance and approbation of the same. [10]

The schoolmaster's duties in the religious/moral realm extended further. The Dorcester regulations held him accountable for his students to pray, and to do so devoutly:

> because all man's endeavors without the blessing of God must needs be fruitless and unsuccessful, therefore, it is to be a chief part of the schoolmaster's religious care to commend his scholars and his labors amongst them unto God by prayer, morning and evening, taking care that his scholars do reverently attend during the same.[11]

Finally, he was to utilize punishment, as appropriate, and without "respect of persons, according to the nature and quality of the offense," recognizing that all things in the school be ordered for the "glory of God and the training up of the children of the town in religion, learning, and civility."[12]

Rules in the New Haven, Connecticut schools of this period contained similar enjoinders for the schoolmaster. In 1648 he was instructed to "every morning begin his work with a short Prayer for a blessing on his Laboures and theire Learning." The "Schollars" were to "behave themselves at all times, especially in Schoole tyme with due Reverence to their Master, & with Sobriety & quietness among themselves."[13]

Meriwether (1907) identifies the general duties of teachers in colonial New England, duties that testify clearly to the importance of moral education in schools at that time. They were:

"To act as court messenger.
To serve summonses.
To conduct certain ceremonials of the church.
To lead the Sunday choir.

To ring the bell for public worship.
To dig the graves.
To take charge of the school
To perform other occasional duties" (p. 16).

TEXTBOOKS—ESPECIALLY THE *NEW ENGLAND PRIMER*

As Gutek (1986) has observed, "In any school system, the reading material conveys the values of the society supporting the school." That adage was true in colonial New England, where the "reading materials stressed Biblical themes and conveyed to the child the concept of the righteous life that should be lived by a good Puritan" (p. 10). Society's values permeated the lives of children, for, as Boorstin (1958) remarks, "From the day he learned his alphabet and read the first syllable in his primer, the New England child was pressed to absorb the truths by which his community lived" (p. 300).

Originating in England, the *New England Primer* was indeed the "most popular text for primary instruction." Expanded to include the "Shorter Catechism" in the 1640s, the *Primer* was the "schoolbook of America" for over a hundred years (Spring, 1986, pp. 4-5). Ford (1962, p. 19) adds that after that century of dominance, it was "frequently reprinted," to the extent that an "overconservative" estimate reached three million copies printed over a span of 150 years. One of the most influential educators and writers, a leading advocate of the secular American public school, Ellwood P. Cubberley (1920), acknowledged in the early twentieth century that the *Primer* "religious throughout, ... exercised a great influence on the New England school character," being used at home, church, and school (pp. 311, 314).

The *Primer* had a number of features. It taught patriotism through the alphabet. So, "Our King the good, No man of blood," became, in the Revolutionary era, "Kings should be good, Not men of Blood" (Ford, 1962, pp. 27-28). It used the alphabet to instruct about biblical themes: "A" In Adam's Fall, We sinned all. "B" Heaven to find, The Bible mind. "C" Christ crucify'd, for Sinners died, and so forth (Ford, 1962, unnumbered). Versions included the Lord's Prayer, The Creed, the Ten Commandments, John Rogers' (the first martyr in Queen Mary's reign) exhortation to his children in 1554, the Shorter Catechism or Catechism, "Milk for Babies," Cotton Mather's "improvement" on the Shorter Catechism, and some had denunciations of the Pope in their pages (Ford, 1962, pp. 39-50). The 1727 version had a section entitled "The Dutiful Child's Promises":

I will fear GOD, and honour the King.
I will honour my Father and Mother.
I will obey my Superiours.
I will Submit to my Elders.
I will Love my Friends.
I will hate no Man.
I will forgive my Enemies, and pray to God for them.
I will as much as in me lies keep all God's Holy Commandments.
I will learn my Catechism.
I will keep the Lord's Day Holy.
I will reverence God's Sanctuary.
For our GOD is a consuming fire (Ford, 1962, p. 53).

Johnson observes that the contents of the various editions may have changed, but "for hundreds of years the teaching of religion and reading united" in the *Primers*. Their precepts were "instilled in minds as yet unformed, and the children were drilled to believe what they were to think out for themselves when they were more mature." The Catechism, which was part of the *Primers* was "treated scarcely less seriously in the schools than it was in the churches, and the teachers drilled their pupils in it as thoroughly as they did in spelling or any other lesson (Johnson, 1904, pp. 69-70, 99). Ford alleges that the *Primer* should have the same epitaph as Webster's Spelling Book of a latter period, i.e., "It taught millions to read, and not one to sin" (Ford, 1962, p. 53).

Other "texts" were used in colonial New England. One of these was the Hornbooks. Consisting of printed paper and then covered with a thin layer of "translucent horn" they were fastened on a paddle-shaped piece of wood. Their contents usually included the alphabet, in capitals and small letters; the vowels; vowel-consonant combinations, the Lord's Prayer, and the Trinitarian Benediction, comprising yet another instance of the tight embrace of religion and education (Cohen, 1974, p. 61).

The Bible was heavily relied on. A variety of "Psalters, a Book of Psalms," and the popular "*Spiritual Milk for Babies, Drawn out of the Breasts of Both Testaments*, all connected with the Scriptures, were widely used in schools throughout the period (Cohen, 1974, p. 63). Less widely used was Michael Wigglesworth's "The Day of Doom," written in 1662. The first and last stanzas of that work are presented below and provide yet another example of the moral thrust in New England colonial education:

Then were brought men with trembling fear,
a number numberless,
Of Blind Heathen, and brutish men
that did God's law trangress.

They using their hands, their caitiff-hands,
and gnash their teeth for terror;
They cry, they roar for anguish sore,
and gnaw their tongues for horror.
Best get away without delay,
Christ pities not your cry;
Depart to Hell, there may you yell,
and roar Eternally.[14]

CONCLUSIONS

Bailyn (1960) writes that the task of the schools in colonial America was "to train the young in purity and loyalty" (p. 39). The schools in New England were, as Gutek concludes, "designed to create educated Puritans who would perpetuate the religious, social, political and economic beliefs of the adults." The ruling groups, "believing that their efforts were divinely sanctioned, proceeded directly to educating the young." All children were to be "able to read and to understand their religion and the laws of the commonwealth." Schooling was an antidote for the children who were "conceived in sin and born in corruption" (Gutek, 1986, pp. 6-9).

It was important, Morgan summarizes, to "teach a child good habits, not because they would save him, but because it was unlikely he would be saved without them. If his education was neglected, his chance of salvation was small, but if education had provided a means of grace, there was every hope that God would use the means" (Morgan, 1966, p. 95). An evil nature could be "trained into good habits only if the training started early" (Morgan, 1966, p. 59). Thus the task of the schools, as well as that of the home and church.

NOTES

1. Cited in Bremmer (1970, p. 17).
2. Quoted in ibid., pp. 18-19).
3. Quoted in Bremmer (1970, p. 19).
4. "Literacy and employment for all children: The Massachusetts Law of 1642." In D. Calhoun (1969, pp. 21-22).
5. "Instructions for the punishment of incorrigible children in Connecticut" (1642). In S. Cohen (1974a, p. 370).
6. "Instructions for the punishment of incorrigible children in Massachusetts" (1646). (1974a). In S. Cohen (1974a, pp. 370-371).
7. "Connecticut School Law of 1690." In S. Cohen (1974a, pp. 394-395).

8.   "Massachusetts School Law of 1648" (1974a). In S. Cohen (1974a, p. 402).

9.   Quoted in Bemmer (1970, p. 80).

10. Quoted in Cohen (1974a, p. 398).

11. Ibid., p. 399.

12. Ibid.

13. "Rules of the Hopkins Grammar School of New Haven" (1648). In S. Cohen (1974a, p. 400).

14. Quoted in Cohen (1974a, pp. 371, 376).

CHAPTER 2

THE REVOLUTIONARY ERA

INTRODUCTION

Welter (1962) asserts that it was the actions of leading public men like John Adams and Francis Marion who "attributed the movement toward independence to the literacy and intelligence of the American people" (p. 23). This chapter will show that the basis of moral education had shifted from theocratic Massachusetts in the colonial era to the position that there was an inexorable link between republican government, democracy, popular education, and virtue and knowledge in the period of the Founding Fathers. Attention will be focused on the positions of Thomas Jefferson, Benjamin Rush, and Noah Webster, to be followed by a general discussion of the period.

THOMAS JEFFERSON

Lee (1961), in his "Introduction" to *Crusade Against Ignorance: Thomas Jefferson on Education*, alleges that:

> There is no grasping the Jeffersonian educational ideas in their fullness without first sensing the essence of Jeffersonianism as a philosophy of politics, morality, and human destiny. For the realization of the political, moral, and ethical ideas of Jefferson's faith was utterly dependent upon enlighten-

Moral Education in America's Schools: The Continuing Challenge, 9–18
Copyright © 2005 by Information Age Publishing
All rights of reproduction in any form reserved.

ment and education—and the nature of that education was determined by the demands and challenges of those ideals. (p. 9)

Jefferson's God was, essentially, "the Enlightenment"; he was a believer in "deistic humanism" (Lee, 1961, pp. 10-11). He interpreted Christianity as a "humanistic moral code" (Tyack, 1967, p. 90), looking to schools to provide "educated and virtuous lawmakers" (Kaestle, 1982, p. 6). Schools and colleges became, for Jefferson, "in a manner and to a degree not heretofore conceived in Western civilization, the most vital pillars of human happiness and security" (Lee, 1961, p. 18). His famous biographer, Dumas Malone, referring to his "More General Diffusion of Knowledge" bills in 1779 and 1817, wrote that "In the light of history, nothing else that he did or proposed during his entire career showed him more clearly to be a major American prophet."[1]

Writing to Peter Carr in 1787 Jefferson claimed that the individual is "endowed with a sense of right and wrong…. This sense is as much a part of his nature as the sense of hearing, seeing, feeling, it is the true foundation of morality."[2] This sense can be improved with exercise, especially by the study of history in the primary schools which would "improve the citizens' moral and civic virtues and enable them to know and exercise their rights and duties," leading to individual and social human happiness (Urban & Wagoner, 2000, p. 72). Education can improve society as it "engrafts a new man on the native stock, and improves what in his nature was vicious and perverse into qualities of virtue and social worth."[3] In the primary schools children should have the "first elements of morality instilled into their minds; such as, when further developed as their judgments advance in strength may teach them how to work out their own greatest happiness," which is "always the result of a good conscience, good health, occupation, and freedom in all just pursuits."[4] They should not, however, study the Bible, because their minds were "not sufficiently matured for religious inquiries."[5] The youth could, though, as Cremin reports on Jefferson, "improve, by reading, his morals and faculties."[6]

Universal literacy was necessary for republican virtue, liberty, and for the survival and progress of the republican state. We conclude our brief treatment of Jefferson's views on moral education with a quote from Joel Spring (1986):

education contributes to the balance between freedom and order by providing all citizens with the basic tools of learning, a knowledge of history, and the ability to work out their own happiness. He believed that knowledge, reason, and a developed moral sense would result in a natural order in a free society. (p. 42)

BENJAMIN RUSH

Much lesser known than Jefferson, Benjamin Rush nonetheless was a leading spokesperson for the role of education in curtailing the excesses of popular liberty and for securing the advantages of a republican form of government. He communicated this idea in 1787 in his "Address to the People of the United States":

> To conform the principles, morals, and manners of our citizens, to our republican forms of government, it is absolutely necessary, that knowledge of every kind should be disseminated through every part of the United States.[7]

A year earlier he had stated that independence had resulted in the acquisition of a "new complexion" on the part of education (Cremin, 1980, p. 116); the Revolution was but the "first act of the drama."[8]

Rush's ideas of the Republican venture on which the nation had just embarked called for the instillation of the values of the New Testament in the primary schools, thus differentiating him from Jefferson, and which he felt was indispensable for a republican nation. Without this there can be no virtue, and without virtue there can be no liberty, and liberty is the object and life of all republican governments.[9] A Christian, Rush held, "cannot fail of being a republican," because "every precept of the Gospel inculcates those degrees of humility, self-denial, and brotherly kindness which are directly opposed to the pride of monarchy and the pageantry of the court" (Rush, 1786/1965, p. 11). Again parting ways with Jefferson, Rush advocated the use of the Bible in education, contending that:

> there is no book of its size in the whole world, that contains half so much useful knowledge for the government of states, or the direction of the affairs of individuals as the Bible. (Rush, 1786/1965, p. 13)

Love of family was critical, but love of country and its welfare surpassed all other claims in Rush's opinion:

> Let our pupil be taught that he does not belong to himself, but that he is public property. Let him be taught to love his family, but let him be taught at the same time that he must forsake and even forget them when the welfare of his country requires it. (Rush, 1786/1965, p. 14)

The authority of the masters in the education of youth was to be as "*absolute* as possible"; the government of schools like the government of private families should be *arbitrary*, thereby preparing our youth for the "subordination of laws" and qualifying them for "becoming good citizens of the republic" (Rush, 1786/1965, p. 16). As he put it, education made it possible to "convert men into republican machines," functioning harmoniously in the republican state (p. 17).

Poor children posed a formidable threat to the survival and success of republican government. In 1787 Rush addressed that issue in his plan for free schools for the poor children of Philadelphia:

> Their ignorance and vices when neglected are not confined to themselves; they associate with and contaminate the children of persons in the higher ranks of society.... They give a complexion to the morals and manners of the people. In short, where the common people are ignorant and vicious, a nation, and above all a republican nation, can never be long free and happy. It becomes us, therefore, as we love our offspring and value the freedom and prosperity of our country, immediately to provide for the poor children who are so numerous in the thick-settled parts of the state.[10]

Initiation in the "principles and obligations of the Christian religion" constituted the "most essential part of education" for these youngsters. Such an indoctrination would make them:

> dutiful children, teachable scholars, and, afterwards, good apprentices, good husbands, good wives, honest mechanics, industrious farmers, peaceable sailors, and, in everything that relates to their country, good citizens.[11]

He had proposed a system of public schools for Pennsylvania in 1786, in which he averred that all of the state's citizens, whether they had children or not, would benefit economically from the establishment of such a system. They would also be protected:

> from the ravages of unprincipled and idle boys, and the children of wealthy parents will be less tempted, by bad company, to extravagance. Fewer pillories and whipping posts, and smaller jails, with their usual expenses and taxes, will be necessary when our youth are properly educated, than at present.[12]

This system, steeped in uniformity, would guarantee that in Pennsylvania there would be "one great and equally enlightened family" (Spring, 1986, p. 35).

NOAH WEBSTER

The third, and last of the "Founding Fathers" to receive modest attention in this section is Noah Webster, best known for his work in establishing the American version of the English language. Like Jefferson and Rush,

Webster tied the existence of a republican nation to the education given its citizens, which would make them true patriots, devoted to the ideals and ethics of their country. Commager (1958) accords him the title of "Schoolmaster to America," and goes on to say that he was "clearly the Father of the American language, and he was certainly one of the Fathers of American education" (pp. 1-2).

Webster's speller, first published in 1783, contained a number of moral precepts, which called for good behavior at home and school, and promised sanctions for evildoers. Among them were:

"No man may put off the law of God....
A bad man is a foe to the law....
Do as well as you can, and do no harm....
I will not walk with bad men, that I may not be cast off with them....
This life is not long, but the life to come has no end....
A bad life will make a bad end.... A good boy will do all that is just: he will flee from sin; he will do good, and walk in the way of life....
Be a good child; mind your book, love your school, and strive to learn. A good child will not lie, swear, nor steal—He will be good at home, and ask to read his book; when he gets up he will wash his hands and face clean; he will comb his hair, and make haste to school; he will not play by the way, as bad boys do....
When good boys and girls are at school, they will mind their books, and try to learn to spell and read well, and not play in the time of school....
As for those boys and girls that mind not their books, and love not the church and school, but play with such as tell tales, tell lies, curse, swear and steal, they will come to some bad end, and must be whipt till they mend their ways ..." (Webster, 1831, pp. 55-58).

The Speller also included a "Moral Catechism" which asked questions such as "WHAT is moral virtue?" and answered "It is an honest, upright conduct in all dealings with man." Similar, subsequent questions and answers were presented on Humility, Mercy, Peace-makers, Purity of Heart, Anger, Revenge, Justice, Generosity, Gratitude, Truth, Charity, and Giving Alms, Avarice, Frugality and Economy, Industry, and Cheerfulness (Webster, 1831, pp. 169-179). As Spring observes, Webster considered these necessary for maintaining order in a democratic society (Spring, 1986, p. 38). Public virtue was equated with Christian morality, and a "good citizen is one who lives a Christian life" (Spring 1986, p. 38).

His "On the Education of Youth in America, composed in 1790, is the repository of his views on the crucial role education plays in the republican nation. Education of youth is, he writes in the opening paragraph:

in all governments, an object of the first consequence. The impressions received in early life usually form the characters of all individuals, a union of which forms the general character of a nation.

It was especially critical in the young United States where:

> our constitutions of civil government are not yet firmly established; our national character is not yet formed; and it is an object of vast magnitude that systems of education should be adopted and pursued which may not only diffuse a knowledge of the sciences but may implant in the minds of the American youth the principles of virtue and of liberty and inspire them with just and liberal ideas of government and with an inviolable attachment to their own country.[13]

It was not possible to minimize the importance of education, Webster affirmed, because its "effects are so certain and extensive that it behooves every parent and guardian to be particularly attentive to the characters of the men whose province it is to form the minds of youth." For, the "education of youth, and employment of more consequence than making laws and preaching the gospel, because it lays the foundation on which both the law and gospel rest for success."[14] The only practicable method to reform mankind is to "banish, if possible, every low-bred, drunken, immoral character. Virtue and vice will not grow together in a great degree."[15] Consequently, "society requires that the education of youth should be watched with the most scrupulous attention." Education, to a considerable extent, "forms the moral characters of men, and morals are the basis of government." Education should be the "first care of a legislature"; which calls for supporting the schools and "furnishing of them with the best men for teachers."[16]

Dedication to one's country was critical for Webster. As soon as "he opens his lips," the child should "rehearse the history of his own country; he should lisp the praise of liberty and of those illustrious heroes and statesmen who have wrought a revolution in her favor."[17] In a republican government, such as existed in the United States, "every class of people should *know* and *love* the laws," knowledge of which "should be diffused by means of schools and the newspapers." In the American republic, "whose government is in the hands of the people, knowledge should be universally diffused by means of public schools." Until a system of public schools is developed, he maintained, "mankind cannot know to what a degree of perfection society and government may be carried."[18] Each district should have its own school, he opined, and in it the children should be taught "the usual branches of learning, submission to superiors and to laws, the moral or social duties, the history and transactions of their own country, the principles of liberty and government." Here they should have the "principles of virtue and good behavior inculcated." The "*virtues*" of men are of "more consequence to society than their *abilities*," he contended. It was for this reason the "*heart* should be cultivated more assiduity than the *head*."[19]

Like Washington, Jefferson, and Rush, Webster was opposed to Americans being educated in Europe. A foreign education, he wrote, "is directly opposite to our political interests and ought to be discountenanced, if not prohibited." He averred that it was of "infinite importance" that those who led the country be educated here. Travel to foreign lands was permissible, after a "knowledge of their country is obtained and an attachment to its laws and interests, deeply fixed in their hearts." His meaning, he tells us, is that "*men* should travel and not *boys*."[20]

In basic agreement with Jefferson and Rush as to the "need for the general diffusion of knowledge," Webster, as a Federalist, was concerned with the possible threat of anarchy present in a republican government (Urban & Wagoner, 2000, p. 81). While he could write in 1796 that when people "*understand* public affairs, they *will not do* wrong," later in life he lost his basic trust.[21] Like Rush, he looked to the schools to promote "order" and prevent social disruption. While he was opposed to the reading of the Bible in schools (the practice could breed contempt for the word of God), he did not want it excluded from schools but wanted to "see it used as a system of religion and morality" (Urban & Wagoner, 2000, p. 81).

Finally, one last word about the role of language. As Commager (1958) pointed out above, Webster was clearly the "Father of the American language" (pp. 1-2). So, in addition to schools, teachers, textbooks, and travel, Webster looked to language to develop patriotism. In Europe, he maintained, language was used to divide people. In the United States, it should be used to "bring people together." Improved spelling and pronunciation, as practiced in the spelling bee, he contended, would strengthen democracy (Church & Aedlak, 1976, p. 16).

SUPPORTING EVIDENCE

Considerable additional evidence exists on behalf of the vital role of moral education in sustaining the fledgling republic in the waning years of the eighteenth and beginning years of the nineteenth centuries. Some of that evidence will be presented in this section.

As early as 1777 the State of Vermont enacted provisions for schools. Included was Sec. XLI, which promulgated that "Laws for the encouragement of virtue and the prevention of vice and immorality, shall be made and constantly kept in force."[22] A decade later came the famous Northwest Ordnance, in which Congress proclaimed that "Religion, morality, and knowledge being necessary for good government and the happiness of mankind, schools and the means of education shall forever be encouraged."[23] That same year Vermont again came out on behalf of laws in favor of virtue and for the "prevention of vice and immorality," and added a provision that a "competent number of schools ought to be maintained in each town for the convenient education of youth."[24]

Massachusetts enacted a major piece of legislation on education in 1789. The law called for each town of fifty families to be provided with a School-Master "of good morals," whose responsibilities included teaching "decent behavior" to his students. The select men of the town were charged with insuring that to the best of "their knowledge, he sustains a good moral character."[25] The teacher, who was to be a "person of sober life and conversation," was assigned "carefully to instruct" the children in reading, and writing if so contracted, but also to "instil in their minds a sense of piety and virtue, and to teach them decent behaviour."[26] The Town of Boston that year called on a school committee to examine students, to see if their teacher motivated his students to a "laudable ambition to excel in a virtuous, amiable deportment, and in every branch of useful knowledge."[27]

Concern over the role of education in producing a virtuous citizenry, indispensable in a republican government, was not limited to Massachusetts and Vermont. Welter (1962) reports that seven of the fourteen states that drafted constitutions before 1800 adopted calls for public aid to education (p. 24). He cites Massachusetts as an example, which legislated that schools were necessary for "virtue," as well as "knowledge and wisdom," and for the "preservation" of the citizens' "rights and duties" (Welter, 1962, p. 24). As the nineteenth century began, Governor George Clinton of New York proclaimed that "advantages to morals, religion, liberty and good government" stem from the "general diffusion of knowledge."[28] He was joined by Governor James Turner of North Carolina who urged the establishment of schools to "enlighten the minds of the people, and to preserve the purity of their morals."[29]

Other leaders in the young nation weighed n with their views on education. John Adams called for the establishment of schools to diffuse virtue, wisdom and knowledge as "necessary for the preservation" of Americans' rights and liberties. These schools were to:

countenance and inculcate the principles of humanity and general benevolence, public and private charity, industry and frugality, honesty and punctuality in their dealings; sincerity, good-humour, and all social affections and generous sentiments among the people.[30]

In the latter stages of the eighteenth century the American Philosophical Society, an outgrowth of Franklin's Junto, sponsored an essay contest. The two winning essays recommended "centralization, uniformity, censorship, and controls of the diffusion of knowledge" (Spring, 1986, p. 35). The first essay was by Samuel Harrison Smith, who advocated the erection of a board which would, among other things, judge all literary and scientific productions, and determine what all students at all levels should read. The second winner, Samuel Knox, called for the "same uniform system of the most approved school books," looked to the schools to build a sense of nationalism through unity, and "control the exercise of liberty through the education of a virtuous character." Citizens needed instruction about government and morality, Smith averred:

> It is certainly of the highest importance in a country like this that even the poorest and most uninstructed of its citizens be early impressed with a knowledge of the benefits of that happy constitution under which they live and of the enormity of their being corrupted in their right of suffrage.[31]

CONCLUSION

The leaders of American society after the Revolution were unanimous in their view that a self-governing people needed "universal education" (Cremin, 1980, p. 103). Yet, as Cremin points out, there was "major disagreement" concerning the means to be employed (p. 103). One should not be surprised at either of these realities, given the circumstances of the time, and the fact that, as Kaestle notes, the purpose of education at any time seeks to maintain a balance between freedom and order "by producing virtuous, well-rounded citizens" (Kaestle, 1982, p. 43). All agreed on the necessity of education for the preservation of the republican form of government, the debate involved schooling which would mold virtuous citizens versus schooling that would provide the tools for the exercise of freedom (Kaestle, 1982, p. 45).

NOTES

1. Quoted in Lee (1961, p. 82).
2. Jefferson, "To Peter Carr, with enclosure," in Lee (1961, pp. 145-146).
3. Jefferson, "Report of the Commissioners Appointed to Fix the Site of the University of Virginia." In Lee (1961, p. 119).
4. Jefferson, "Notes on the State of Virginia." In Lee (1961, p. 95).
5. Ibid.
6. Jefferson, quoted in Cremin (1980, p. 110).

7. Quoted in Welter (1962, p. 27).
8. Quoted in Kaestle (1982, p. 6).
9. Quoted in Cremin (1980, p. 118).
10. Quoted in Bremmer (1970, p. 249).
11. Ibid., p. 250.
12. Quoted in Cohen (1974b, p. 757).
13. Webster, "On the education of youth in America." In Rudolph (p. 45).
14. ibid., p. 59.
15. ibid., pp. 63-64.
16. ibid., p. 64.
17. ibid., pp. 64-65.
18. ibid., pp. 67-68.
19. ibid., p. 67.
20. ibid., p. 76.
21. Quoted in Tyack (1967, p. 88).
22. "Constitutional Provisions for Schools in Vermont" (1777). In Cohen (1974b, p. 794).
23. "The Northwest Ordinance and Education." In Cohen (1974b, p. 809).
24. "Constitution of 1787" (Vermont). In Cubberley (1920, p. 420).
25. "An Act to Provide for the Instruction of Youth, and for the Promotion of Good Education." In Cohen (1974b, pp. 794-796).
26. Ibid., p. 797.
27. "The System of Public Education, Adopted by the Town of Boston, 15th October, 1789." In Cohen (1974b, p. 733).
28. Quoted in Welter (1962).
29. Quoted in ibid., p. 25.
30. Quoted in Fraser (2001, p. 18).
31. Quoted in Spring (1986, p. 36).

CHAPTER 3

THE EDUCATION OF URBAN POOR CHILDREN

New York City and the Lancaster Method

INTRODUCTION

The growth of cities which industry brought about in the early days of the nineteenth century had serious consequences for schooling. The story of that education in New York City, in particular, graphically demonstrates the kind of moral education deemed appropriate for the youngsters of the urban poor. The charity schools which were created in these environments are important for a number of reasons. As Spring notes, the "charity school movement is important because it was the first major attempt to use the school as a means of socializing children into an industrious way of life" (Spring, 1997, p. 62). Witnessing the growing problems in New York City, the "hospitals and almshouses were full" because "education had been neglected," Thomas Eddy, a Quaker, led the movement to have the New York Free School Society incorporated by the State of New York. Not only the destitute, but also the laboring class, were becoming "less industrious, less moral, and less careful to lay up the fruits of their earn-

Moral Education in America's Schools: The Continuing Challenge, 19–30
Copyright © 2005 by Information Age Publishing
All rights of reproduction in any form reserved.

ings" (Kaestle, 1983, p. 40). The Free School Society intended to address these serious social needs.

As Bourne (1971) comments, the application to the state was signed by "about one hundred of the most respectable men in the city" (p. 3), who "viewed with painful anxiety the multiplied evils which have accrued, and are daily accruing, to this city, from the neglected education of the children of the poor."[1] These children were not being educated by any of the Charity Schools established by the "various religious societies in this city." Their condition, the memorial maintained, was "deplorable, indeed"; these children, reared by parents who neglected them, and whose "bad example" led to the neglect of education which produced "ignorance and vice, and all those manifold evils resulting from every species of immorality." It was the lack of a "*virtuous education*," early in life, that was at fault.[2] This the Society, if incorporated, promised to address by establishing free schools in the city.

Subsequent to state approval, The President of the New York Free School Society, DeWitt Clinton, addressed the public in 1805 on behalf of the Society. Clinton pointed out that, despite the efforts of the churches, there still remained a large number of children living in "total neglect of religious and moral instruction, and unacquainted with the common rudiments of learning, essentially requisite for the due management of the ordinary business of life."[3] This neglect, he averred, was due either to the "extreme indigence of the parents of such children, their intemperance and vice; or to a blind indifference to the best interests of their offspring." The "consequences," he maintained, must be obvious to the "most careless observer."[4] Children so "brought up in ignorance, and amidst the contagion of bad example, are in imminent danger of ruin," and likely to become the "burden and pests of society." They must receive "early instruction," combined with "fixed habits of industry, decency, and order," which are the "surest safeguards of virtuous conduct." When parents are "either unable or unwilling to bestow the necessary attention on the education of their children," then it becomes the "duty of the public, and of individuals, who have the power, to assist them in the discharge of this important obligation."[5] These considerations had led to the formation of the Society and to seeking the sanction of the state, which had occurred. Clinton informed his readers that care would be exercised in the "selection of teachers, and, besides the elements of learning usually taught in schools, strict attention will be bestowed on the morals of the children." All "suitable means," he assured his fellow New Yorkers, would be called on to "counteract the disadvantages resulting from the situation of their parents."[6]

ENTER THE LANCASTER METHOD

Quaker philanthropists were common in England and the United States at this time. One of their instruments for humanitarian reform was education which divorced "doctrinal religion from charity schooling" (Kaestle, 1973, p. 35), Thomas Eddy was a Quaker who had witnessed the workings of the Lancaster method in England, and he led the push to bring that system to the United States (p. 36). As Ravitch (1974) observes, the system worked and it was cheap (p. 12).

By using monitors, older students, the system allowed for one teacher to "teach" hundreds of pupils. (The first schools in New York City were for boys only; schools for girls followed at a later date.) The teachers had a minimal role, supervising, organizing, and rewarding. Lancaster reserved the "teaching" to the monitors, who gave exams, promoted deserving students, assigned new students, and took care of paper, slates and books (Ravitch, 1974, p. 13). Lancaster (1973) said, the "surest way to cure a *mischievous* boy was to make him a *monitor*" (p. 64). Repeated offenders in his schools were to have a "wooden log" placed around their necks, and if that failed, then the offender's legs were to be fastened "together with wooden shackles," and made to walk until he was "exhausted." Lancaster also used the method of putting misbehaving students in baskets and suspending them from the ceiling, while classmates smiled "at the bird in a cage" (Lancaster, 1973, pp. 80-81). Learning Scripture occupied a prominent place in Lancaster's schools; he believed that if students had, "Deism would have had fewer converts" (p. 85).

Lancaster highlighted the beneficial aspects of his program for poor urban youth:

> The predominant feature in the youthful disposition is an almost irresistible propensity to action; this, if properly controlled by suitable employment, will become a valuable auxiliary to the master; but, if neglected, will be apt to degenerate into rebellion. *Active youths, when treated as cyphers, will generally show their consequence by exercising themselves in mischief* ... In education, nothing can be more important than economy of time,... but it is most peculiarly necessary in primary schools, and in the instruction of the poor. (Kaestle, 1973, p. 64)

His method of education appealed to society not only because of its claims of effectiveness in the moral realm but also because it was so inexpensive. By using student monitors and cards he provided "A Method of Teaching to Spell and Read Whereby One Book Will Serve Instead of Six Hundred Books." The cards he recommended made it possible for "*two hundred boys* may all repeat their lessons from *one* card, all in the space of *three hours*" (Kaestle, 1973, pp. 68-69). Emulation and reward served as motivating tools (p. 70). His plan was so efficient that he penned that "*any boy who can read, can teach—ALTHOUGH HE KNOWS NOTHING ABOUT IT*" (p. 74).

Kaestle (1973) remarks that while the system made learning the rudiments inexpensive, the rudiments "were not, after all, the main points of elementary schooling for the working class, moral education was" (p. 8). As he put it:

> The central intent of the curriculum, seen both explicitly in the teaching materials and implicitly in the procedures of the schools, was to inculcate the values of obedience, subordination, promptness, regularity, cleanliness, thrift, and temperance.... The school, with its neat, uniformed rows and its regimented activity, would teach poor children the discipline so sorely lacking in the chaotic world of poverty outside its doors. School officials constantly testified that manners were improved and crime reduced by the stable of Lancasterian schools. (pp. 8-9)

A system of emulation and rewards was used to inculcate the desired behaviors. For several decades monitors used tickets to reward good behavior, tickets which could be used to purchase toys, and fines were employed to punish bad behavior. For instance, a fine of four tickets was assessed for "Talking, playing, inattention, out of order," and a fifty ticket penalty was levied for "Fighting" (Ravitch, 1974, pp. 14-16).

The "proper moral and religious training" that made the "good life" attainable was "synonymous with democratic tolerance" and was superior to the "divisive sectarianism of the church schools" (Ravitch, 1974, p. 18). Lancaster's backers believed that "monitorial instruction and scriptural education constituted a world-wide solution to mass education" (Kaestle, 1973, p. 37). The system was not devoid of religious activity. For instance, Tuesday afternoons were set aside for religious instruction. Bourne (1971) reports that an "association of more than fifty ladies of the first position and character," who belonged to different denominations, "volunteered their services" and taught the children "in their respective catechisms" (p. 27). On Sunday mornings the students met at the school and were escorted by monitors to their respective churches. The Scriptures were read daily in the schools (pp. 26-27). Ravitch (1974) provides an example of a moral lesson that was used in the monitorial schools:

Teacher: Children, who is good?

Answer: The Lord is good.

  T: To whom should we be thankful?

  A: Be thankful unto him.

  T: Whose name shall we bless?

A: Bless his name …
T: God always sees you. (*Slowly, and in a soft tone.*)
S: God always sees me.
T: God hears all you say.
S: God hears all I say (pp. 18-19).

THE MORAL EDUCATION PLAN

According to Kaestle, New York City's social situation in the early days of the nineteenth century was simply deplorable, with "low wages and foul tenements" degrading the urban working class. Reformers, among whom were the leaders of the New York School Society, attributed the grinding poverty of that class and the growing crime in the City to "faults of character" (Kaestle, 1973, p. 34). Ravitch maintains that the Society's trustees believed that "scrupulous nonsectarianism, coupled with inculcation of what they took to be commonly accepted moral and ethical values," would enable the schools to "teach children of all religious groups," and hence combat the vices of ignorance and crime (Ravitch, 1974, p. 19). Katz contends that the system, which had "minuscule cost" attached to it, was a "mechanistic form of pedagogy, which reduced education to drill," and seemed fitting because the schools served lower-class children who were "unfinished products, needing to be inculcated with norms of docility, cleanliness, sobriety, and obedience," which they did not get at home (Katz, 1971, p. 10). The moral virtues which the schools were to communicate were class-bound, Katz argues, and had clear social class goals:

> It is not difficult to see a very particular ideal of an urban working class implicit in those pedagogical arrangements. As a result of such schooling, the working class would be alert, obedient, and so thoroughly attuned to discipline through group sanctions that a minimum of policing would ensure the preservation of social order. But, and this is important, programmed from an early age to compete with one another, working-class children would not grow up to form a cohesive and threatening class force. The zealous amateurs of the New York Public School Society, it thus becomes apparent, did not design their system for their own children or for the children of their friends. Rather, they attempted to ensure social order through the socialization of the poor in cheap, mass schooling factories. (Katz, 1971, p. 11)

The particular form of moral or character education to be transmitted was founded on military discipline, which like factory discipline, "would train the children of the poor how to act inside and outside of school."

The character traits the children of the working class, urban poor were in desperate need of, especially promptness and obedience, were deemed "beneficial to the child as well as the society" (Kaestle, 1973, p. 17). The "regimentation of the students" in the Lancasterian system was "symbolically and psychologically appropriate to the moral mission of the schools," Kaestle declared. By imposing order on chaos, it brought the pupils into an "obedient subordination." This "philosophy of order" went hand in hand with order in urban society, indeed it was an "attempt to promote" such order (Kaestle, 1983, pp. 165-166). As Spring (1997) notes, a student's submission to this "factory system of education" was supposed to indelibly impress the virtues of "orderliness and obedience" on the student's mind. Then, when he entered the world, armed with the "virtues of submission, order, and industriousness," he could function in the "world of business" (p. 66). As Spring put it, the "Lancasterian system was supposed to help the pauper child escape poverty and crime by imparting formal knowledge and instilling the virtues needed in the world of work." A child made moral in this framework makes him or her "useful to and functional in society" (Spring, 1977, p. 66).

CLINTON'S ADDRESSES OF 1809 AND 1819

In 1809, speaking at the opening of a new school building in New York City, Clinton heaped lavish praise upon the accomplishments of the Lancaster movement. "Ignorance," he held, was the "cause as well as the effect of bad governments," and was prevalent in the Old World, especially in England.[7] Referring to the millions England had spent on the "cultivation of arts and sciences," he argued that:

> If one tenth part of that sum had been applied to the education of the poor, the blessings of order, knowledge, and innocence would have been diffused among them, the evil would have been attacked at the fountain-head, and a total revolution would have taken place in the habits and lives of the people, favorable to the cause of industry, good morals, good order, and rational religion.[8]

Referring to the fund, "established for sinking vice and ignorance," Clinton remarked that the citizens had "every reason" to believe that it will "remain unimpaired and in full force and vigor to the latest posterity," for the "propagation of knowledge and the diffusion of virtue among the people."[9] Citing the deplorable problems of moral mass depravity in London, he alleged that:

There can be no doubt that hundreds are in the same situation in this city, prowling about our streets for prey, the victims of intemperance, the slaves of idleness, and ready to fall into any vice, rather than to cultivate industry and good order.[10]

How, then, he asked, "can it be expected that persons so careless of themselves, will pay any attention to their children?" Many of the children of these unfortunates, when interrogated, have replied that they were "without home and without friends." In this "state of turpitude and idleness, leading lives of roving mendicancy and petty depredation, they existed, a burden and a disgrace to the community."[11]

Turning to Joseph Lancaster and the method he had developed, which had been adopted in New York's Free Schools, Clinton claimed that "many boys in our school have been taught to read and write in two weeks, who did not before know the alphabet." He went on to laud the method's many accomplishments, especially those of the moral order:

> when I contemplate the habits of order which it forms, the spirit of emulation which it excites, the rapid improvement which it produces, the purity of morals which it inculcates—when I behold the extraordinary union of celerity in instruction and economy of expense— ... I confess that I recognize in Lancaster the benefactor of the human race. I consider his system as creating a new era in education, as a blessing sent down from heaven to redeem the poor and distressed of this world from the power and dominion of Ignorance.[12]

A decade later Clinton addressed the "Parents and Guardians of the Children belonging to the Schools under the care of the New York Free-School Society." He advised these people that the schools had been established for the promotion of the "moral and literary improvement" of the students, and were still trying to do all they could to "advance the welfare of both children and parent."[13] He wrote to "impress" on their minds, "the importance of the establishment," which is intended to promote "not only the good of your children, but their happiness and yours, both here and hereafter." Clinton instructed the parents that it was of:

> great importance that the minds of your children should be early cultivated and moral instruction inculcated, and that, by example as well as precept, you should use all endeavors to preserve them in innocence.[14]

It was the parents' duty to "improve every opportunity," to lay the foundation of "usefulness and respectability, both in civil and religious society." He reminded the parents that the Free School their child(ren) attended "holds out much encouragement," and they were "bound by every moral obligation to avail themselves of the advantages" which were present for their children, especially that they be "improved in morals and manners."[15]

Condescendingly, he pointed out that "Many of you have not been favored with the privileges your children now enjoy—that of a gratuitous education." The school "may be productive of great good to you, and to your children especially, if, on your part, there is a disposition to promote it."[16] "You know," he intoned:

> that many evils grow out of idleness, and many more out of the improper use of spirituous liquors; that they are ruinous and destructive to morals, and debase the human character below the lowest of all created beings; we therefore earnestly desire you may be watchful and careful in this respect, otherwise in vain may we labor to promote the welfare of your children.[17]

"Temperance and economy" are indispensable virtues in the promotion of the comfort and welfare of families, Clinton averred. But "without cleanliness, your enjoyments as well as your reputation will be impaired." They must be "clean and decent," especially when sent to school:

> where it is expected they will appear with their hands, faces, and heads perfectly clean, and their clothing clean and in good order. The appearance of children exhibits to every observing mind the character of the mother.[18]

Parents were instructed to observe the Sabbath, because "public worship is a duty we owe to our creator." Parents should model good behavior in observance of Sunday and should support Sunday schools for their children. Overall, they should focus on the religious duties of "that day, which ought to be appropriated to public worship, retirement, and other duties connected with the improvement of the mind."[19] Further, they should "omit no opportunity to instruct" their children "early in the principles of the Christian religion," so that they may understand the "unspeakable love and infinite wisdom of their Almighty Creator."[20]

Clinton called attention to the need of "every Christian to be frequent and diligent" in the reading of the Scriptures to their families. In the eyes of the Society's trustees, "education calculated to form habits of virtue and industry, and to inculcate the general principles of Christianity," establishing their children "in the nurture and admonition of the Lord," were more primary than other school learning.[21] As he approached the conclusion of his remarks, he saw fit to speak of the debt the parents and guardians owed those affiliated with the Free School movement:

> It may not be improper to state to you, that the establishment of the New York Free School has been attended with much labor and personal exertions on the part of its friends and patrons; great expense has also accrued,

and continues to be the case, where so many buildings are erected and so many teachers employed; and as all this is done in order to promote the good of your children, and to improve their condition, you cannot but feel a weight of obligation to the friends and patrons of so valuable an institution.[22]

Before ending his patronizing address, Clinton reminded his readers that it was impossible to include "minutely every thing" that might have a "bearing on your religious and moral character." He then closed with a list of rules that parents and guardians were to see that the children in their charge strictly observed.[23]

JOSEPH LANCASTER AND THE SPREAD OF HIS MONITORIAL SCHOOLS

Lancaster came to the United States from England in 1818. Kaestle observes that by then the "Lancaster system was such a rage in American educational circles that a certain amount of respect for the founder was assured" (Kaestle, 1973, p. 41). He shortly found out that he was no more indispensable in the States than he was in England, however. He did run the Lancaster school in Philadelphia in 1819 (p. 41). His career was cut short when he was killed by a run-away horse in New York City in 1838, following a period when he had been "constantly complaining of ingratitude and deceit," and his "vale of sorrows" in both the United States and England (pp. 42-43).

The movement spread to other American cities. For instance, in 1817 the Philadelphia Society for the Establishment and Support of Charity Schools promoted the Lancaster method. It described the system as the "best mode yet discovered of spreading the benefits of education, either in the hands of individual Tutors or School Societies."[24] The method was used, and praised, in the Model schools in Pennsylvania in the 1820s (Ellsbree, 1939, p. 145).

Boston's mayor, Josiah Quincy, lauded the system, particularly in comparison with the "old system," especially in matters of morals or character. The advantages he claimed for it were:

> it keeps attention awake and interested, by permitting no moment of idleness or listlessness; its effect on the habits, character and intelligence of youth is highly beneficial; disposing their minds to industry, to readiness of attention, and to subordination, thereby creating in early life a love of order, preparation for business and acquaintance with the relative obligations and duties, both of pupil and instructor.[25]

CONCLUSION

Kaestle (1973) summarizes somewhat favorably the role that Lancaster's monitorial system played in the annals of American education:

> In the history of the real school systems which have dealt with our social problems, forging compromises and collective solutions, facing crushing numbers of students with inadequate resources, mediating, and sometimes institutionalizing, social prejudices and interest group competition—in this history Lancaster and his monitorial system assume an important role. (p. 46)

Commenting on the critical importance of moral character of the people in the survival of the nation, Bourne (1971) writes that:

> the foundation of character is laid in the moral nature. The heart is exercised while the mind is yet just unfolding its earliest powers.... But the permanence of a popular form of government in this country depends more upon the pure and elevated moral character of the people than upon its intelligence.... The only strong, sufficient and reliable bond of union and guaranty of our national permanence is in the virtues of the nation the moral training of the people becomes an act of self-preservation *for* the State. (p. xix-xx)

Leadership of the right kind of men was necessary, because "Thousands of parents are intemperate, vicious, thriftless, and improvident" (Bourne, 1971, p. xx). These people need "higher ground," which will come from the agreement that the "doctrine of public education" is that "morality shall be taught in all our common schools, if for no other reason than because it is essential to the safety of the state" (pp. xxii-xxiii). And it will be much cheaper than to "pay five times the amount to punish and incarcerate one in fifty of the population over twelve years of age for crimes against virtue, order, and human life" (p. xxiii).

Moral education was the keynote of the Lancaster system. Free from subservience to any sect, Lancaster argued, and some leading New Yorkers (and others) agreed, his system provided that indispensable moral education for the nation's urban poor children. As he put it:

> a reverence for the sacred name of God, and the Scriptures of Truth, a detestation of vice; a love of veracity; a due attention to duties to parents, relations, and to society; carefulness to avoid bad company; civility without flattery; and a peaceable demeanor; may be inculcated in every seminary for youth. without violating the sanctuary of private religious opinion in any mind. (Lancaster, 1973, p. 63)

Looking back at the workings of the Lancaster method in New York and other American cities, Gutek (1986) observes that the plan "may have been the model for the factory like urban schools that emerged in the United States in the late nineteenth century" (p. 64). Katz (1971) takes the Society to task for its highhanded operations in which it assumed "exclusive control" over the poor children, not permitting their parents any participation in "the direction of the course of studies, the management of the schools, or ... the selection of teachers." The Society, he writes, ordered parents with "no action or cooperation" to "submit their children to the government and guidance of others, probably strangers," who were in "no way accountable to the parents" (pp. 11-12).

Ellwood P. Cubberley, that eminent stalwart of public education, had a much more benign view of the New York Free School Society and its schools, seeing them as a "great improvement' over what went on before, replacing "idleness, inattention, and disorder" with "activity, emulation, order and a kind of military discipline which was of much value to the type of children attending these schools" (Cubberley, 1919, p. 93). Cubberley saw a precursor role for these schools, in that they "exerted a very important interest in and a sentiment for free schools." They helped people realize the "advantages of a common school system, and become willing to contribute to the support of the same" (p. 94).

Cubberley ventures that it was "not strange that the new plan aroused widespread enthusiasm in many discerning men, and for almost a quarter of a century was advocated as the best system of education then known" (p. 94). The movement died in this country in the 1840s, going out, as Kaestle (1973) described it, with a "fizzle, not a bang" (pp. 44-45).

NOTES

1. "To the Representatives of the People of the State of New York, in Senate and Assembly, convened: The Memorial of the Subscribers, Citizens of New York." In Bourne (1971, p. 3).
2. Ibid.
3. "Address of the Trustees of the Society for Establishing a Free School in the City of New York for the Education of such Poor Children as do not Belong to, or are not Provided for, by any Religious Society." In Bourne (1971, p. 6).
4. Ibid., pp. 6-7.
5. Ibid., p. 7.
6. Ibid.
7. "De Witt Clinton's Address." In Bourne (1971, p. 15).
8. Ibid., p. 16.
9. Ibid., p. 17.

10. Ibid.
11. Ibid.
12. Ibid., p. 19.
13. Clinton, "To the parents and guardians of the children belonging to the schools under the care of the New York Free-School Society," in Bourne (1971, p. 36)
14. Ibid.
15. Ibid.
16. Ibid., p. 37.
17. Ibid.
18. Ibid.
19. Ibid.
20. Ibid.
21. Ibid., p. 38
22. Ibid.
23. Ibid.
24. Quoted in Cohen (1974b, pp. 980-981).
25. Quoted in Cohen (1974b, p. 989).

CHAPTER 4

HORACE MANN'S COMMON SCHOOL

INTRODUCTION

Horace Mann is known as the "Father of the Common School." Mann quit the profession of law and, as quoted in Cremin (1959, p. 3), took himself "to the larger sphere of mind and morals." He is the best known of a number of political leaders of the time who "supported the establishment of common schools as part of their political platform" (Gutek, 1986, p. 93). Originally Calvinist, he wrote to his sister in 1836 that his "nature revolts at the idea of belonging to a universe in which there is to be never-ending anguish ... while we are on earth, the burden of our duties is toward man."[1] Concerned over the growing social disorder in the United States, and especially in Massachusetts, he accepted the position of Secretary of the State Board of Education in Massachusetts and announced that "Henceforth, so long as I hold the office, I devote myself to the supremest welfare of mankind upon earth.... I have faith in the improvability of the race." Adults, Mann maintained, were "castiron; but children are wax" (Mann, quoted in Spring, 1997, p. 101). Spring comments that Mann believed that he was entering a "field of endeavor that promised universal salvation" (p. 101). The priority of the common school, under the leadership of Horace Mann, was moral education.

Moral Education in America's Schools: The Continuing Challenge, 31–48
Copyright © 2005 by Information Age Publishing
All rights of reproduction in any form reserved.

THE ENVIRONMENT

The Massachusetts legislature had enacted a statute that forbade the use of any text in public schools that was "calculated to favor any particular religious sect or tenet" (Michaelsen, 1970, p. 72).The law of 1827 was intended to impress on students a host of moral virtues:

> the principles of piety, justice, and sacred regard to truth, love to their country, humanity, and universal benevolence, sobriety, industry, and frugality, chastity, moderation, and temperance, and those other virtues, which are the ornament of human society, and the basis upon which the republican constitution is founded. (McCluskey, 1958, p. 21)

Other states reflected a groundswell toward common schools at this time. For instance, Thaddeus Stevens of Pennsylvania held that support of common schools was a necessity "if an elective republic is to endure for any great length of time" (Stevens, 1974b, p. 1065). Superintendent Pierce of Michigan penned that the primary schools were the "chief support of all our free institutions" (Pierce, 1974b, p. 1025). Henry Barnard, Mann's counterpart in Connecticut, maintained that his state would become "more elevated by intelligence, morality and religion" with the advent of the common school (Barnard, 1971, p. 72).

Whigs and Unitarians occupied prominent positions in the common school reform. For instance, in its first year nine of the ten members of the State Board of Education, all appointed by the Governor, were Whigs; seven were Unitarians, there was one Episcopalian and two Congregationalists (Williams, 1937, p. 118). Mann, Williams contends, "saw the schools and the universal education of the people as the only hope of Massachusetts." The schools were to be "of the people, by the people, and for the people, of the *whole* people, by the *whole* people, for the *whole* people" (Williams, 1937, pp. 124, 345).

Not everyone agreed with Williams' assessment of the common schools, nor did they support the movement. Mann had his well-documented conflicts with the Boston schoolmasters, with Catholics, and with others. Most notable among the others were the Reverend Frederick A. Packard, editor of the American Sunday School Union—a tussle over books—and with the Calvinist Reverend Matthew Hale Smith, who alleged that the Board had "contributed substantially to the precipitous decline in the morals of youth and the rapidly accelerating incidence of juvenile delinquency" (Michaelsen, 1970, pp. 74-74).

The plight of America's cities was well-known. Morgan (1936) relates that "Fear, greed, and confusion were everywhere. Unemployment, misery, and distress prevailed ... the time had come for an educational revival" (p. vii). Social critics pointed to the growing tide of immigration and migration, the growth of unfettered industry, with a body of hostile workers, which collectively posed a threat to the stability and peace of the nation's urban centers. Katz argues that to Mann the results of urbanization were poverty, crime and vice. Civilization was threatened by the rapid and uncontrollable growth of cities, and Mann viewed it as an urgent duty for the schools to save "a considerable portion of the rising generation from falling back into the conditions of half-barbarism or of savage life." The increase in the concentration of population, combined with the multiplication of "artificial wants" led to the increase of "temptations," which must be countered with an increase of "guards and securities," lest "society will deteriorate." Education was chief among these guards and securities (Katz, 1968, p. 41). Sectarian schools could not answer this need, because they were "particularly divisive," hence the requirement to find a common nonsectarian morality for the schools to espouse (Church & Sedlak, 1976, p. 90).

A VIEW OF MANN'S PHILOSOPHY

A brief treatment of Mann's philosophy as it relates to moral education is in order before focusing on his views toward and efforts to implement moral education during his twelve year career as Secretary of the State Board of Education. Cremin maintains that Mann saw public education as a "moral enterprise," in which "education, philanthropy and republicanism can combine to allay all of the wants and shortcomings which have traditionally beset human civilization." This "popular education" was the "only foundation on which republican government can securely rest" and was "essentially one of moral education" (Cremin, 1959, pp. 5, 7).

Schooling, Mann believed, was to elevate morality, to bring about a needed revolution in character, which would result in the enthronement of the "ideas of justice, truth, benevolence, and reverence ... in the hearts of the people and made ascendant over conduct" (Cremin, 1980, pp. 138-139). This moral revolution was necessary for the survival of humankind; as Mann put it, "I think I restrict myself within bounds in saying that so far as I have observed in this life, ten men have failed from defect in morals where one man has failed from defect in intellect."[2]

The mixture of children from all social classes in the common school would bring about the kindling of a "spirit of mutual unity and respect which the strains and cleavages of adult life could never destroy," Mann believed. Hence social harmony was the "primary goal of the school" (Cremin, 1959, p. 8). Social harmony would inevitably lead to the larger goal of social progress, brought about by popular education as the "great equalizer," a vivid reflection of Mann's "limitless faith in the perfectibily of human life and institutions" (p. 8) There was "no end to the social good which might be derived from the common school" (p. 9).

Mann presented two solutions to the question of what can be the moral foundations of a common educational program in a religiously diverse society. This question, Cremin (1959) notes, was "central to the common school and remained so ever since" (p. 12). The first of these two solutions was to accept "common principles" from all creeds that all could agree with, such as the "Fatherhood of God" (p. 13). The second prong was to be found in the doctrine of phrenology. Phrenologists held that thirty-seven faculties made up the mind, and these "govern the attitudes and actions of the individual." Desirable actions should be cultivated through exercise and undesirable wiped out by disuse. As a phrenology adherent, Mann believed that "morals can be taught outside of their historic context in particular religious doctrines." Thus:

> *public*—or common—schools can teach such publicly accepted virtues as brotherly love, kindness, generosity, amiability, and others; leaving to home and church the task of teaching the differing *private* sectarian creeds which sanction these virtues. (Cremin, 1959, pp. 13-14)

Public control of schooling would be maintained through civic agencies, thus guaranteeing adherence to its "ultimate purpose, which for Mann was always first and foremost moral" (Cremin, 1959, p. 20).

A word about poverty and its impact on people's morals. Mann believed that poverty and ignorance threatened the self-preservation of mankind, and it behooved the upper classes to see to the education of the lower if they wished to be safe:

> As a famine teaches mankind to be industrious and provident, so do these great developments teach the more favored classes of society that they can never be safe while they neglect the welfare of any portion of their social inferiors.[3]

Pauperism, Mann felt, would be eliminated within "two or three generations by more and better public schools" (Curti, 1959, p. 122). The elimination of poverty was crucial because poverty bred barbarity ("poverty casts its victims into heaps, and stows them away in cellars and garrets").[4]

HORACE MANN'S POSITION ON MORAL EDUCATION

As Secretary of the State Board, Mann made twelve annual reports. He also wrote and lectured on his beloved common school, and the prominent place moral education held in it.

The Early Years, 1837-1840

In his first report in 1837, Mann addressed the fundamental role of moral education in the context of the needs of the common schools. He wrote that the schools' graduates "may be emancipated" only after that state had "secured for all its children, that basis of knowledge and morality, which is indispensable to its own security" (Mann, 1838, p. 55). The "elevation of the common schools" was the only "remedy and preventive" of the polemics which arose from separate sectarian schools, which had led to such "disastrous consequences" as "social, interminable warfare" in England and would do so in Massachusetts (p. 57).

Mann, addressing the role of teachers in the common schools, reminded his readers that the law of the Commonwealth stated:

> It shall be the duty of all instructors of youth, to exert their best endeavors to impress on the minds of children and youth, committed to their care and instruction, the principles of piety, justice and a sacred regard to truth, love to their country, humanity and universal benevolence, sobriety, industry and frugality, chastity, moderation and temperance, and those other virtues, which are the ornaments of human society, and the basis upon which a republican constitution is founded; and it shall be the duty of such instructors, to endeavor to lead their pupils, as their ages and capacities will admit, into a clear understanding of the tendency of the above mentioned virtues to preserve and perfect a republican constitution, and secure the blessings of liberty, as well as to promote their future happiness, and also to point out to them the evil tendency of the opposite vices. (Mann, 1838, p. 59)

Teachers, Mann argued, should be appointed who would represent a "fulfillment of the elevated purposes contemplated by the law." Yet, they should avoid converting the school into an "engine of religious proselytism" (Mann, 1838, pp. 60-61). No one, he maintained, could deny the "indispensableness of moral instruction and training":

> Entirely to discard the inculcation of the great doctrines of morality and of natural theology has a vehement tendency to drive mankind into opposite extremes.... Against a tendency to these fatal extremes, the beautiful and sublime truths of ethics and of natural religion have a posing power. (p. 62)

It was the duty of common school teachers to systematically instruct their students in their familial and civic duties. Accordingly, he wrote:

> Let education, then, teach children this great truth, written as it is on the fore-front of the universe, that God has so constituted this world, into which He has sent them, that whatever is really and truly valuable may be possessed by all, and possessed in exhaustless abundance. (Mann, 1855a, p. 58)

In a lecture delivered in 1838 Mann spoke to the blessings of teaching:

> but to breathe pure and exalted sentiments into young and tender hearts.... To be the former of wise and great minds, is as much more noble than to be wise and great, as the creative is higher than the created....The tendencies of virtue are self-perpetuating and self-increasing. (Mann, 1855b, pp. 74-75)

That Mann regarded teaching as a sacred calling is clear from his words that "our duty to these children *shall be done,* shall we proclaim, in the blessed language of the Savior; —IT IS NOT THE WILL OF YOUR FATHER WHICH IS IN HEAVEN THAT ONE OF THESE LITTLE ONES SHOULD PERISH" (Mann, 1855b, p. 113). Education, he contended, was "such a culture of our moral affections and religious susceptibilities, as, in the course of Nature and Providence, shall lead to a subjection or conformity of all our appetites, propensities, and sentiments to the will of Heaven."[5] Writing in the *Common School Journal,* which he founded and for which he served as editor, Mann propounded the perspective of that journal, a perspective that embraced moral education. It will, he said:

> explain, and as far as possible, enforce upon all parents, guardians, teachers, and school officers their respective duties toward the rising generation. It will also address to children and youth all intelligible motives to obey the laws of physical health, to cultivate "moral behavior," ... and to advance moral and religious sentiments into ascendancy and control over animal and selfish propensities ... it will be kept entirely aloof from partisanship in politics, and sectarianism in religion, vindicating, and commending to practice, only the great and fundamental truths of civil and social obligation, of moral and religious duty. (Mann, 1974b, p. 1080)

Mann's third annual report dealt mainly with the necessity of having free libraries in a republican government (Cremin, 1959, p. 44). In 1839 he also delivered a lecture on "The Necessity of Education in a Republican Government," in which he put forth some of his views on moral education. If we look at a human as a "citizen in a free government," and "consider how a virtuous or a vicious education tends to fit or unfit him ... you will catch one more glimpse of the importance" of education. But if we expand our views to include the "immortal destinies" of humankind then we will be "awed, amazed, overpowered, by the thought, that we have been created and placed in a system where the soul's eternal flight may be made higher or lower by those who plume its tender wings and direct its early course" (Mann, 1855c, pp. 119-120). The moral responsibility incumbent on society to provide an uplifting kind of education to its children was an awesome responsibility with dire consequences if neglected:

> If this dread responsibility for the fate of our children be disregarded, how, when called upon, in the great eventful day, to give an account of the manner in which our earthly duties have been discharged, can we expect to escape the condemnation: "Inasmuch as ye have not done it to one of the least of these, ye have not done *It* to me." (Mann, 1855c, p. 162)

Mann focused more of his attention on moral education in 1840. In his fourth report, a goodly portion of which dealt with teachers, he opined that the "school room and its play-ground, next to the family table, are the places where the selfish propensities come into most direct collision with social duties." Thus the importance of the "manners of the teacher," if "a right direction" is to be given the growing mind (Mann, 1841, p. 57). "On the indispensable, all-controlling requisite of moral character," Mann wrote that he had "but a single suggestion to make," in addition to those that had been made throughout the reports. The suggestion related to the responsibility to those who give "letters of recommendation, or certificates of character, to candidates for schools" (pp. 57-58). He recognized the potential problems associated with declining to recommend a candidate for teaching based on lack of knowledge or of a teacher candidate's character or evidence of bad character, but felt that the "vast moment" of the "moral influence of teachers upon the rising generation" should not be sacrificed to any other consideration. Only those with good character should "be installed over the pure minds of the young, as their guide and exemplar." Indeed, "if none but teachers of pure tastes, of good manners, of exemplary morals, had ever gained admission into our schools, neither the school rooms, nor their appurtenances would have been polluted, as some of them now are" (p. 59). With a "single voice," Mann declared, the school committees have urged, insisted, demanded, "as a single voice coming from a single heart," that "the great axioms of Christian morality shall be sedulously taught, and that the teachers shall themselves, be patterns of the virtues, they are required to inculcate" (p. 59).

The year 1840 also witnessed several lectures that Mann gave on education, in which he emphasized the moral character of education. In one, he maintained that education was carrying on God's word; it was not *"optimal"* but was *"indispensable,"* it was not "merely *commended* to us as a means of promoting public and private welfare, but *commanded,* as the only safeguard against such a variety and extent of calamities as no nation on earth has ever suffered" (Mann, 1855d, p. 165).

The Middle Years, 1841-1844

Mann's fifth annual report in 1841 once again dealt with the process of approving teacher candidates. The first and "indispensable condition of approval" was *"moral education"* (1842, p. 40). He also lectured on the overall responsibility of the "Common School system," to cultivate in students a:

> sacred regard for truth; to keep them unspotted from the world, that is, uncontaminated by its vices; to train them up to the love of god and the love of man; to make the perfect example of Jesus Christ lovely in their eyes; and to give to all so much religious instruction as is compatible with the rights of others and with the genius of our government... which, in a Protestant and republican country, is the acknowledged birth-right of every human being. (1855e, p. 263)

Mann's sixth report, issued in 1842, was concerned in the main with health and physical education (Cremin, 1959, p. 54). One of his compatriots in the common school movement penned that year that *"The Common School is common, not as the school for poor men's children, but as the light and the air are common. It ought to be the best school because it is the first school; and in all good works the beginning is one half"* (quoted in Tyack, 1967, p. 125).

Cremin (1959) points out that Mann went abroad in 1843 to visit the schools of Europe. He returned with glowing comments about the Pestalozzian method that infuriated the Boston schoolmasters (p. 54). His belief that morality and religion were inseparable is clear from the following statement in his seventh report:

> But, it will be said that this grand result, in Practical Morals, is a consummation of blessedness that can never be attained without religion; and that no community will ever be religious, without a Religious Education. Both of these propositions, I regard as eternal and immutable truths.[6]

Mann treats a number of subjects in his eighth report that deal with what Cremin (1959) calls the "multifarious problems which beset a growing public school system" (p. 56). He concludes this report with a section on vocal music, which, he asserted, promotes health, intellectual exercises, and above all, advances "social and moral influences" that "far transcend, in value, all its physical or intellectual utilities" (Mann, 1845, pp. 124-126). Music held a "natural relationship or affinity with peace, hope, affection, generosity, charity, devotion. There is also a natural repugnance between music and fear, envy, malevolence, misanthropy" (p. 126).

Vocal music, accompanied by appropriate song books, were of crucial, indispensable importance in the moral development of children:

> The literary character and moral sentiment of the poetry which children learn, will have an abiding effect upon them through life—or rather, it would be more correct to say, they will constitute a part of their moral nature, during their existence. While all poetry for children, therefore, should be intelligible and comprehensible by them, it should be select in diction, beautiful and graceful in style, and harmonious in versification. It should be such, in all points, as, in after-life, will never offend a mature and cultivated taste. In sentiment, it should inculcate all kindly and social feelings; the love of external nature; regard and sympathy for domestic animals; consideration and benevolence towards every sentient thing, whether it flies, or creeps, or swims; all filial, all brotherly and sisterly affections; respect for age; compassion for the sick, the ignorant, the destitute, and for those who suffer under a privation of the senses or of reason; the love of country, and that philanthropy which looks beyond country, and holds all contemporaries and all posterity in its wide embrace; a passion for duty and a homage for all men who do it; and emphatically should it present such religious views as will lead children to fulfil the first great commandment–to love the Lord their god with all their heart, and with all their soul, and with all their mind. (pp. 131-132)

The Later Years, 1845-1848

As Cremin (1959) has observed, Mann's ninth annual report, which covered the year 1845, focused on the primacy of moral over intellectual education (p. 57). In the report, Mann attested to the tie-up between the common school and republican government:

> The great moral attributes of self-government cannot be born and matured in a day; and if school children are not trained to it, we only prepare ourselves for disappointment, if we expect it from grown men.[7]

Schools were called on to avoid the extremes of despotism and license, else they will remain unfitted until they have become "morally acclimated to our institutions, to exercise the rights of a freeman."[8]

Mann credited the State Board with contributing to the moral training of children:

> Directly and indirectly, the influences of the Board of Education have been the means of increasing, to a great extent, the amount of religious instruction given in our schools.

Moral training, or the application of religious principles to the duties of life, should be its inseparable accompaniment. No community can long subsist, unless it has religious principles as the foundation of moral action, nor unless it has moral action as the superstructure of religious principle.[9]

He asked the Board a series of questions that included a volley that zeroed in on the effectiveness, or lack thereof, of moral education in the Commonwealth's schools:

Has the moral nature of the young been so neglected that the groups of happy children now sporting around us, will, as so many of their fathers have done, go forth to depredate upon the property of the community, to embezzle private funds, to commit peculation upon private revenues, to become traitorous recipients of honorable trust, to corrupt innocence, to fill the land with the woes of intemperance, to vilify sacred reputations, to destroy innocent lives, to crowd prisons and other receptacles of crime and infamy, and at last, after inflicting a life of curses upon a world they should have blessed, to lie down in a dishonored grave?—or, on the other hand, have the reason and conscience of these children been so successfully cultivated, that, when they come upon the stage of life, they will be able to shake off the gigantic evils which have fastened themselves upon society, and are impairing the value of all that makes life desirable? (Mann, 1846, p. 20)

The primacy of the moral over intellectual education was repeated in a different vein later in this report. Mann (1846) wrote:

It becomes then, a momentous question, whether the children in our schools are educated in reference to themselves and their private interests only, or with a regard to the great social duties and prerogatives that await them in after-life. Are they so educated that when they grow up, they will make better philanthropists and Christians, or only grander savages?—for, however loftily the intellect of man may have been gifted, however skillfully it may have been trained, if it be not guided by a sense of justice, a love of mankind and a devotion to duty, its possessor is only a more splendid, as he is a more dangerous barbarian. (pp. 60-61)

Mann reported that "nothing has given me so much pleasure" as reading the Reports of the school committees that have given "prominence" to the "subject of Moral Education; and the sincerity, the earnestness and the persistence with which they have vindicated its claims to be regarded as an indispensable part of all Common School instruction" (1846, p. 65). Notwithstanding all of the efforts on behalf of moral education in the schools, Mann wondered whether there were not "moral means for the renovation of mankind which have never yet been applied?" He worried that a "large class of men seem to have lost that moral sense," and inquired if "some more powerful agency cannot be put in requisition to impart a higher moral tone to the public mind;—to enthrone the great ideas of justice, truth, benevolence and reverence, in the breast of people, and give them a more authoritative sway over conduct, than they have ever yet possessed" (pp. 67,69).

He opined that it was "too obvious to need remark, that the main tendency of institutions and of a state of society, like those here depicted, is to cultivate the intellect and inflame the passions, rather than to teach humility and lowliness of the heart." The present century had added to that tendency: "In the Moral Price Current of the nation, has not Intellect been rising, while Virtue has been sinking in value?" (Mann, 1846, p. 75). And, he asked, who will say:

> even of the most favored portions of the country, that their advancement in moral excellence, in probity, in purity, and in the practical exemplification of the virtues of a Christian life, has kept pace with their progress in outward conveniences and embellishments? Can Virtue recount as many triumphs in the moral world, as Intellect has won in the material? (pp. 75-76)

Turning to the schools, Mann asked what could be done? The first thing was to choose school committee members who would "scrutinize as diligently the moral character of the proposed teacher, and his ability to impart moral instruction, as they do his literary attainments." Freedom from vice on the part of teachers was not enough. A teacher needed a "positive determination towards good, evinced by his life, as well as by his language." Society could be "happy without knowledge; but it is not in the power of any human imagination to picture to itself a form of life, where we could be happy without virtue" (Mann, 1846, pp. 77-78).

One last episode in Mann's ninth report, which emphasized the primacy of the moral over the intellectual in the common schools, will have to suffice. Moral virtues, he contended, cannot be "exhibited on the black-board, but they are graven upon the heart." They were "written in the Book of Life." Disdaining vulgar display, they were "lowly and retiring." The installation of true virtue in the character of students was the preeminent charge of the teacher (pp. 80-81).

Cremin (1959) observes that Mann's tenth report consisted in a "general discourse on the Massachusetts schools" (p. 59). Free schools were "indispensable to the continuance of a republican government," which was superior to all other forms of government, a reality in which citizens "religiously believe." The "only basis of republican institutions," free schools produced an educated people which was a "more industrious and productive people." They led to the instillation of the "higher instincts" of character in the young.[10] Indeed, the child has a "far higher claim" to be "rescued from the infamy and perdition of vice and crime" via the common school than to have "shelter to protect him from the destroying elements." Likening the denial of an education to infanticide, Mann claimed that: "All moralists agree, nay all moralists maintain, that a man is as responsible for his omissions as for his commissions ... they who refuse to enlighten the intellect of the rising generation, are guilty of degrading the human race!" They were "training up incendiaries and madmen to destroy property and life, and to invade and pollute the sanctuaries of society."[11] Mann held that a society had the moral responsibility for the education of all of its children, with terrible retribution to come if it didn't make:

> provision for the free education of all its children, dares the certain vengeance of Heaven; and in the squalid forms of poverty and destitution, in the scourges of violence and misrule, in the heart-destroying corruptions of licentiousness and debauchery, and in political profligacy and legalized perfidy,—in all the blended and mutually aggravated crimes of civilization and of barbarism, will be sure to feel the terrible retributions of its delinquency.[12]

Why, Mann asked, should a society preserve the "natural life" of an infant, if it did not provide him or her with free schools? Every state, he argued, "is bound to enact a code of laws legalizing and enforcing Infanticide, or a code of laws establishing Free Schools!"[13]

The year 1846 was not a happy one for common school advocates in New England. Connecticut, where Mann's colleague, Henry Barnard, occupied a position parallel to that of Mann's in Massachusetts, abolished its state board of education. Mann greeted that action with unbounded dismay, terming it a paralysis of moral good and an undoing of extensive moral influence which the common schools had provided in that state,[14]

In his introduction, Cremin (1959) writes that Mann's words in this report show that Mann believes that education is the "centre and circumference" of the "wheel of Progress" (p. 78). Indeed, Mann himself gives his topic the title of "THE POWER OF COMMON SCHOOLS TO REDEEM THE STATE FROM SOCIAL VICES AND CRIMES" (Mann, 1848, p. 39). Subsequently, Mann argues that the "redeeming and transforming influences" of the "Common school system" will "expel ninety-nine hundredths of all the vices and crimes under which society now mourns and agonizes." The "crowning beauty" of the system was that "Christian men of every faith may cordially unite in carrying forward the work of reform" (p. 87). Instructors at all levels in Massachusetts were to:

> exert their best endeavors to impress on the minds of children and youth, committed to their care and instruction, the principles of piety, justice, and a sacred regard to truth, love to their country, humanity and universal benevolence, sobriety, industry and frugality, chastity, moderation and tem-

perance, and those other virtues which are the ornament of human society, and the basis upon which a republican constitution is founded; and it shall be the duty of such instructors to endeavor to lead their pupils, as their ages and capacities will admit, into a clear understanding of the tendency of the above mentioned virtues to preserve and perfect a republican constitution, and secure the blessings of liberty, as well as to promote their future happiness, and also to point out to them the evil tendency of the opposite vices. (pp. 89-90)

Unfortunately, according to Mann, the "people did not yet seem to see" the savings that virtue-producing education would provide, namely, the "cost of legislating against criminals"; the "building of houses of correction, and jails and penitentiaries"; constituting a "beneficent kind of insurance" (Mann, 1846, pp. 101-102). Manufacturers, in particular, would benefit because the "children who had enjoyed such a school development and training, as we are now supposing," would "go into the mills, after the completion of their educational course, with physical and intellectual ability to help, and with a moral inability to harm, which, of itself, would far more than compensate for the loss of their previous absence" (p. 117). For, with workers so educated, a manufacturer could have:

all his operatives transformed at once into men and women of high intelligence and unswerving morality; to have them become so faithful and honest, that they would always turn out the greatest quantity and the best quality of work, without the trouble and expense of watching, and weighing, and counting, and superintending; that they would be as careful of his machinery as though it were their own; that they would never ask or accept more in payment than their just due; that they would always consult their employer's interest, and never sacrifice it from motives of personal ease, or gain, or ill will. (p. 117)

In his conclusion to this report Mann delivers what he terms a consideration which he "cannot forbear to introduce" for all those who "desire to ameliorate the condition of mankind," viz., that "Education encompasses, pervades, and overrules all their efforts; grants them whatever triumphs they may achieve, and sets bounds to their successes which they cannot overpass" (p. 133). Without education, the appeals of advocates of moral reform and missionary societies fall on "stony hearts" and speak to "adders' ears." But by uniting on behalf of "universal education," only then can "the wheel of Progress move harmoniously and resistlessly forward" (pp. 134-135).

It is Cremin's (1959) contention that Mann's final report, his twelfth, written after he had won election to Congress, was "far and away the most inclusive and searching of the twelve documents" (p. 79). That Mann regarded popular education as a moral enterprise, with far-reaching consequences to government, is clear from his utterance that "Never will wisdom preside in the halls of legislation and its profound utterances be recorded on the pages of the statute book, until Common schools ... shall create a more far-seeing intelligence and a purer morality than has ever existed among communities of men" (Mann, 1849, p. 84). The common school had the potentiality of becoming the "most effective and benignant of all the forces of civilization."[15] This was especially true for a republican government, in which the "legislators are a mirror reflecting the moral countenance of their constituents." In fact, he wrote, "woe to the Republic that rests upon no better foundation than ignorance, selfishness, and passion."[16]

"Community without a conscience would soon extinguish itself," he maintained. Using history, which recorded the failings of humankind to prove his point, Mann argued that "there is one experiment which has never yet been tried"; *"Train up a child in the way he should go, and when he is old he will not depart from it."*[17] Education had "never yet been brought to bear with one hundredth part of its potential force, upon the natures of children, and, through them, upon the character of men, and of the race." Looking at the common school, he penned as follows:

> Here, then, is a new agency whose powers are but just beginning to be understood, and whose mighty energies, hitherto, have been but feebly invoked; and yet, from our experience, limited and imperfect as it is, we do know that, far beyond any other earthly instrumentality, it is comprehensive and decisive.[18]

Mann recognized that "grave charges" had been brought against the common school, on the grounds that it excluded religion, and its "common exponent," the Bible, or at least the tendency to "derogate from its authority, and destroy its influence."[19] He contended that there had never been any thought to "exclude the Bible or religious instruction" from the schools. Rather, it was sectarianism which was to be kept out of popular education. It was this exclusion that led the advocates of "parochial or sectarian schools," which constituted a "rival system" to free schools, the latter designed for the "whole people," to claim that the common school was "anti-Christian."[20]

Since common schools were aimed at benefitting all people, taxes could be levied in their support, which was not possible for schools designed to serve but a fraction of the populace. This taxation was legitimate, since the common school served as a *"preventive* means against dishonesty, against fraud, and against violence; on the same principle that ... taxed to support criminal courts as a *punitive* means against the same offenses."[21]

The Bible, Mann wrote, was in the schools by "common consent." It was there because "Christianity has no other authoritative expounder." The Bible had been "restored" in the common schools; sectarian instruction had been, "at least to a great extent, ceased to be given." Thus, the common schools were indeed religious, because:

> If the Bible, then, is the exponent of Christianity; if the Bible contains the communications, precepts, and doctrines, which make up the religious system, called and known as Christianity; if the Bible makes known those truths, which, according to the faith of Christians, are able to make men wise unto salvation; and if this Bible is in the schools, how can it be said that Christianity is excluded from the schools; wherever the Bible might go, there the system of Christianity must be.[22]

The moral, nonsectarian Christian education as espoused by Mann imposed duties on teachers. Mann wrote that Massachusetts law "explicitly and solemnly" enjoined all teachers to:

> impress on the minds of children and youth committed to their care and instruction, the principles of piety, justice, and a sacred regard for truth, love to their country, humanity and universal benevolence, sobriety, industry, and frugality, chastity, moderation, and temperance, and those other virtues which are the ornament of human society, and the basis upon which a republican constitution is founded.[23]

These "virtues and those duties towards God and man, are inculcated in our schools," Mann held, and the common school system called on "resident ministers of the Gospel" to assist in bringing a youngsters to the practice *of* the virtues enumerated above.[24]

CONCLUSION

In their excellent work on the history *of* American education, Wayne Urban and Jennings Wagoner (2000) write that moral education comprised the "heart of the curriculum" for Mann (p. 103). The common school, they state, aimed to educate workers to a particular brand of morality, however, one that:

> infused with respect for property, for the work ethic, and for the wisdom of the property owners. This respect and docility were equated with morality, implying that those workers who acted in opposition to owners of capital and property were immoral. Strikes and other crimes could be avoided if common schools flourished. (p. 107)

Rush Welter (1962) put it this way, "The one major point in democratic criticism of the existing social order that Mann refused to accept was the charge that some men are poor because other men are rich" (p. 100).

Joel Spring (1997) argues that the "primary result" of the common school reform was not educating an ever-increasing percentage of children, but rather bringing "education into the service of the public goals of government and creating new forms of school organization." The common school movement, he maintains, "established and standardized state systems of education designed to achieve specific public policies" (p. 97). For Mann, the common school movement was similar to a "religious crusade," with the "salvation of society" as its goal (p. 99). It consisted of:

> a common piety rooted in Scripture, a common civility revolving around the history and the state documents of a Christian Republic, and a common intellectual culture conveyed via reading, writing, spelling, arithmetic, English grammar, geography, singing, and some health education. (Cremin, 1980, p. 140)

The movement for Mann was, as Jonathan Messerli (1972, p. 249) put it, a "holy and patriotic crusade."

The crusade was necessary in Mann's view, Michael Katz argues, because urbanization had resulted in poverty, crime, and vice. Civilization itself was threatened by the rapid and uncontrollable growth of cities, which made it an urgent duty to save a "considerable portion of the rising generation from falling back into the conditions of half-barbarous or of savage life."[25] A common school education would make it possible to educate leaders so they will avoid "demagoguery and mob rule," threats that were posed by the populous cities. The values to be stressed in these schools in order for these catastrophies to be avoided in urban areas were "hard work, effort, honesty, diligence, thrift, literacy, respect for property, and respect for reason" (Gutek, 1986, pp. 96-97).

The common school was THE answer to the urban problems of poverty and all forms of social evil. Cubberley (1919) maintains that Mann was the "first prominent educator in America to meet and answer the religious onslaught" pushed by the denominationalists (p. 195). Mann described his religious crusade that was embodied in the common school system:

> Reverently, it recognizes and affirms the sovereign rights of the creator; sedulously and sacredly it guards the religious rights of the creature; while it seeks to remove all hindrances, and to supply all furtherances to a filial and paternal communion between man and his Maker.... It is a *Free* school system. It knows no distinction between rich and poor, of bond and free, or between those who, in the imperfect light of this world, are seeking through different avenues to reach the gate of heaven. Without money and without

price, it throws open its doors, and spreads the table of its bounty, for all the children of the State. Like the sun, it shines, not only upon the good, but upon the evil that they may become good, and, like the rain, its blessings descend, not only upon the just, but upon the unjust, that their injustice may depart from them and be known no more.[26]

Considering statements such as the above, Merle Curti (1959) writes that:

> In short, Mann's moral earnestness and faith in individualism led him to believe that, were character training resorted to in accordance with the principles of phrenology, the old-time New England virtues of honesty, frugality, and uprightness would prevail even in a changing and unfriendly world. (p. 123)

The common school version of education would rid the world of "all-encompassing misanthropy, the Law of Caste, which includes within itself every form of inequity, because it lives by the practical denial of Human Brotherhood" (Curti, 1959, p. 122).

Curti contends that Mann and his contemporaries overemphasized the effectiveness of moral behavior implanted by reason. Mann didn't seem to realize, Curti states, that "abstract training in virtues in schools could not, in the majority of cases, compete successfully with incompatible practices in the everyday world." Mann also "failed to understand" that the competitive system for profits was too strong for rational morality to survive in the lives of most people (p. 125).

Writing in 1911, Hinspale presents a relative naive assessment of the effect, then and in the future, of Mann's moral and universal education:

> He may have exaggerated the healing power of knowledge; nevertheless, if the public schools, at any time, become weak and sickly, a new baptism in the thought of him who did so much to extend, and improve them will be their best restorative.... But his great theme was the relation of intellectual and moral knowledge to human well-being, individual and social. Here his faith never faltered, his ardor never cooled. In no other name did he trust for the safety of society. A confirmed rationalist, he looked with supreme confidence to the healing power of popular intelligence and virtue. (pp. 280, 274)

But Mann's vision did endure in American society, for, as Spring (1997) notes, "Since the mid-1800s, the school has continually been seen as a means of eliminating poverty, crime, and social problems" (p. 106).

In his justly-lauded book, *Piety in the Public School*, Michaelsen (1970) concludes that Mann believed that the common school was the one institution that could achieve moral advancement and that its primary task was moral in nature. He opines that Mann's motto might well have been "Common religion for the common school" (pp. 76-79). Or, perhaps his motto should be cast in his own words in his valedictory address at Antioch College in 1852: *"Be ashamed to die until you have won some victory for humanity."*[27] Whatever motto is selected, there is no doubt that for Horace Mann and the common school with which he is justly associated that moral education, as he conceived it, was more than prominent, it was pre-eminent and indispensable.

NOTES

1. Mann, quoted in Spring (1997, p. 100).
2. Mann, quoted in Filler (1965, p. 15).
3. Mann, quoted in Filler (1965, p. 18).
4. Mann, quoted in Katz (1968, p. 41).
5. Mann, quoted in McCluskey (1958, p. 41).
6. Mann, quoted in McCluskey (1958, p. 43).
7. Mann, quoted in Cremin (1959, p. 57).
8. Ibid.
9. Mann, quoted in McCluskey (1958, p. 43).
10. Mann, quoted in Cremin (1959, pp. 61, 75).
11. Ibid., p. 75.
12. Ibid., p. 76.
13. Ibid., p. 77.
14. Mann, quoted in Cubberley (1920, pp. 567-568).
15. Mann, quoted in Cremin (1959, p. 80).
16. Ibid., pp. 91-92.
17. Ibid., p. 100.
18. Ibid., p. 101.
19. Ibid.
20. Ibid., p. 102.
21. Ibid., p. 103.
22. Ibid., pp. 105-106.
23. Ibid., p. 106.
24. Ibid., p. 107.
25. Mann, quoted in Katz (1968, p. 41).
26. Mann, quoted in Cremin (1959, pp. 111-112).
27. Mann, quoted in Cohen (1974b, p. 115).

CHAPTER 5

THE ANTEBELLUM STATE NORMAL SCHOOL

INTRODUCTION

It is evident from the writings of Horace Mann, Henry Barnard and their cohorts that the creation of a special institution, controlled by the civil state, was viewed as an indispensable partner to the common school in the education of children. There were institutions, such as academies, which prepared teachers prior to the introduction of the state normal school. Indeed, normal schools did not prepare the majority of teachers even in Massachusetts throughout the nineteenth century. The private institutions, if the academies may be called such, and the liberal arts colleges were not seen as satisfactory by Mann et al. Teachers institutes that lasted for a few weeks, when under the control of the state, were accepted as sort of a "fall back" to the normal school, whose terms usually ran for at least a year. Mann and his allies looked to Europe for models of institutions designed solely for the preparation of teachers for public schools, institutions that would instill the moral virtues necessary for a republican democracy. Hence the rise of the normal school.

Moral Education in America's Schools: The Continuing Challenge, 49–57
Copyright © 2005 by Information Age Publishing
All rights of reproduction in any form reserved.

EARLY BEGINNINGS

In 1820 the Rev. James Carter, who has been called the "Father of the Massachusetts School System and of Normal Schools" proposed an "institution for the training of teachers" (Cubberley, 1919, p. 287). Several years later, in 1825, Walter E. Johnson called for the establishment of "schools for teachers," such as existed in Prussia, where "its beneficial influence is seen in every aspect of society."[1] Carter echoed similar sentiments the next year in his "Plan for a Teacher-Training Seminary" in which he declared that the said institution would be a "very important part of the free school system," which should "emphatically be the State institution" and "under the direction of the State." It would serve as an "engine to sway the public sentiment, the public morals, and the public religion, more powerful than any other in the possession of government."[2] As Merle Borrowman (1965) observed, the American normal school, "inspired by European models," developed as an "intimate companion to the American common school" (p. 19).

The pressure to create state normal schools increased along with that for the common school. For instance, in 1838 Calvin Stowe argued that the "management of the human mind, particularly the youthful mind, is the most delicate task ever committed to the hand of man." This task should not be "left to mere instinct," he contended, for teachers should have "at least as careful a training as our lawyers and doctors," and that training should be under the direction of the civil state.[3] Meanwhile, in Massachusetts, Edmund Dwight offered $10,000 for the establishment of a normal school, if the legislature would provide a matching sum. In 1838 the State Board of Education petitioned the legislature successfully for such an appropriation (Glenn, 1988, p. 137). Two years later, Mann, speaking at the dedication of a building for the normal school in 1840 in Bridgewater maintained:

> I believe Normal schools to be a new instrumentality in the advancement of the race.... Without them Free schools ... would be shorn of their strength and their healing power, and would at length become mere charity schools.... Neither the art of printing, nor the trial by jury, nor a free press, nor free suffrage, can long exist, to any beneficial and salutary purpose, without schools for the training of teachers.[4]

A contemporary of Mann's, the Rev. Charles Brooks, was of like mind. Brooks claimed that "Teachers, yes I say teachers, have an inconceivable and paramount agency in changing the destinies of the world." Competent teachers, "whose learning is sanctified by piety, and whose characters are all radiant with love, will assuredly impart their nobility of soul to their pupils." Further, their "spiritual magnetism" will reflect through their "daily lessons some moral suggestion, moral hint, moral maxim, or moral query, thus giving moral polarity to everything."[5]

The first such institution opened in Lexington, Massachusetts on July 3, 1839 with "three young ladies enrolled as students" (Harper, 1939, p. 7). The Rev. Cyrus Peirce, a veteran educator, was the school's principal. That the moral role of the school was uppermost in Peirce's mind is clear from his "Journal" entry of March 4, 1840 in which he preaches that "if children are taught but One thing, let it be their duty.... If you make them anything, make them good!" (O'Leary, 1950, p. 28).

THE POSITION OF HORACE MANN

Widely regarded as the "Father of the Common School," Horace Mann was firmly committed to the position that the civil state had to be in control of the education of teachers if the goals of the common school were to be met. He accepted teacher institutes as an alternative to normal schools, should the latter be unattainable. Nonetheless, state-run normal schools remained the ideal place for teachers for the common school to be prepared in order for the moral goals of public education to be met. Mann's writings, especially his Annual Reports to the Board, provide ample evidence in support of this contention.

Writing on the "History, Regulations and Curriculum of the First Normal Schools: Narrative and Documents," Mann held that to be admitted to the normal school candidates "must furnish satisfactory evidence of good intellectual capacity, and of high moral character and principles."[6] He had elaborated on the moral responsibilities of teachers earlier in his "First Annual Report" to the State Board in 1837, referring to the law in Massachusetts that required:

> all instructors of youth, to exert their best endeavors to impress on the minds of children and youth committed to their care and instruction, the principles of piety, justice and a sacred regard to truth, love to their country, humanity and universal benevolence, sobriety, industry and frugality, chastity, moderation and temperance, and those other virtues, which are the ornament of human society, and the basis upon which a republican constitution is founded; and it shall be the duty of such instructors, to endeavor to lead their pupils, ... into a clear understanding of the tendency of the above mentioned virtues to preserve and perfect a republican constitution, and secure the blessings of liberty, as well as to promote their future happiness, and also to point out to them the evil tendency of the opposite vices.[7]

In that "First Report" Mann alleged that the lack of proper teachers was due to insufficient compensation, thus hurting the "sacred cause of education." Addressing the exclusion of denominational religious instruction from the schools, he averred that its very absence "enhances and magnifies, a thousand fold, the indispensableness of moral instruction and training." Improperly prepared teachers, obsessed with the "culture of the intellect mainly," failed to recognize that "children have moral natures and social affections." The same could be said for some of the manuals in use in the schools, which deal with commas and spelling but omit teaching the "laws of forbearance under injury, of sympathy with misfortune, of impartiality in our judgments of men, of love and fidelity to truth...."[8]

Mann's "Second Report," like the First, continued to use religious/moral language in describing the activities of teachers and the schools. He termed females engaged in teaching to be participating in a "divinely appointed ministry" in the "sacred temple of education."[9] He elaborated on the reasons why women teachers were better for children than men in his "Fourth Report," in addition to emphasizing the indispensability of the teacher being a moral person. Women are "more mild and gentle," he wrote. They are "endowed by nature with stronger parental impulses," and their "minds are less withdrawn from their employment." They are "also of purer morals" than men, far less likely to engage in "profanity" and "intemperance."[10] The woman teacher's influence "is of a moral character," flourishing "amid peace and union." She will transfer into the "minds of her pupils, purer elements, both of conduct and character, which will extend their refining and harmonizing influences far outward into society, and far onward into fraternity."[11] All youths will be taught "good behavior" from teachers who "must be virtuous," possessing the "all-controlling requisite of moral character."[12] School committees, he averred, are "sentinels stationed at the door of every schoolhouse in the state, to see that no teacher ever crosses the threshold, who is not clothed, from the crown of his head to the sole of his feet, in garments of virtue."[13] The consequences of moral teachers were momentous: "If none but teachers of pure tastes, of good manners, of exemplary morals, had ever gained admission into our schools," the schools would not now be "polluted" as some of them are, with "ribald inscriptions" and "cravings of such obscene emblems" that would "make a heathen blush."[14]

Mann's "Fifth Report" did not refer to normal schools. However, he addressed the matter of the moral character of teachers when he wrote that "the school committee shall require full and satisfactory evidence of the good moral character of all instructors who may be employed in the public schools of their town...."[15] Mann highlighted the theme of moral responsibility that is incumbent on all society in his "Sixth Report," issued in 1841, with remarks taken from his Fourth of July address in Boston:

Remember the child. Remember the youth. Remember that whatever station in life you may fill, these mortals—these immortals—are your care. Devote, EXPEND, consecrate yourselves to the holy work of their improvement.... Learn only how the ignorant may learn; how the innocent may be preserved; the vicious reclaimed; ... *And go forth,* and TEACH THIS PEOPLE. For, in the name of the living God, it must be proclaimed that licentiousness shall be the liberty; and violence and chicanery shall be the law; and superstition and craft shall be the religion; and the self-destructive indulgence of all sensual and unhallowed passions shall be the only happiness of that people who neglect the education of their children.[16]

This charge fell squarely on the students at normal schools, who besides preparing to be the teachers of the commonwealth's children were receiving state funds to meet this challenge. They should apply themselves to their task so "they can answer the just expectations of the public, and discharge, with religious fidelity, the momentous duties to which they are called." For the "noble office of improving others," their primary obligation, their "first step of preparation is self-improvement. For those who serve at the altar of this ministry, 'the first act of worship is the purification of the worshipper.'"[17]

Lawrence Cremin (1959), referring to Mann's "Ninth Report," asserts that the report's central theme was the "primacy of moral over intellectual education" (p. 59). In the report, Mann had written that "if securing the good will of scholars is preliminary to their attainment of *knowledge*, far more important is it to the cultivation of their *moral* sentiments, and to the growth of *good habits*.[18] The connection between religious principle and moral training were "inseparable" in Mann's view: "No community can long subsist, unless it has religious principle as the foundation of moral action; nor unless it has moral action as the superstructure of religious principle."[19] Teachers, he claimed, must use morally correct motives to inspire students to moral action. Through good teachers, appropriately prepared, the state will "proclaim, in the blessed language of the Savior,—'It is not the will of your Father which is in heaven that one of these little ones should perish'" (Mann, 1969, pp. 103, 113).

The importance of the normal school and its impact on moral education had an effect on Mann's personal life. His wife, Mary Peabody Mann, penned that her husband felt free to go on their honeymoon in 1843 because he had set in "operation the most adequate means—the normal school," and put them in the hands of men who "saw the importance" of moral education in "human culture" (Glenn, 1988, p. 139). In his Twelfth, and final Report, Mann testified to the crucial role normal schools played in his overall plan for moral education in Massachusetts: "Without them, all the labors and expenditures would have yielded but a meager harvest of success," and "common schools will never prosper without normal schools" (Mann, 1849b, p. 27).

THE CANDIDATES

Candidates for admission to state normals were expected to display good moral character. For instance, in his "Fifth Report" Mann wrote that "moral character is made a first and indispensable condition of approval" of applicants. If the applicant lived close to the normal school, Mann said her character would be known; testimonials were required for those who lived at a distance (Mann, 1842, pp. 40-41). The Massachusetts Board of Education agreed. For example, in its "Seventh Report," it pronounced that "no persons" were admitted into the Lexington Normal School who did not "present certificates" and "furnish other probable evidence of their possessing ... a good moral character" (Board, 1844, p. 5).

A quality moral character in candidates was also required for admission in other states. For instance, in Connecticut under the leadership of Henry Barnard, the first imperative was "purity and strength of moral and religious character" (Harper, 1939, p. 53). In New York in 1850, candidates had to present "testimonials of good moral character." Those scrutinizing the applicants were instructed not to pay any attention to the "political opinions of applicants"; rather, the "selection should be made with reference to the *moral worth* and abilities of the candidates."[20]

INSTITUTIONAL PRACTICES

Charles Glenn observes that "Contemporary descriptions of normal schools during the nineteenth century, ... almost never fail to stress the *moral* content of the formation of future teachers." In support of this statement, Glenn quotes Samuel Grixley Howe, director of the Institution for the Blind in South Boston and an ally of Mann's as a member of the Board of Education, who wrote in 1840 that the normal school at Lexington was functioning effectively because "the moral nature is as much cultivated as the intellectual" (Glenn, 1988, pp. 134-135). Cyrus Peirce, the institution's principal, maintained in 1841 that "there are no subjects in which scholars manifest more interest than in questions of morals." One biography of Peirce stressed the "especial attention he had paid to the *moral* culture of his pupils" (p. 135). The emphasis on moral education at Lexington resulted, Glenn alleged, in its graduates' convictions as "clear and as winning as those of a teaching sister in a Catholic school" (p. 135).

Normal schools, referred to by some as "teacher seminaries," attracted the attention of the State Board of Education in its "Second Report." Referring to its curriculum the board avowed that "The principles of Christian ethics and piety, common to the different sects of Christians, will be carefully inculcated; and a portion of Scripture will be daily read in all the Normal schools established by the board" (Board, 1839, p. 6). All teachers in the state were instructed by the Board in its "Eighth Report" that Massachusetts law required them to impress on their students' minds, "the principles of piety" and "those other virtues which are the basis, upon which a republican institution is founded," virtues that were to be inculcated in the normal schools (Board, 1845, p. 16).

THE "CALLING" OF TEACHERS

We have seen how Horace Mann viewed teaching as essentially a moral enterprise, and the institutions that prepared them were expected to communicate Mann's program of moral public education. Mann was far from alone. Merle Borrowman points out that Cyrus Peirce, a Unitarian minister, felt "called" to lead a noble experiment. As Borrowman phrased it, "In its singleness of purpose, its evangelical zeal, and even its commitment to dogma, his normal school resembled the divinity schools that trained the missionaries of militant fundamentalists" (Borrowman, 1965, p. 54). While no one knows if the twenty-five adolescent girls in his first class felt a "calling," Borrowman contended that we do know that most of them "left as dedicated missionaries of public education" (p. 54). As Mary Swift, Peirce's assistant at Lexington, put it, the teaching of children is a "most serious, noble, and inspiring work" (p. 55). She looked to the teachers to remove negative impressions of the public schools by "elevating their moral standards." To do this she held that teachers "must think seriously upon the subject, and influence the pupils both by example and precept," a view for the normal schools to impart.[21]

Henry Barnard, Mann's counterpart in Connecticut, looked on teaching as second only to the ministry as a means of service (Thursfield, 1945, p. 131). Some, such as William Ellery Channing, a Unitarian minister and ethical leader, believed teaching was "a more holy calling" than the ministry (p. 131). Barnard, along with other early schoolmen, equated "professionalization with the 'awakening' of moral character," as Paul Mattingly has observed.[22] Teachers needed, and normal schools should inculcate in them during their preparation, "moral and religious purity," and "strength of character," along with good manners, "the *manners* as well as the *matters* of the Golden Rule."[23]

WOMEN TEACHERS

Horace Mann had extolled the virtues and the superiority of women teachers in both his Second and Fourth reports, as we saw above. He had company. Catherine Beecher, writing of women in general, said that "In matters pertaining to the education of their children, ... they have a superior morality." Turning to teaching, she contended that women teachers had a "crucial responsibility" in the republic to "create the elevated morality and social unity on which the successful operation of republican institutions ultimately depended." They were, she maintained, "divinely ordained and equipped by nature" to carry out this task.[24]

Henry Barnard was of like mind. Writing in 1853 he argued that women teachers were suited by nature to "bring the influences of home and society, of religion and free institutions," into the classroom. He sought women teachers of "the requisite tact, patience, mentality" to accomplish this goal (Steiner, 1919, p. 79). "Their more gentle and refined manners, purer morals" were irreplaceable assets (Downs, 1977, p. 68). Writing more than a century later, Joel Spring is less charitable in his assessment of why women were sought as teachers. As "republican mothers, and vessels of virtue," women were considered the "ideal teachers for a system of schooling that emphasized moral development." The low salaries and status of women in society, along with the "emphasis on moral exhortation" in the schools, contributed to the low status of teaching, Spring believed (1997, p. 133).

CONCLUSION

From the above, it is clear that moral education was a constant feature of the antebellum state normal school. Indeed, in the eyes of Mann and his colleagues, it was a *sine qua non* for the institution that was established for the precise purpose of preparing teachers for the common schools. Indeed, were the normal schools to abstain from fulfilling their "sacred" ministry, the very mission of the common school itself would be aborted.

NOTES

1. Quoted in Calhoun (1969, p. 175).
2. Quoted in Cohen (1970, pp. 1304-1305).
3. Quoted in Calhoun (1969, p. 197).
4. Quoted in Glenn (1988, p. 138).
5. Quoted in Ibid., p. 137.

6. Horace Mann, quoted in *The First State Normal School in America*. Cambridge, MA: Harvard University Press, 1926, p. 261.

7. Mann, in the *First Annual Report of the Board of Education together with the First Annual Report of the Secretary of the Board, Covering the Year 1837*. Boston: Dutton and Wentworth, State Printers, 1838b, p. 59.

8. Ibid., pp. 60, 62, 64.

9. Quoted in Cremin (1980, p. 146).

10. Mann, in the *Fourth Annual Report of the Board of Education, together with the Fourth Annual Report of the Secretary of the Board, Covering the Year 1840*. Boston: Dutton and Wentworth, State Printers, 1841b, p. 45.

11. Ibid., p. 46.

12. Ibid., pp. 56-58.

13. Ibid., p. 59.

14. Ibid.

15. Mann, in the *Fifth Annual Report of the Board of Education, together with the Fifth Annual Report of the Secretary of the Board, Covering the Year 1841*. Boston: Dutton and Wentworth, State Printers, 1842b, p. 40.

16. Mann, in the *Sixth Annual Report of the Board of Education together with the Sixth Annual Report of the Secretary of the Board, Covering the Year 1842*. Boston: Dutton and Wentworth, State Printers, 1843, p. 16.

17. Ibid., pp. 29, 42.

18. Mann, in the *Ninth Annual Report of the Board of Education, together with the Ninth Annual Report of the Secretary of the Board, Covering the Year 1845*. Boston: Dutton and Wentworth, State Printers, 1846b, p. 86.

19. Ibid., p. 157.

20. "An Account of the New York State Normal School at Albany 1850." In S. Cohen (1970, p. 1344).

21. "The First Term of a Student at the Lexington, Massachusetts Normal School 1839." In S. Cohen (1970, p. 1332).

22. Quoted in Downs (1977, p. 63).

23. Ibid., p. 67.

24. Quoted in Cremin (1980, p. 147).

CHAPTER 6

ANTE- AND POSTBELLUM SCHOOLING IN THE SOUTH

Virginia—A Case Study

INTRODUCTION

Charles William Dabney (1969) notes that Thomas Jefferson's "A Bill for the More General Diffusion of Knowledge," which was an inherent part of his political views, called for the Platonic concept of service to the state (pp. 4-9). Jefferson's bill, as we know, was not adopted. Rather, the Virginia General Assembly established the Literary Fund in 1810 "for the encouragement of learning." The Literary Fund, designed to provide education for the children of the indigent, was to play a prominent role in the moral education of poor white children for decades to come.

CHARLES FENTON MERCER

Charles Fenton Mercer was born in Fredericksburg, Virginia in 1778 to a prominent Virginia family (Garnett, 1909, p. 200). A Federalist who became a Whig, Mercer was active in many civic causes. He served in the Virginia House of Delegates from 1810 until 1817 when he was elected to Congress.[1] Mercer, while in the House of Delegates, sought to establish a

Moral Education in America's Schools: The Continuing Challenge, 59–73
Copyright © 2005 by Information Age Publishing

state system of primary schooling for all white Virginia children.[2] Mercer's plan was defeated, in part due to opposition from Jefferson who did not want primary education supported at the state level (V. Dabney, 1971, p. 246).

In spite of this defeat, Mercer clung to his belief of the value and importance of popular education to the republic, including its role of inculcating moral virtue. His sentiments are best expressed in his *A Discourse on Popular Education*, which was delivered at the commencement exercises of Princeton University, his alma mater, in 1826. The main theme of that *Discourse* is that the nation's happiness and well-being are based on the diffusion of virtue and intelligence among all of its citizens, a goal that can only be achieved by a system of public education. Inequality of knowledge, like the inequality of wealth, threatened the social order. A system of popular education would "operate, if not immediately, in diminishing, ultimately, as the most powerful check" on pauperism (Mercer, 1826, pp. 10-14). The "'Wealth of Nations' cannot be reckoned as a merchant counts up his ledger," Mercer said. In a republic it resides in the presence of moral virtue and intelligence among all its citizens. In America, "intelligence and moral" worth constituted "our only nobility" (pp. 36-38, 40, 76).

The role of the primary schools was to "supply those means of intelligence and moral culture, of which no member of society should be destitute," and these means should be "within reach of every citizen." Mercer pointed to the dire social consequences that were present in England due to the absence of a system of popular education. His travels in Europe led him to lament that "Alas! that any people should prefer vindictive to preventive justice; houses of correction to the village or city schools" (1826, pp. 43, 74). Mercer argued that all citizens had a "common interest" in the "improvement of mankind," just as they have such an interest in the "common defense of a common territory, against a common enemy." Public monies, obtained by taxation, were indispensable in war; likewise, they were indispensable in popular education which was necessary for the moral well-being of the community, state, and nation (pp. 20, 68).

SUPPORT FOR POPULAR EDUCATION GROWS

It was also in 1826 that William Maxwell delivered an oration at Hampden-Sydney College in Virginia in which he proclaimed that the way to improve the commonwealth was "a more general and generous education … extending to all classes and conditions … in our state" (Maxwell, 1826). A little over a decade later, another Hampden-Sydney graduate, Benjamin Mosby Smith, who had been commissioned by Governor David

Campbell to study the Prussian Primary School System, made his report to the Virginia legislature. Among the reasons for his recommendation that a state primary school system be established was the benign moral influence it would have on Virginia, with the result that whatever the cost of that system of schooling might be, it would be offset by money saved through less crime, fewer prisons, and the contribution to wealth that the schools would make. The curriculum and life of the schools would be vitalized by Religion, "not of a sect, but of the Bible" (Smith, 1839, pp. 2, 31-34).

HENRY RUFFNER

Born in 1790 in western Virginia, Henry Ruffner was ordained a Presbyterian minister and later was appointed president of Washington College in 1836 (C.W. Dabney, 1969, p. 81; Ruffner, 1904, pp. 31-90, 105). As president, Ruffner was active both outside and inside the college. He set out to teach the "Christian religion ... not ... the peculiar dogma of any sect or school of theology" (Ruffner, 1904, pp. 33ff.). Charles William Dabney (1969) has observed that Ruffner was "active in speaking and preaching wherever he could advance the cause of education or religion" (p. 81). For some of that era, such as Ruffner, there was often little, if any, distinction between the two.

In his inaugural address at Washington College, Ruffner had advanced the cause of universal public schooling for white Virginians as necessary to produce "virtuous and intelligent citizens." Such an education, he averred, would make citizens capable of forming their own opinions on matters of civil policy and not leave them prey to "deceptive demagogues" (Crenshaw, 1983, pp. 247-248). He repeated this theme in an address to the Agricultural Society in Rockbridge County in 1839. Farmers, "enlightened yeomanry," would serve as agents for social peace and betterment by virtue of their literary skill, knowledge of history and geography, and their political philosophy gleaned from their common school education (Ruffner, 1840, p. 1).

Educational conventions had become a way of life around 1840 in western Virginia. It was at one of these, at Lexington, in which Henry Ruffner unveiled his comprehensive "Plan" for popular education in Virginia. Moral concerns were uppermost in this Plan. The sectional superintendents were to be men of "high standing for purity of character, learning, and sound judgment" (Ruffner, 1901, p. 384). The state superintendent was to be "regular and industrious in his habits, observant and judicious, pure in morals, sound in his religious principles, but free from sectarian bigotry" (p. 385). School officials should exercise supervision over teachers, noting that at present "immoral or incompetent men … now go about as schoolmasters—some of them lazy, drunken, unprincipled vagabonds—who impose on illiterate and incautious parents by crafty pretensions, and gain employment by offering to work cheaply" (p. 386). Ruffner demanded that future teachers be of "unblemished moral character" with "sound principles of Christian piety," have an "aptness to teach and to govern his scholars without unnecessary harshness," and be of "regularity and industry in the management" of their teaching (p. 386).

Ruffner, like Jefferson and Mercer before him, was unsuccessful in his attempt to establish a universal public system of primary schooling for white Virginians that would bring prosperity, virtue and wealth to the commonwealth, and put an end to crime, vice, and poverty. A system of public education set up to accomplish those moral goals would await the end of the Civil War and Reconstruction.

WILLIAM HENRY RUFFNER AND PUBLIC SCHOOLING IN VIRGINIA

The issue of slavery had cast a long shadow over all social matters, including the educational, in ante-bellum Virginia. The place of the freedmen in Virginia society after the War was also critical. Schools opened by the Freedmen's Bureau, as well as those begun by the freedmen themselves, showed the "extraordinary eagerness of the Freedmen for the advantage of schools" (Alderson, 1952, p. 87). However, history reveals that the freedmen were to be denied their legitimate aspirations for adequate schooling in Virginia as well as the rest of the former Confederacy. In Virginia, the constitution of 1869, which replaced the so-called "Underwood Constitution" of 1868 that was sponsored by the "Radicals", was approved and Virginia was readmitted to the Union in 1869 (pp. 65-79). The new constitution called for the establishment of a system of public schools, and William Henry Ruffner, Henry's son, was chosen the first state superintendent—with the backing of Robert E. Lee—by the General Assembly in 1870.[3]

Prior to Ruffner's selection, several individuals had played a leadership role in establishing free schools in Virginia. Among these was Barnas Sears, a Baptist clergyman, who was the agent of the Peabody Fund, former state superintendent of schools for Rhode Island and former president of Brown University. Sears argued for common schools as necessary for the moral, intellectual, political, and economic benefit of Virginia (Sears, 1868, pp. 3-18). Sears was joined by others, such as the editors of *The Educational Journal of Virginia*, who called for the establishment of free schools in that publication's first issue in 1869 in order to overcome igno-rance and preserve and develop the common weal.[4]

Opposition

Ruffner, as state superintendent, contended that the state had the right to educate, a right that was not accepted by many Virginians. Public taxa-tion, he declared, should be used to support these schools, which com-prised the moral foundations of society. Public schools, separate for both whites and African Americans, would be the guardians of morality. His chief opponents, Bennett Puryear of Richmond College and J. William Jones, a Baptist clergyman who wrote under the *nom de plume* of "Civis," charged that the state schools were secular and therefore must be immoral (Fraser, 1970, p. 415). They were joined in the assault by the Rev. Robert Lewis Dabney, a former colleague and friend of Ruffner, a Presby-terian, of the Union Theological Seminary in Richmond (Wilson, 1981, pp. 77-89; Overy, 1967). Basically, these men argued that the state did not have the right to educate. That right belonged to parents, and the usur-pation of that right by the civil state would destroy the family's role in society and lead to the substitution of the secular state in its stead (C.W. Dabney, 1969, pp. 153-157).

The Education of the Freedmen

The education of the freedmen was at issue. Ruffner supported it (but in separate schools); his protagonists opposed it. Ruffner encouraged white southerners to instruct the freedmen "with a view to elevate their character, and to adapt them to the successful discharge of the new duties imposed upon them by their changed condition." He exhorted the local superintendents of schools to "lead a educational revival among the peo-ple" and compared their endeavor to a religious crusade.[5] Ruffner believed that racially-mixed schools would be the death blow to public education in the South. The absence of the "power of common school education" had contributed to the presence of slavery (Ruffner, 1880, p. 3). He characterized African Americans in Virginia as "an enigma, and yet part of my work." The African American "craves education," he said; wants "to do right ... and is the most amicable of races"; their civilization was "progressing"; and, finally, "as a class they are in character weak and ignorant—and hence to that extent a dangerous element in society." The only way of "making them safe members of society" was by "educating them" (p. 10). An advocate of separate schools for the races, Ruffner defended his "middle of the road" position and claimed that "aversion felt for the negroes," as expressed by one of his opponents, would "lash into fury all the violent passions of war."[6] Virginia had the option of educating the African American, which would provide economic benefit and social peace, or it faced violent racial conflict.[7]

Dabney and "Civis" were Ruffner's chief foes in the schooling of African Americans. Dabney maintained they were unfit for the voting franchise, and possessed it only due to the efforts of radical Republicans. The education the freedmen were receiving was "utterly deceptive, farcical and dishonest," he claimed (R.L. Dabney, 1876, p. 251ff.). Educated African Americans, he contended, would develop "foolish and impossible aspirations." They would become surly and insolent and disinterested in their true calling, manual labor. Miscegenation constituted an even greater danger. He charged that the goal of the state board of education was to bring about the "amalgamation" of the races. He urged that Virginia thwart the efforts of congressional Radicals that would lead to the mingling of the blood "which consecrated the battle fields of the Confederacy, with this sordid, alien taint." He predicted that "Yankees" would eventually experience the "curse of mixed blood" that, like a cancer, would spread across and "putrify" the entire nation (p. 251ff.).

"Civis" joined Dabney in his opposition to the schooling of African Americans. He averred that African Americans were not equal to whites; "mixed" race schooling would lead to "corruption of blood" and would "Constitute a crime against decency and morals ... against God and nature."[8] He elaborated at length against schooling of African Americans, while calling himself a "friend of the negro, but a friend to him in his proper place of subordination." He did not hesitate to invoke the deity in support of his doctrine of inequality between the races:

> The line of demarcation between the races is not accidental or the result of outward surroundings; it has been fixed by the finger of God....

> The law of nature, which is always the law of God, is inequality, not equality; diversity, not uniformity; and the happiness of the whole animal kingdom is best subserved by this arrangement....

> *The whites and negroes cannot live together as equals.* Why cannot this be done? our modern reformers ask. I answer because God, for wise reasons not difficult to be understood, has made it impossible. It is forbidden by a law of nature.[9]

Attack against Ruffner and the Public Schools

The attacks against the education of the former slaves led into an overall assault against Ruffner and public education that erupted full-scale in 1875. Professor Bennett Puryear of Richmond College announced that the provision for public schools amounted to state paternalism and tended to "relax individual energy and debauch private morality." He maintained that the entire system of public education violated the American principle that allowed each citizen to conduct his own affairs without undue government interference. Charging that the "public school is atheism or infidelity" in that it replaced parental control of the child with state control, Puryear condemned the whole enterprise as a "negation of God's authority." Further, he held that education was both unnecessary and unwise for those who were destined to perform the menial tasks of society; if an exceptional child should spring from the lower social levels, he believed, private charity could provide for his education.[10]

"Civis" expanded upon Puryear's criticisms. He declared that the political principles "which are invoked in the support of the public school are foreign to free institutions and fatal to liberty." The "education of children is not the business of government, but the sacred and imperative duty of parents." State involvement in education, he wrote "is a wicked and dangerous denial of the reciprocal relations and obligations of parent and child, as proclaimed by nature and taught with solemn emphasis over and over by God, by Christ and his Apostles."[11]

It was the criticisms of his former classmate and fellow Presbyterian clergyman, Robert Lewis Dabney, which particularly stung Ruffner. Dabney blasted the public school system as a "quixotic project ... the cunning cheat of Yankee state-craft." He condemned the "unrighteousness" of a system that "wrung by a grinding taxation from an oppressed people" huge sums for use in the "pretended education of freed slaves." Expenditures for public education were even more deplorable, he wrote, at a time "when the state can neither pay its debt nor attend to its own legitimate interests." Asserting that many white Virginians were keeping their children home to work, "to raise ... taxes to give a pretended education to the brats of the black paupers" who "loaf and steal," he maintained that the freedmen's low character, ignorance, low morals, dependent nature, and his lack of ambition could not be cured by education (R.L. Dabney, 1876, p. 251ff.).

Dabney's anti-public school argument was founded on the theory of the family as the independent and basic unit in society. He held that parents were, or ought to be, the sole responsible agents of the family; it was the state's duty to protect the family, not to interfere with it, nor usurp one of its fundamental rights, the rearing of children. Christianity was indispensable in this process, he argued: "There can be no true education without moral culture and no true moral culture without Christianity." Teachers had to be professing Christians, because teaching was a "spiritual function," since the "soul is a monad and its training cannot be divided, it cannot be equipped as to its different parts at different times and places." The state, as a secular institution, is "totally disqualified to conduct schools for all the people." The state should assume an ancillary role, and should limit its educational activities to encouraging "individual and voluntary efforts and aid those whose poverty and misfortunes disable them from properly rearing their own children" (C.W. Dabney, 1969, p. 155).

Ruffner Responds

Ruffner replied to each of the objections posed by Puryear, Dabney and Civis. He pressed on in his goal of making public education viable in the Commonwealth of Virginia.

With regard to the schooling of African Americans, Ruffner expressed the belief that education would "foster among the Negroes a pride of race which would have a purifying and stimulating power and will gradually overcome that contemptible ambition to associate with white people, which has been instilled into their minds by the blundering policy of the Northern people and the Federal government."[12] Education of the freedmen would improve their efficiency in labor, lead to responsible citizenship, and reduce their pauperism and criminal acts. Universal education would benefit them, as it would whites (Ruffner, 1871b, pp. 108ff.). Two decades earlier, in 1852, he had declared that the "Negro has abundant capacity for all the ordinary affairs of self-government, and may attain to as high a degree of civilization as any other race." He reminded his fellow Virginians that "the Negro is our brother and our ward; and God will hold us responsible for his training and for his end, temporal and eternal. He may, by suitable effort, become a blessing and an ornament to the earth" (Ruffner, 1852, pp. 8, 48).

Given the strong opposition to the mixed school clause in Virginia, Ruffner endeavored to show that forced integration would undo the progress that had been made in the South since the end of the Civil War. Only the "disintegrating work of time" could eliminate the antipathies southern whites held toward African Americans, he averred (Ruffner, 1874, p. 86ff.). Ruffner also advanced a moral reason for opposing mixed schools. He wrote in 1874 that African Americans as a class "move on a far lower moral plane than whites." With this observable gap in manners between the two races, he concluded that it was understandable that whites in the South would "refuse to associate their children with [African Americans] in the intimate relations of a school. He opined that the wide moral and social differences between the races made the attempt to mix them in the schools both "vain and foolish ... base and malicious." White parents simply would not assent to mixed schools in the South. To him the choice was simple: dual schools or no schools (p. 88ff.).

The Social Benefits of Public Schooling

According to Ruffner, the "true end and aim of education is the development of character in its broadest sense."[13] Character education included the duties of citizenship. Youth were to leave school "fully rounded in character, and well-equipped morally as well as mentally for all the duties of citizenship" (Ruffner, 1871b, p. 58). The "enlightened public opinion" which would result from civic-oriented schooling of this nature would produce political stability, because it would lead to the election of legislators who would pass laws that would guarantee civic welfare (p. 58). The opposite result, founded on "unlettered masses," who in his words "have already been irrational, corrupt and dangerous," would inevitably bring social ruin on Virginia, such as had befallen France with the Paris Commune.[14] It could not be otherwise, he maintained, because the uneducated were incompetent to vote or to judge, and were inherently "unable to furnish the moral support needed for the proper execution of the law." Ignorance necessarily lowered the moral tone of society, because candidates for public office would need to descend to the lowest level in order to gain the votes of an uneducated electorate. Once elected, these office-holders would be responsive to their constituencies, enact unwise legislation, and thereby endanger the public's security and moral tone.[15]

Crime reduction made up another social benefit that resulted from public schooling. Schools, along with churches and families, would produce individuals who both recognized and abided by the moral law. While he acknowledged that some crimes, such as forgeries, were "rendered possible by education alone," Ruffner nonetheless contended that toleration for this type of crime would be reduced by teaching "practical ethics" in the schools (Ruffner, 1876a). Education would be most effective in diminishing crime among that segment of the community, the "criminal masses, who people the prisons and give work to the executioner." These, he averred, were the offenses which "chiefly affect the peace and safety of society, and occasion the greatest outlay of criminal expenses." On several occasions he mused over the money that could be saved if the number of prisons and prisoners could be reduced, a goal that was attainable via universal free public education, which required a much smaller outlay of funds than did prisons (Ruffner, 1876a).

Education, universal and free, would increase respect for property on the part of those so educated; it would also lead to an increase of quality products. This was so because schooling would inculcate in the common man, future laborers, "more character, ability and faithfulness." The "security of property," he maintained, had a "close ratio" to the "degree of enlightenment possessed by the masses of the people." The "quickening power of education on the people who work with their hands" would manifest itself in skills development, increased general intelligence, and greater honesty. Ruffner placed the development of these traits in a "life and death" international scenario, because the United States relied on skilled, intelligent, honest laborers to compete successfully with the rest of the world (Ruffner, 1878a, pp. 64C-64J). The universal literacy created by free public schooling would "powerfully aid in the work of civilizing, enlightening, and purifying society; and thus giving character and stability to the State" (p. 64B).

Moral Education in the Public Schools

Robert Michaelsen (1970) has described Ruffner's position on the role of the public school in moral education as "common religion for the common school" (p. 85). Ruffner himself stated that public schools "may formally teach the recognized morality of the country, and the will of God as the standard and ultimate authority of all morality, but distinctively religious teaching shall be left to volunteer agencies."[16]

Ruffner called for "systematic moral training" in both public and private schools, utilizing the same methods.[17] His version of "common religion" was not "dogmatic religion," but rather comprised the "cardinal religious doctrines, and a complete code of the highest and purest morality.," i.e., the "existence and government of God," which "constitutes its great controlling feature, and from that is developed the whole code of moral duties" (Ruffner, 1871c, p. 57). Ruffner admitted that while the "State cannot properly teach religion ... it does not follow, however, that all incidental allusions or observances of a religious character should be forbidden." Indeed, he supported such activities whenever they "can be introduced in an edifying and inoffensive way," provided that they did not contravene "individual rights of conscience" (p. 56). Religious truths, he averred, could be taught "educationally, not theologically, in schools." He stood for a "religious common law accepted by everybody," which in his words "will yet be embodied in the textbooks in every school without offense" (p. 56). The presence of this "common religion" enabled public schools to be "morally elevating," not simply "morally neutral." The "common religion" was, in his words, "highly ethical," able to train the child in "habits of reticence, order, industry, truth, self-sacrifice, and good behavior, including good manners" (Ruffner, 1878b, p. 60).

Schools were to be a "place of safety, refinement, and moral as well as intellectual culture" (Ruffner, 1876b). A "sound educational training" was for the child "earth's greatest blessing."[18] Common school education was not a substitute for formal religion, but was its "handmaid."[19] Universal free public schools would bring about, in a few years, a "doubling" of Sunday schools and an increase in the "power of the pulpit." This would happen, he argued, by the very nature of the educational process.[20]

Ruffner's view of common religion was that it was not sectarian, even though it taught the principles and morals of religion. Responding to charges that public schools were harmful to the work of churches, he asked how that could be, "unless reading is a diabolical art?"(Ruffner, 1878c, p. 61). Rather, he held, common schools complemented the roles of church and family. For instance, he reasoned that since God had intended the Bible and its reading to be for all people, how could illiterates fulfill God's plan? Thus, schools, by producing universal literacy, were instrumental in carrying out the divine plan, and illiteracy was seen as one of the great "hindrances to the progress of the Gospel" (Ruffner, 1871c, p. 59).

Ruffner advocated the use of traditional Protestant practices in the schools, viz., Bible reading, psalm singing, and recitation of the Lord's Prayer. He cited as "models" the public schools he had observed in Pennsylvania and Connecticut that had a "full and hearty Christian tone."[21] Yet he advocated the discontinuance of these practices if citizens objected. If discontinued, how could the schools be Christian then? He replied that there was "no need to legislate Christianity into the schools of a Christian people; it will go in of itself as do salt and leaven."[22] He maintained that this common religion, with its systematic moral training, which "indoctrinates the child in respect to all his terrestrial relations, without weakening the celestial," was indispensable if Virginia and the nation were to be Christian (Ruffner, 1878d, p. 64A). Church schools educated about one-twentieth of the school-age population, he observed, while private schools educated only those who could pay the required tuition. Public schools, on the other hand, provided moral, universal education for all.[23]

An ordained Presbyterian clergyman, Ruffner advocated what Sadie Bell has called the "Presbyterian emphasis in the teaching of a common religion" in public education (Bell, 1930, pp. 348-364). Not all clergymen agreed with Ruffner's position. Civis, for example, argued that public education as advanced by Ruffner imperiled, rather than protected the civil welfare.[24] Dabney contended that the family and church were God's chosen instruments for the education of youth. These agencies, acting in accord with God's plan in education, would bring about the advancement of the common good, something the secularist state could not achieve.[25] Episcopalian clergy joined in the criticism. Bell argues that Episcopalians felt that the "public schools would be withdrawn wholly from religious influence" under Ruffner's plan (Bell, 1930, p. 422). An Episcopalian clergyman of that period in Virginia, the Rev. Kinloch Nelson, depicted the public schools as "essentially communistic" (V. Dabney, 1971, p. 381).

Moral Education and Public School Personnel

None of Ruffner's goals described above were within Virginia's grasp, however, unless all of those persons entrusted with the responsibility of conducting schooling were paragons of the very virtues they were to imbue in their youthful charges. According to Ruffner, this moral requirement embraced school trustees, who needed "suitable character and habits," which were to include such qualities as "honesty, prudence, moral judgment and humility" plus the traits of "common sense and business habits."[26] Trustees were admonished to utilize the utmost care in selecting the teachers, avoiding choosing relatives and friends, even if they were the "best available" for a position. This challenge, termed their "greatest temptation," called for the "sternest of virtues" and constituted the real test of their "honor."[27]

Ruffner repeatedly called for the state superintendent to avoid getting entangled with politics. He was more explicit in his comments on the moral role of the local superintendent, going so far as to base the "value of the school system in every county" on the character of the county superintendent.[28] Not only was the local superintendent of schools to be "free from immoralities," he was also o be "morally above suspicion," with "nothing in his habits of speech or conduct which could be offensive to good people."[29]

The character of teachers was extremely crucial to the success of public schooling. The teacher's character "determines the character of the nation," Ruffner wrote. The public's educational concern was above all with "moral work from moral teachers."[30] The only way that education could produce the desired effects portrayed above was if schools were taught by "carefully selected (Christian) teachers, supervised by Christian men."[31] The "fundamental question" for Ruffner was "*who is to form the character of the people? The answer is—the teacher!*" Accordingly, he campaigned for the establishment of normal schools designed to train teachers, to replace the variety of institutions at which pre-service teachers were enrolled (Ruffner, 1878a, p. 64A). His quest for appropriate teacher education included both whites and African Americans, the latter located at Hampton Institute.

CONCLUSION

Affected by place and time, Ruffner championed universal public education as a moral and social necessity. The same reasons existed for educating African Americans as for educating whites: members of both races could "be made more intelligent, more moral, more industrious, and more skillful."[32] Public schools were in fact moral agencies for both races. Every teacher, he maintained, "has an *ethical* work to perform, which is second only to the work of the Christian pastor." He hastened to add, however, that the "school teacher's business is Christian ethics, not Christian theology."[33]

Ruffner was in solid company with nineteenth century educational reformers who fervently believed that the common school could be infused with a "common religion" that would unite "not only all professing Christians and Jews, but unbelievers of every grade."[34] Instilling this "common religion" into the public schools enabled them to be "morally elevating," not simply "morally neutral" (Ruffner, 1878a, p. 60). Believing that the "true end and aim of education is the development of character in its broadest sense,"[35] he worked tirelessly toward the goal of having all children in public schools where they would be "fully rounded in character, and well-equipped morally as well as mentally for all the duties of citizenship" (Ruffner, 1871b, p. 58).

NOTES

1. *Dictionary of American Biography*, Vol. VI. New York: Scribner's, 1933, p. 539.
2. *Journal of the House of Delegates of the Commonwealth of Virginia*, December 8, 1816. Richmond: Thomas Ritchie, 1816, p. 65.
3. *Report of the Commissioner of Education for the Year 1900-1901* (1902, Vol. II, p.2451). Washington, DC: Government Printing Office.
4. Free Schools in Virginia. (1869, November). *The Educational Journal of Virginia, 1*(1), 19-20.
5. W.H. Ruffner, *The Educational Journal of Virginia* 2 (February, March, May 1871): 155ff, 191, [272], [280] (December 1870):72ff; Fraser (1970, pp. 326, 321; 1971, p. 267).
6. W.H. Ruffner, "Dr. Dabney emotional." The Public School System, 1st Series, Ruffner Papers, Historical Foundation of the Presbyterian and Reformed Church, Montreat, North Carolina.
7. Ibid., p, 6;. W.H. Ruffner, "Education of the Negroes." In *Dr. Ruffner and the Public Schools.* Ruffner Papers, Historical Foundation, Montreat; W.H. Ruffner (1871a, pp. 154-155).
8. Civis (J. William Jones), "The public school in its relation to the Negro." *The Southern Planter and Farmer, I*, (December 1875), p. 1; Ibid., II (January 1876), pp. 8-14; Ibid., (May 1876), pp. 15-17.

9. Civis, "The public school in its relation to the Negro." Reprint from *The Southern Planter and Farmer* (1877), pp. 4, 8ff., 16, in Ruffner Papers, Historical Foundation, Montreat.

10. Cited in Fraser (1970, pp. 414ff.).

11. Civis, "The public school in its relation to the Negro." Reprint from *The Southern Planter and Farmer* (1877), p. 3, in Ruffner Papers, Historical Foundation, Montreat.

12. Quoted in C.W. Dabney (1969, p. 155).

13. William Henry Ruffner, "What are normal schools in fact?" p. 12, Ruffner Papers, Historical Foundation, Montreat.

14. William Henry Ruffner, "The political value of popular education." In *Dr. Ruffner and the Public Schools*. Ruffner Papers, RGF, 444, 4, 15, Historical Foundation, Montreat.

15. Ibid.

16. William Henry Ruffner, "The Bible in the public schools." *Ruffner Papers*, Historical Foundation, Montreat.

17. William Henry Ruffner, "The moral effect of education." In *Dr. Ruffner and the public schools*. RGF, 446, 4, 15, Ruffner Papers, Historical Foundation, Montreat.

18. William Henry Ruffner, "Teaching of the ignorant." In *Dr. Ruffner and the public schools*. Ruffner Papers, RGF, 446, 4, 15, Historical Foundation, Montreat.

19. William Henry Ruffner, "The moral effect of education." In Ibid.

20. Ruffner, quoted in Fraser (1970, p. 337).

21. William Henry Ruffner, "What are normal schools in fact?," p. 8, Ruffner Papers, Historical Foundation, Montreat.

22. William Henry Ruffner, "The Bible in the public schools." Ruffner Papers, Historical Foundation, Montreat.

23. William Henry Ruffner, "Universal education possible only in the public school system." In Dr. Ruffner and the public schools, Ruffner Papers, RGF, 444, 4, 15, Historical Foundation, Montreat.

24. See Civis, "The public school in its relation to the Negro," *The Southern Planter and Farmer* I (December 1875); II (January 1876); III (February 1876); IV (May 1876), for an explication of this position.

25. For a summary of Dabney's position in this regard, see Dabney (1969, pp. 154-161).

26. William Henry Ruffner, "School trustees: Their duties and temptations." Ruffner Papers, RGF, 444, 3, 50, Historical Foundation, Montreat.

27. Ibid., pp. 14-15.

28. William Henry Ruffner, Circular, July 20, 1876, Richmond.

29. Ibid.

30. William Henry Ruffner, "Dr. Dabney emotional." The Public Free School System, 1st Series, Ruffner Papers, Historical Foundation, Montreat.

31. William Henry Ruffner, "The Bible in the public schools." In *Virginia school doctrines* (Vol. I, 2nd Series, May 8, 1876b). Ruffner Papers, Historical Foundation, Montreat.

32. William Henry Ruffner, "The public free school system." Reprint of articles in the *Richmond Dispatch and Enquirer*, April and May 1876, Ruffner Papers, Historical Foundation, Montreat.
33. Ibid., pp. 27ff.
34. Ibid., p. 28.
35. William Henry Ruffner, "What are normal schools in fact?," p. 12. Ruffner Papers, Historical Foundation, Montreat.

CHAPTER 7

THE NINETEENTH CENTURY PAROCHIAL SCHOOL

INTRODUCTION

Catholic schools existed in what became Florida and Louisiana as early as the seventeenth century. Other Catholic schools, also established for religious/moral reasons, began prior to the nineteenth century (see Buetow, 1970). Those schools established in the wake of the common school movement in the nineteenth century are, however, the focus of attention in this chapter. These schools, founded and maintained at a tremendous cost by the Church, were to preserve the faith of a poor, immigrant population, besieged at first by Protestantism and later threatened, according to Catholic belief, by what the bishops felt were the menacing values of secularism. Accordingly, the bishops understandably turned to parish schools as the indispensable vehicle by which Catholic faith and morals would be preserved in Catholic children, thus insuring the future of the Church in the nation.

How did moral education fit into the mission of the nineteenth century parochial school? First, it is important to note that the Catholic Church does not distinguish between religious and moral education as some do. It does not look to the school to direct students' moral education, and the alliance of home and Church to be in charge of students' religious education. This chapter will focus on the official teaching of the Catholic

Moral Education in America's Schools: The Continuing Challenge, 75–87
Copyright © 2005 by Information Age Publishing
All rights of reproduction in any form reserved.

Church as it related to the moral education of youthful Catholics in the nineteenth century parochial (parish elementary) school.

EARLY STIRRINGS

Bishop John Carroll of Baltimore made the first official comment of the American hierarchy on education in 1792. His remarks were of a general nature, pertained to the life-long benefits of a Christian education, and reminded parents that by properly rearing their children they were serving God by preserving religion and simultaneously benefitting the nation "whose welfare depends on the morals of its citizens."[1] As the number of Catholics increased in the new nation, four other dioceses were added to Baltimore, making up the Province of Baltimore in 1808 (McCluskey, 1972, p. 51). That Council's "Pastoral," issued in 1829, attempted to motivate parents to see to the religious education of their children by reminding them of the words of Christ: "Suffer the little children to come unto me"; described Hell as "this is too frequently the necessary consequence of an improper education"; and warned parents that if they did not implement proper values in their children "What will it avail them to gain the whole world if they lose their souls?"[2]

The "Pastoral" of the 1833 Council referred to the strenuous efforts put forth by the bishops on behalf of Catholic children to "provide schools ... united to a strict protection of their morals and the best safeguards of their faith."[3] In 1840, shortly after the establishment of the common school by Horace Mann and others in Massachusetts, the hierarchy referred for the first time to difficulties with the public schools. They complained of textbooks and even of the very system itself being directed against the Catholic Church, which, in their words, made it "no easy matter thus to preserve the faith of your children in the midst of so many difficulties."[4]

Three years later the bishops were more forceful in their accusations against public education, viewing it as a serious threat to the faith and morals of Catholic children. They exhorted parents to vigilance and reminded them of the seriousness of the obligations that emanated from their state in life:

> We have seen with serious alarm, efforts made to poison the fountains of public education, by giving it a sectarian hue, and accustoming children to the use of a version of the Bible made under sectarian bias, and placing in their hands books of various kinds, replete with offensive and dangerous matter.... Parents are strictly bound, like faithful Abraham, to teach their children the truths which God has revealed; and if they suffer them to be led astray, the souls of the children will be required at their hands. Let them,

therefore, ... see that no interference with the faith of their children be used in public schools, and no attempt made to induce conformity in any thing contrary to the laws of the Catholic Church....[5]

THE MID-19TH CENTURY: THE STRIFE INTENSIFIES

The bishops returned to Baltimore for the first national or plenary council in 1852. Assembled in solemn congregation, they again reminded parents of their God-delegated custodianship over the morals of their children and both warned and advised them accordingly:

> What terrible expectation of judgment that will fill his soul, should his children perish through his criminal neglect, or his obstinate refusal to be guided in the discharge of his paternal duties, by the authority of God's church. To avert this evil give your children a Christian education, based on religious principles, accompanied by religious practices and always subordinate to religious influence. Be not led astray by the false and delusive theories which are so prevalent, and which leave youth without religion, and consequently, without anything to control the passions, promote the real happiness of the individual, and make society find in the increase of its members, a source of security and prosperity. Listen not to those who would persuade you that religion can be separated from secular instruction.[6]

The Church's leaders then gave specific instructions to parents how they could raise their children in accord with the "Science of the saints," thereby avoiding having them filled with moral error and immoral vices:

> Encourage the establishment and support of Catholic schools; make every sacrifice which may be necessary for this object; spare our hearts the pain of beholding youth whom, after the example of our Master, we so much love, involved in all the evils of an uncatholic education, evils too multiplied and too obvious to require that we should do more than raise our voices in solemn protest against the system from which they spring.[7]

THE ETHNIC QUESTION

Two of the five ecclesiastical provinces of the Catholic Church in the United States, Cincinnati and St. Louis, were created shortly before the First Plenary Council of Baltimore in 1852. These were to form the two bases of the "German triangle" in the midwest. The bishops of Cincinnati were quick to speak out on behalf of the importance of Catholic schools in protecting the faith and morals of Catholic children. In 1855, the First Provincial Council of Cincinnati declared:

We admonish pastors of souls again and again to strive by all the means in their power to prevent the boys and girls entrusted to them from frequenting those schools which they cannot attend without grave danger to their faith and morals.[8]

The bishops acknowledged with gratitude the record of the German parishes to establish and support Catholic schools, and they set them up as models to be emulated by their English-speaking brethren:

Our excellent German congregations leave us nothing to desire on this subject. The children attend at Mass every morning, they sing with one accord the power of God, they go from the church to the school. They are accustomed to cleanliness and neatness of dress, to diligent and affectionate respect for their parents, the Reverend Clergy, and their teachers. We have nothing more at heart than that the pupils of our English schools should imitate their example.[9]

Three years later the bishops of this province met again, enjoining that the matter of establishing Catholic schools was so serious that Church authorities were to "provide a Catholic school in every parish or congregation subject to them, ... under pain of mortal sin."[10] Moral necessity required attendance at Catholic schools, the bishops of the Cincinnati province averred in 1861, because of the moral evils present in the public schools:

Under the influence of this plausible, but most unwise system of Common school education, the rising generation has been educated either without any definite principles at all, or with false, at least, more or less exaggerated and fanatical principles. The system itself, if carried out, is well calculated to bring up a generation of religious indifferentists, if not of practical infidels; and if not carried out, its tendency is to develop false or very defective, if not dangerous, religious principles.[11]

THE EPISCOPAL CAMPAIGN CONTINUES

In 1866 the American bishops returned to Baltimore for the Second Plenary Council. The bishops here reaffirmed the teachings on moral education of Baltimore I and then added that "religious teaching and religious training should form part of every system of school education" so that the young could be reared morally.[12] Directing their attention to the authority the voice of the Church should have on its followers in matters of faith and morals, the bishops proclaimed:

The Catholic has a guide in the Church, as a divine institution, which enables him to discriminate between what the Law of God forbids or allows; and this authority the State is bound to recognize as supreme in its sphere— of moral, no less than dogmatic teaching.[13]

In 1864, in the midst of mighty struggles with civil authorities in Europe, Pope Pius IX issued his controversial "Syllabus of Errors." In this document the Pope condemned a number of political, philosophical, and educational positions; one of these was Proposition 48, which dealt with the instruction of youth:

48. This system of instructing youth, which consists in separating it from the Catholic faith and power of the Church, and in teaching exclusively, or at least primarily, the knowledge of natural things and the earthly ends of social life alone, may be approved by Catholics.[14]

Catholic bishops in the United States supported the Pope's statements. In 1872, Archbishop J. B. Purcell of Cincinnati wrote, tying enrollment in Catholic schools to parents' reception of the sacraments:

The Catholic school is the nursery of the Catholic congregation. The one should stand under the protecting shadow of the other. This duty they do not discharge who do not send the children under their care to a Catholic school when in their power. We see not how they, who willfully and deliberately neglect this duty, can worthily approach, or be conscientiously admitted to the sacraments.... their (the children's) souls while yet pure, their parents will not sacrifice for the kind of education received in Godless or sectarian schools.[15]

Bishop St. Palais of Vincennes, Indiana, presented his objections to the kind of moral/religious education (or absence thereof) in the public schools in a series of statements:

1. We object to the public schools on account of the *infidel* source from which they originated.

2. We object to these schools because the teaching of religion is excluded from them, and such exclusion will *inevitably* produce religious indifference, if not infidelity.

3. We object to these schools because religious instruction which is necessarily connected with the acquirement of secular knowledge cannot be introduced in them without interfering with the conscientious rights and wounding the most delicate feelings of the pupils.

4. We object to these schools again because the promiscuous assembling of both sexes of a certain age is injurious to the morals of the children, and because we dread association which might, in time, prove pernicious to them and distressing to their parents.[16]

Several other Ohio bishops addressed the necessity, on the grounds of preserving their faith and morals, of Catholic children attending Catholic schools during this period. Bishop Rosecrans of Columbus equated, in terms of Catholic doctrine, such attendance with belief in the Divinity of Jesus and of the Real Presence of Christ in the Eucharist.[17] Bishop Gilmour of Cleveland argued that the school should be built before the church in a new parish, contending that "There is little danger of the old losing their faith, but there is every danger that the young will." He reminded Catholics in his diocese that there must be "no division" on the school question, since the "public schools are organized and managed for the benefit of Protestants."[18] Archbishop Elder, Purcell's successor in Cincinnati, was very forceful in his support of the Church's official position on the necessity of the Catholic school to inculcate morals in Catholic youth. He declared that the Church's teaching on the matter was so clear "that there is nothing for a Catholic to do but obey them, or renounce his religion: 'He that will not hear the Church, let him be to thee as the heathen and publican'."[19]

Agitation on behalf of building Catholic schools in another predominantly German state, Wisconsin, was also strong. In his Lenten Pastoral of 1872 Archbishop Henni of Milwaukee reminded his flock of the moral necessity of having parish schools: "Every congregation, therefore, is *in duty bound—a duty its members owe both to God and society*—to have its own *parish school* established." The reason, he maintained, was "because the attendance at Public Schools *generally* results in the ruin of the tender soul."[20] Bishop Heiss, to be Henni's successor in Milwaukee, as the sitting ordinary of the Diocese of LaCrosse, worried over the moral condition of the majority of Catholic youth in his diocese:

> We grieve in our inmost heart when we look on the children growing up in our diocese!—for, far the greater number of them are either without any school, or go to the Public Schools, where so many of them imbibe in their tender souls the poisonous germs of infidelity and immorality.[21]

Kilian C. Flasch, who like Henni and Heiss had been born in Bavaria, was Heiss' successor in LaCrosse. He reemphasized the the indispensability of Catholic schools for Catholic children to receive the religious/moral education which was their divine right. He wrote:

The place where this divine right is secure to the children is the Christian school. There is mockery to say that the parents should instruct their children in catechism at home and prepare them for the holy sacraments. They have neither the time, nor the patience, and frequently not the ability, for such a task. (Biechler, 1958, p. 1)

In 1873, Bishop James Gibbons of Richmond, destined to become Cardinal Archbishop of Baltimore, demonstrated that support for the view that Catholic schools were indispensable agents in the religious and moral education of Catholic youth was not limited to German-American bishops from the midwest. He noted that the inevitable consequence of separating the "religious and secular" education of Catholic children was the loss of Catholic faith." Without such school attendance, Gibbons claimed, "twenty years hence, it will be much easier to find churches for a congregation, than a congregation for churches."[22]

THE GROWING NATIONAL STRUGGLE

The indispensable function of the parochial school in the moral/religious education of Catholic youth was the focal point of controversy in the last three decades of the nineteenth century. It was spurred first by the "Instruction" of the Vatican congregation reponsible for Catholic matters in mission countries, which the United States was at the time. The document, promulgated in 1875, declared that the perversion of the faith for Catholic children in public schools must be rendered remote if Catholics were to attend such schools as dictated by natural and divine law. Bishops were urged to found Catholic schools, and the laity, especially the wealthy and influential, were instructed to support them financially. The goal was to avert "with God's help," the dangers to faith and morals that Catholic children faced in the public school system. Parents, who did not see to the sufficient training of their children in morals as well as faith, at home or via a Catholic school, could not be "absolved" from that sin.[23] Writing about a decade later, Catholic author James Conway penned that the "Instruction" meant that "Catholics everywhere should have their own schools," in order to avoid the "corrupting influences of the public schools" (Conway, 1884, p. 667)

Michael Muller expressed the most extreme Catholic view on the moral corruption that would result from attendance at public schools on the part of youthful Catholics and on the concomitant necessity of Catholic schools for the proper moral education of these youngsters. In 1872, he wrote that the public school system aimed to bring about:

> A generation without belief in God and immortality, ... a generation that looks upon religion, marriage, or family and private property, as the greatest enemies to worldly happiness—a generation that substitutes ... a community of goods for private property, a community of wives for the private family; in other words, a generation that substitutes the devil for God, hell for heaven, sin and vice for virtue and holiness. (Muller, 1872, pp. 72-73)

The system was so harmful that in it, the child "unlearns ... whatever principles of religion he may have learned from his parents." As baleful as these effects were for boys, they were moral disasters for girls, who lost their divine calling "due to the godless system of education" (Muller, 1872, pp. 89-93, 106-108). The civil state, sans any moral right, was responsible for imposing this "wicked, detestable, irreligious system," which was "diabolical in its origin, and subversive of all political, social and religious, order" on Christians (p. 140). Even more detestable was that Catholics were forced to pay taxes to support this "*prolific mother of children of anti-Christ*," which would deliver "hell upon earth" (pp. 164-168, 199).

The remedy for this aberration of moral education for Muller was clear: the teachings of the Christian religion, hence the inculcation of the tenets of moral education, in denominational schools supported by the government (pp. 214, 237). Contact with public schools would inevitably result in moral contamination for Catholic youth, he averred; the only hope for maintaining the faith and morals of Catholic children lay in Catholic schools. Parents and pastors who did not adhere to this position would be guilty of trampling on the blood of Christ and on judgment day would be cast outside into the darkness where there will be the "weeping and gnashing of teeth" (pp. 367, 407-409).

THE THIRD PLENARY COUNCIL OF BALTIMORE

In 1883 three American bishops were called to Rome where they were presented with an agenda which the Vatican wanted an American episcopal council to implement (McAvoy, 1957, p. 28). As the church historian Peter Guilday (1932) has observed, the progress of public schools in the United States led to the bishops' belief that the problems related to the moral/religious education of Catholic children in these schools was the "dominant anxiety of our prelates and clergy" (p. 237). The school question was to be the paramount concern of the Third Plenary Council of Baltimore.

The bishops decreed that the Catholic laity were to playa crucial role in the coming combat; to carry out this role they needed a moral and religious education, upon which civilization depended.[24] The three educational agencies of home, Church, and school must all contribute to this lofty cause, but this cooperation was impossible in schools in which religion was excluded as a matter of public policy.[25] The school that "principally gives the knowledge fitting for practical life, ought to be preeminently under the holy influence of religion," the prelates declared. Every Catholic child ought to have available a school with such an education, and it was the responsibility of Catholic communities to provide same, and the duty of parents to see that their children attended such schools unless the requisite moral and religious education could be obtained elsewhere.[26]

Conway (1884) can hardly be accused of stretching a point when he wrote of the consensus that existed among the American Catholic hierarchy on the vital importance of Catholic schools to the Church:

> There is hardly a bishop living today in the United States who has not condemned the existing system of public schools in the strongest terms, and earnestly exhorted the clergy and the faithful entrusted to this charge to provide for Catholic schools for the education of the Catholic youth. (p. 669)

It is clear that the spiritual leaders of the Catholic Church felt that attendance at Catholic schools was the vehicle for Catholic children to love their religion, learn its religious and moral teachings, and then followed them when they left school and entered the world, a world which the bishops saw as inimical to their faith and morals.

THE NATIONAL IMPACT OF BALTIMORE III

In the last quarter of the nineteenth century Catholic leaders identified the "American" secular public school as their chief educational threat, it having replaced the Bible-based, pan-Protestant common school of earlier in the century. Jenkins (1886) was not alone is fearing a repetition of the European situation with its "God-hating European societies with God-eliminating systems of popular instruction" (p. 6). Schools such as these would produce indifferentists and infidels, an inevitable outcome because "creedless, neutral schools breed creedless children," and "indifference to God and virtue is the surest precursor to infidelity in practice" (p. 8). Problems for Catholic children in public schools were unavoidable because they were "in constant association with ill-bred, unbelieving and immoral companions" that included "Jews, Gentiles, heathens of the low and degraded classes of society; for none are, or can be, excluded from public instruction" (pp. 16-18).

Catholics asserted that the failure of the Protestant-oriented common schools to produce good citizens had forced their proponents to abandon their original rationale and seek a new purpose for them. As one Catholic writer explained it:

> The failure of public schools to train their pupils in good morals and virtuous habits, along with secular instruction, is so evident that, contrary to the very arguments which were used when the public schools were first projected and introduced, their defenders now assert that it is not part of the purpose and object of public schools to teach morality or train their pupils in virtuous habits; that their purpose included nothing more than that of imparting secular knowledge and promoting intellectual development. (Wolff, 1886, p. 740)

Ideally, for the orthodox Catholic, the entire environment of the school should be religious. Only then would the students learn and then exhibit moral and religious behavior:

> The eyes should be chastened by the contemplation of pious objects; the ears should be trained to the melody of the sacred song; the lips should be taught to lisp the holy name; the tiny hands to fold themselves in prayer, the whole person to compose itself to Christian modesty; the imagination should be stored with pious and chaste representations; the memory should become the treasury of holy recollections. The practice of religion should, at this age, be made sweet and easy by frequent and appropriate exercises of devotion. Oh, the teachers that took half as much pains for the religious training of children as the godless kindergarten does for their secular drill. (Conway, 1884, p. 661)

Attacks on the alleged immoral consequences of public schooling led some to contend that the Catholic clergy was "engaging in a systematic and general attack upon the public school system," a charge that was denied by Cardinal Gibbons of Baltimore. This acknowledged leader of American Catholicism yet wrote that "The second evil that bodes mischief to our country and endangers the stability of our Government arises from our mutilated and vicious system of public school education."[27] It was "mutilated," he opined, because the "religious and secular education of our children cannot be *divorced* from each other without inflicting a fatal wound upon the soul." The result of such a "separation is to paralyze the moral faculties and so foment a spirit of indifference to matters of faith."[28]

Gibbons was far from alone in his criticisms of the moral ills that were inherent in public education as it existed. One Catholic writer described these schools as "heartless," because they relied on a diet of "parched rationalism in science, on which the heavenly dews of religion do not fall"; of being "headless," precisely because they were "heartless," and since they operated without religion were also "Godless" (McSweeney, 1888, pp. 435-437). Catholics thus had no moral alternative but to erect their own schools and assume the resulting financial burdens in order to "save their children from perversion" (Shea, 1888a, p. 691). The public schools, heralded by some as the "mainstay of the republic" (Dwight, 1888, p. 546), must by the "ultimate decision of results, show their inferiority in all that constitutes moral excellence" (Shea, 1888a, p. 696). One writer cast the struggle in the context of the Catholic schools serving as a defense against yet another onslaught of paganism:

> The Catholic Church, which in the centuries of the past preserved society from the efforts of ruthless barbaric invasions, is determined to defend it now from greater and more destructive enemies—from irreligion and pagan infidelity. She will do this now, as in the past, by her schools. (Baast, 1888, p. 609)

The Catholic historian John Gilmary Shea (1888b) expressed the commonly held Catholic belief that education without religion, and hence without morality, was harmful not only to the individual but also to society: "Education when based on religion and morality is a good; without such control it may be and must be a curse and not a blessing to any community" (p. 358).

One of the American hierarchy's staunchest supporters of Catholic schools and committed opponent of Catholic children attending public schools was Bishop Bernard McQuaid of the Rochester, New York diocese. In the wake of Baltimore III McQuaid intensified his efforts in both arenas. When some people accused Catholics of trying to destroy the public school system, McQuaid claimed that this charge was merely an attempt to draw attention away from the defects of the system itself, wherein lay its real danger: "It is a system liable to blunders innumerable, to inefficiency of accomplishment, and to the perpetrating of injustice." Its underlying principle was "unadulterated communism," which consisted of "state paternalism," which usurped the primacy of parental rights by the creeping tentacles of state authority (McQuaid, 1889, pp. 179-381, 390).

CONCLUSION

The tremendous effort put forth by Catholics on behalf of their schools in the nineteenth century, especially considering the dearth of financial resources available to them, is impressive, indeed. The effort testifies to the widespread, but not unanimous, belief by Catholic officialdom that such attendance was necessary for the religious and moral welfare of young Catholics and for the existence of the Church itself in the future. In many dioceses, failure by parents to send their children to Catholic schools resulted in the application of ecclesiastical sanctions by Church authorities. One such sanction was the assessment of a reserved sin, forgivable only by the bishop of the diocese. These penalties document further the dedication to the proposition that attendance at Catholic schools was indispensable to the religious and moral state of the young. The schools were an indispensable vehicle that would bring about loyalty to the Church, influence their graduates to be active in their parishes as adults, produce vocations to the religious life, and live a moral life that would result in benefit to civil as well as ecclesiastical society and lead to their eternal salvation. which was the goal of their existence on earth.

NOTES

1. John Carroll, "Pastoral Letter," (1792), in McCluskey (1964, p. 48).
2. "Pastoral Letter," First Provincial Council of Baltimore (1829), in McCluskey (1964, pp. 52-53).
3. "Pastoral Letter," Second Provincial Council of Baltimore (1833), in McCluskey (1964, p. 56).
4. "Pastoral Letter," Fourth Provincial Council of Baltimore (1840), in McCluskey (1964, p. 61).
5. "Pastoral Letter," Fifth Provincial Council of Baltimore (1843), in McCluskey (1964, p. 63).
6. "Pastoral Letter," First Plenary Council of Baltimore (1852), in McCluskey (1964, pp. 79-80).
7. Ibid., pp. 80-81.
8. "Pastoral Letter," First Provincial Council of Cincinnati (1855), in Burns and Bernard (1937, p. 138).
9. Ibid.
10. "Pastoral Letter," Second Provincial Council of Cincinnati (1858), in Bums (1912, p. 186).
11. "Pastoral Letter," Third Provincial Council of Cincinnati (1861), in Jenkins (1886, p. 34).
12. "Pastoral Letter," Second Plenary Council of Baltimore (1866), in McCluskey (1964, p. 82).
13. "Pastoral Letter," Second Plenary Council of Baltimore (1866), in Guilday (1954, p. 206).
14. Pope Pius IX, "Syllabus of Errors," quoted in Helmreich (1964, p. 5).
15. Quoted in Jenkins (1886, pp. 82-82).
16. Quoted in ibid., p. 89.
17. Quoted in ibid., p. 86.
18. Quoted in ibid., pp. 84-85.
19. Quoted in ibid., p. 86.

20.   Quoted in ibid., p. 100.
21.   Quoted in ibid., p. 99.
22.   Quoted in Jenkins (1886, pp. 121-122)
23.   "Instruction of the Propaganda de Fide" (1875), in McCluskey (1964, pp. 122-126).
24.   "The Pastoral Letter of the Third Plenary Council of Baltimore," in Guilday (1954, p. 244).
25.   Ibid., p. 245.
26.   Ibid., pp. 246-247.
27.   Gibbons, quoted in *The Catholic Citizen,* October 22, 1887, pp. 3, 1.
28.   Ibid., p. 1.

CHAPTER 8

THE BIBLE AS A TEXTBOOK OF MORAL EDUCATION

INTRODUCTION

The Bible (King James version) played a central role in the moral education scheme of Horace Mann, as we have seen in Chapter Four. It was also featured in the ideas of Noah Webster, as shown in Chapter Two. It was so important as a moral agent in the life of the schools and society in the nineteenth century that it merits its own chapter. Witness the American Bible Society, founded in 1816, which had as a main purpose the Bible's use as a school book (Butts, 1953, p. 172). It was featured in the weighty moral education task of the public schools, which was, in the words of Calvin Stowe in 1835, "no longer a mere question of benevolence, of duty, or of enlightened self-interest, but the intellectual and religious training of our foreign population has become essential to our own safety; we are prompted to it by the instinct of self-preservation" (McClellan, 1999, p. 35). Also in 1835, the Rev. Lyman Beecher, in his *Plan for the West*, urged New England Protestants to take an interest in education in the west, the "great experiment ... whether the perpetuity of our republican institutions can be reconciled with universal suffrage ... can the nation ... be so imbued with intelligence and virtue ... bring about a perpetual self-preserving energy." The west would be the scene of the "conflict of institutions for the education of her sons, for purposes of superstition, or evangelical light; of despotism, or liberty."[1] Considerable

Moral Education in America's Schools: The Continuing Challenge, 89–107
Copyright © 2005 by Information Age Publishing

attention will be focused on the state of Wisconsin in this chapter, because it was in that state that the devotional use of the Bible, as an agent of moral education, was for the first time ruled illegal in the public schools.

EARLY SUPPORT

In 1839 the Baltimore City Council left no doubt as to its position on how it viewed the moral educative role of the Bible in its public schools: "The chief object in adopting the use of the sacred volume was, to endeavor, by every available means, to imbue the minds of the scholars with that moral influence which its inspired pages are so well calculated to impart."[2] The Board declared that it would never support sectarianism in its schools but believed that the "Holy Scriptures have provided an invaluable blessing to the Christian world"; it therefore indulged "in the hope that a salutary influence will be diffused in the schools from that pure and sacred source."[3] The Board was joined that year by American Bible Societies who pledged that the Scriptures would be read in every classroom in the nation, and repeated that commitment again in 1840 (Billington, 1938, p. 145).

Confronted by clashes with Roman Catholics over the use of the King James version in schools, one minister in New York proclaimed in 1840 that "*I would rather be an infidel than a papist*" (Billington, 1938, p. 147). Rev. Horace Bushnell declared that same year that securing the Bible its "proper place" must be a major concern for all Christians, a "sacred duty" to which all "sectarian claims must be sacrificed.... It must be enough to find a place for the bible as a book of principles, as containing the true standards of character and the best motives and aids to virtue."[4] Other conflicts with Catholics occurred over the place of the Bible as a book of moral education in the schools. These clashes led the Ohio Presbyterian and Congregational Convention in 1844 to state that the "liberty to *worship* God according to the dictates of conscience," which had been conceded by the Constitution, "cannot, by any principle of legitimate interpretation, be construed into a right to embarrass the municipal authorities of this Christian and Protestant nation in the ordering of their district schools."[5]

WISCONSIN AT THE TIME OF STATEHOOD

As the Wisconsin Territory moved towards statehood in the mid 1840s the idea of assimilating common schools began to grow. The Constitutional Convention of 1846 deleted the words "no book of religious doctrine or belief" from its education plank and replaced them with "no sectarian instruction shall be used or permitted in any common school in this state," an indication that the Bible was not considered sectarian instruction (Quaife, 1919, pp. 538, 744).

The voters rejected the 1846 Constitution but approved a revised version in 1848. This Constitution, established with gratitude to "Almighty God for our freedom," guaranteed the rights of religious liberty and conscience, and denied preference to any "religious establishment or modes of worship." It also established free district schools that were not allowed any "sectarian instruction" (Quaife, 1928, pp. 227, 714; Kliebard, 1969, p. 112). The founders did not prohibit a "book of religious doctrine or belief" because that would have excluded the Bible (Whitford, 1869, p. 343). Moral education was uppermost in the minds of the state's leaders as is clear from Governor Nelson Dewey's words to the legislature in 1848 that included the recommendation that they "educate people in the scale of moral excellence and intellectual improvement."[6] The Senate Education Committee, responding to his message, spoke of the state's responsibility to exercise a "benign influence over the moral tone of its whole people."[7] The role of the Bible in contributing to the moral temper of the times is reflected in the requirement in Wisconsin's *Statutes* that the master give his apprentice, "at the expiration of his or her service, a new Bible." The *Statutes* also required keepers of prisons, at "county expense," to have a copy of the "Bible or New Testament" available during prisoners' confinement, and mandated enabling the inmates to consult "any minister of the gospel" for instructing them in their "moral and religious duties." The "family Bible" was the first item of personal property of an executed prisoner's that could not be seized or sold by the state.[8] The *Statutes* also held the State Superintendent of Schools responsible to "discourage the use of sectarian books and sectarian instruction in the schools."[9]

Early Wisconsin school superintendents support the view that the Bible occupied an exalted place in moral education in Wisconsin schools and that it was not considered to constitute sectarian instruction. In 1850, Superintendent Eleazar Root declared that since "under our laws the bible is not regarded as a sectarian book," it could be used in any school district in the state.[10] Less than a year later he ruled that the Wisconsin constitution prohibited all sectarian instruction in the common schools, but "it does not prohibit simply the reading of the Bible in school, for the Bible under our law is not regarded as a sectarian book."[11] Root believed that it was permissible for a teacher to pray in school, because praying was "one of the most beneficial exercises that can be introduced." Schooling, he held, would be incomplete if it focused on the memory and intellect and neglected a "just knowledge and love of those wholesome truths which form the basis of all religions."[12] The Bible was the source of these truths.

Azel P. Ladd succeeded Root, an Episcopal clergyman. Ladd argued that "there can be no doubt, under our laws, of the Bible being a lawful book to be read in common schools."[13] It was not to be read as a mere textbook, however. It was to play a prominent role in the moral function of the common schools:

> The moral sense and the affections are means which a kind creator has provided for educating the character of youth. The child should be taught to rely on his own consciousness of right as his rule of conduct.... He should be taught to despise and shun falsehood, dishonor, and whatever is vicious or base—to admire and practice truth, temperance, and whatever is virtuous and noble. He should be taught to love virtue for its loveliness, to hate evil because of the evil, and not from a selfish hope of reward or a coward fear of punishment.[14]

THE PRE-CIVIL WAR CLIMATE

The effect of reading from the Bible each morning was described as "most salutary" by a teacher in southern Indiana in 1849. She felt she couldn't "commence the duties of the day without it." It provided the foundation for her to "often talk with them [the children] about the lesson, endeavoring to impress on their minds the serenity of having a new heart—of loving the Savior, and in general I am listened to with much apparent interest."[15] The teacher's role in the overall religious mission of the common schools was a holy one. Moral education was the overriding goal of the schools in the Midwest as well as in the East. Ministers occupied key positions of leadership, for instance, Caleb Mills, Superintendent of Schools in Indiana and his counterpart in Michigan, John D. Pierce, were ordained ministers (Blinder, 1974, p. 71). The teacher's responsibility was ordained by God:

> As certainly as God has traced this way for the development of the mind, so certainly the teacher should follow it in his method. The organization of the child's mind is not altered when he is sent to school; it remains the same. And as God was the teacher of the child til now, so he will remain his teacher, and the school-teacher ought to be his assistant. (p. 71)

Accepting this divinely-issued charge, teachers in tax-supported schools daily guided their students in sound moral character, utilizing Bible-reading, prayers, and hymns that were common to all Protestant creeds. They were to place the children in "pleasant, healthful surroundings," and expose them to "examples of morality" that were provided through "Biblical and secular literature" and the "behavior of virtuous parents and teachers." As a result, the child was to be "virtuous, obedient, thrifty, diligent, and loyal to faith and state," quite similar to his predecessor in colonial Massachusetts (Binder, 1974, p. 73). Carl Kaestle points out that the increase in Catholic population led Protestants to close their ranks on educational issues, including Bible-reading in the schools. The Superintendent of Schools in Brooklyn maintained in 1851:

> That there is one God; that we are His creatures, dependent on Him for our mercies, and accountable to Him for our conduct; that we are sinners and need a Savior; and that One "mighty to save" has been provided. These are truths freely admitted and incidentally taught throughout our public schools.[16]

The case of Thomas Wall, a Catholic youth who was whipped for, among other things, allegedly causing a "disturbance during daily Bible reading," is instructive for several reasons. One of those was expressed by Henry Durand, that it was "not the Protestant Bible, but the Christian Bible" that was being read. As Durand put it in 1859, "our children are to learn piety from it, not sectarianism, or creeds, but pure religion, undefiled before God." The Bible, he said, "will remain the rule and guide of our faith, the Great Charter of our liberties."[17] The Rev. J. E. Rankin of Vermont lent his support to the use and importance of the Bible in public schools in 1860 when he held that the "right to keep the bible in its original position of dignity and authority" was an "inalienable right of Protestant Vermont," reflecting both the Protestant domination of public schooling and the identification of Protestantism with Americanism.[18] Illinois' superintendent added in 1861 that "moral education should be based on those 'original, immutable, and indestructible maxims of moral rectitude' on which people of all faiths agreed."[19]

Wisconsin's population reveals a trend toward heterogeneity in the 1850s. With that trend came challenges to the Protestant hegemony in public schools, a hegemony that was highlighted by the character-building reading of the King James version of the Bible. Responding to a controversy over the practice of Bible-reading in 1858 Superintendent Lyman C. Draper (1858) contended that the common sense of the people of Wisconsin would not consent to the banishment of the Bible from its schools:

> and thus repudiate its unequalled teachings of virtue and morality as unfit for the instruction and guidance of the children of their love—children who, at no distant day, must become the rulers and law-givers of the State, and custodian of all that we now hold dear and sacred, our homes, our country, Christianity and the Bible. (pp. 242-243)

The teacher's most ennobling action, Draper averred, was to teach moral virtue, devoid of any sectarian comments. At all costs the Bible should be read, "reverently and impressively, and the blessing of the God of the Bible will never fail to attend it" (p. 243). Religion, and the Bible, and consequently moral education, obviously held a prominent place in Draper's view of common public schools:

> But, you may ask, may not a majority of the School Board, if they see fit, utterly refuse to tolerate the Bible, prayer and moral instruction in the public school? We might obstinately and insanely refuse food for our perishing bodies, as well as for our craving immortal minds, but we should only spite and injure ourselves by so rash and suicidal an act, The District Board, too, under the advice of the Superintendent of Public Instruction, has power to determine the text-books to be used; and I should ever feel bound to regard with special favor the use of the Bible in public schools, as preeminently first in importance among textbooks for teaching the noblest principles of virtue, morality, patriotism and good order—love and reverence for God—charity and good will to man. (p. 244)

Draper was consistent. On the eve of his retirement from office, he pleaded "earnestly for moral, and as earnestly for deprecating sectarian, instruction in our public schools," and for the "sacred preservation of the School fund, consecrated to the education of our children."[20] A majority of the state's inhabitants still agreed with the position espoused at the Wisconsin Teachers Convention in 1859 that it was the function of the public school to inculcate the "broader and sublimer sentiments" of religion and morality in their youthful charges and that "The Bible is preeminently the book of God, and as such it belongs, by divine grant, to every human being. It has an equal right to the school-room with the air which the same God has made" (Kinney, 1859, p. 71). The "wedding" between the moral and the intellectual in public schools, with the former having ascendancy, was the theme of E. P. Larkin's article in 1859:

> I have no hesitation in saying that if we could have but one, moral and religious culture is even more important than a knowledge of letters; and that the former cannot be excluded from any system of popular education without infinite hazard. Happily, the two are so far from being hostile forces in the common domain, that they are natural allies, moving on harmoniously in the same right line, and mutually strengthening each other. The more virtue you can diffuse into the hearts of your pupils the better they will improve their time, and the more rapid will be their proficiency in the common studies. (Larkin, 1859, p. 103)

THE WAR AND ITS AFTERMATH

Moral education remained paramount in the concern of Wisconsin's superintendents as the Civil War began and it continued so throughout the 1860s. Josiah Pickard, superintendent from 1860-1864 was concerned about the pernicious effects of the "school in the street" on the moral character of the young.[21] A year later he spoke of the "vital interest" the state had in the training of students' moral faculties, and remarked that the "chief obstacles" to the progress of the common schools in the state were "bad morals and bad manners."[22] In 1863 Pickard observed that the permanent existence of the nation depended on "a large, liberal and truly Christian basis" of the public schools.[23]

Reading the Bible remained in the forefront of moral education in the schools during this period. It continued to be listed as a text to be used in "Moral Instruction,"[24] and its devotional reading was held not to constitute sectarian instruction.[25] The consensus regarding the Bible's fundamental role in infusing Christian principles into all public school children, without engaging in sectarianism, was expressed in the *Wisconsin Journal of Education* in 1864:

> There is enough—thank God there is enough—of common Christian ground in the Bible, for all sects to meet on and cultivate the spirit of Christian truth, love and brotherhood, without impaling themselves on sectarian points of irrevocably diverging into sectarian by-paths.[26]

John McMynn, who in 1861 had described the mission of teachers as one of "imparting moral and religious instruction, and in Christianizing the people,"[27] became superintendent in 1864. He recommended Francis Wayland's *The Elements of Moral Science* as a textbook. Wayland's work referred to "The Bible, The Bible, The Religion of Protestants," and then stated that "what is contained here alone is binding upon conscience" (Wayland, 1963, p. 129). This book advised its readers that the Bible contained the will of God which served as an indispensable guide to a person seeking to know her or his moral duties. The New Testament, Wayland averred:

> being thus intended for the whole human race, and being a final revelation of the will of God to man, may be supposed to contain all the moral precepts both of natural religion and of the Old Testament, together with whatever else it was important to our salvation that we should know. (p. 132)

McMynn felt the common schools were the instrument Christianity demanded to save the republic and to promote morality and the good of all. An editorial in the *Wisconsin Journal of Education* in 1865 looked to the

schools to contribute to the cause of religion and morality "without usurping the office of preacher… by imparting the leading truths of the Bible,
and thus laying the foundations for parent and minister of the gospel to
build upon."[28]

Devotional Bible-reading in schools became a subject for court decisions as the practice was challenged in several states in the union in the
1860s. In one such decision in 1866, the Massachusetts Supreme Court
came out in strong, forthright support of the practice:

> No more appropriate method could be adopted of keeping in the minds of
> both teachers and scholars that one of the chief objects of education, as
> declared by the statutes of this commonwealth, and which teachers are espe-
> cially enjoined to carry into effect, is to impress on the minds of children
> and youth committed to their care and instruction the principles of piety
> and justice, and a sacred regard for truth.[29]

Just three years later the National Teachers Association, the forerunner
of the National Education Association (NEA), proclaimed that the "Bible
should not only be studied, venerated and honored as a classic for all
ages, people, and languages … but devotionally read, and its precepts
inculcated in all the common schools of the land." Shortly after espousing
this statement, they voted against allowing any "partisan or sectarian
principles in our public schools, or the appropriation of public funds for
the support of sectarian schools" because it was a "violation of the fundamental principles of our American system of education" (Tyack & Hansot,
1982, pp. 74-75).

The Bible as a book of moral education in schools received the backing
of yet another court decision, this time by the Superior Court in Cincinnati, in the case of *Minor* v. *Board of Education* in 1870. Justice Hagans,
writing for the majority, penned that the Holy Bible impresses on the:

> children of the common schools, the principles and duties of morality ad
> justice, and a sacred regard for truth, love of country, humanity, increased
> benevolence, sobriety, industry, chastity, moderation, temperance and all
> other virtues, which are the ornaments of human society.[30]

American Protestants would have agreed with the position of conservative
R. W. Clark, who wrote in 1870 about the Bible's basic function in American public schools:

> In a Protestant nation, the Protestant Bible should be used in the public
> schools, and thus carry out the public choice according to the public con-
> science, in the system of education for freedom's sake, and in this, its
> authority is as legitimate as in any civil legislation.[31]

In 1870 Samuel Fallows was installed as superintendent of schools in Wisconsin. A colonel in the "God and Morality" regiment of the Union Army in the Civil War, Fallows was a Methodist minister and the secretary of the Wisconsin Methodist Conference for several years before becoming superintendent (Agnew et al., 1960, p. 126). That same year the state's Methodists issued a forceful statement on the relation of the church to the common schools. They declared that the common school system was the offspring of the Bible; that popular education existed only among Evangelical Protestants who alone were capable of furnishing the inspirational base for the system's existence; and that Protestant Christianity had special duties to maintain it.[32] Taking note of claims made by Catholics that the devotional reading of the Bible was a sectarian practice and made the schools sectarian, the Methodists replied that the Bible was "the voice of the nation"; and they asked if the "cherished convictions of a great people" should be "sacrificed to the abnormal prejudices and caprices of exceptional individuals" whose objective is to destroy the system.[33] The Methodists resolved that:

> in the Common schools no part of the mind or character shall be neglected—least of all that which is highest and most important. As the religious principles of the Bible have been the basis and inspiration of the system from the beginning, so they should continue to inform and animate it, and that not in the interest of any sect or party, but of a broad, Catholic, symmetrical culture, embracing especially those moral and religious elements which humanity is known to crave and profit by.[34]

CONFLICT INTENSIFIES

Challenges to the place of the Bible and its longtime featured role in moral education intensified in the 1880s. Referring to challenges to its prominence posed by some Catholics, one minister stated that "'The roots of the American government run into the Bible, and with the Bible our government stands or falls." Those who object to its reading in the schools, he averred, "are simply not good Americans."[35] In an address to the NEA in 1888 George Atkinson proclaimed that the nation, "beset by anarchism, its moral fabric unraveling," needed the authoritative discipline provided by the Bible. Therein could be found the principles of rectitude, which were "axioms, self-evident truths, needing only to be stated in order to be admitted. Of such quality are the Decalogue, the Proverbs, the aphorisms of Jesus in the Sermon on the Mount, and in His parables."[36]

It was in the 1880s that the first successful legal challenge to the moral educative role of the Bible in schools was mounted. That confrontation occurred in the state of Wisconsin, culminating in the state's outlawing the use of the Bible in the common schools of that state. The claims made in the Bible's defense are of particular interest for this chapter.

The struggle commenced with the charge leveled by some Catholics in Edgerton, Wisconsin that the devotional reading of the Bible constituted sectarian instruction, violated the rights of conscience of the Catholic students in the school, and hence was in violation of the law.[37] The School Board responded that the practice was not sectarian instruction, that the Bible was an indispensable text, unable to be replaced by any other book, and that it was a crucial part of the students' education.[38] John R. Bennett was the presiding judge over the 12th Circuit Court, Rock County, Janesville, Wisconsin. He upheld Bible-reading, saying it did not constitute sectarian instruction, that "sectarianism" came from "creeds which imperfectly define the great spiritual truths of the Bible, and which rituals only imperfectly express" and not from the Bible itself (Bennett, 1889, pp. 56-67). Referring to the Bible as a unique book, Bennett reminisced that, it was the only book left in the schools since he was a boy, and described it as a "good, true and ever faithful friend and counselor" (pp. 69-77).

The case was appealed to the Wisconsin Supreme Court. A. A. Jackson represented the Edgerton School Board. He argued that the framers of Wisconsin's constitution had intended to "educate and make intelligent and independent the common people and leave them free to form their own religious opinions and choose their own form of worship." This they had done, and had chosen to read and interpret the Scriptures for themselves in forming their consciences.[39] The Bible, he averred, could not constitute sectarian instruction because it belonged to all people and was responsible for civil liberty:

> Did they [the framers] intend that coming generations should be kept in ignorance of the principles upon which the nation had been founded; that their children should remain in ignorance of the biblical history and chronology; that the youth of this land should be kept in ignorance of the grand system of morals inculcated by the Bible; that its sublime poetry should be kept from places of education.[40]

Indeed, it would be unlawful to exclude the Bible from schools because it was "THE BOOK" to be used in teaching morals and the fundamentals of the Christian religion.[41] Jackson concluded his presentation with a plea to the Court not to abandon the Bible that had been of such value to the country and individual, the banning of which would result in incalculable injury to both:

Shall this wonderful book that has commanded the admiration of men wherever it is known, whose teaching is the rule of action of people of this great nation, that has molded the form, and aided in a most remarkable degree the wonderful growth and development of this nation, and that has been, and is a guide in life, a consolation in death, be excluded from the schools where our children are taught.[42]

THE DECISION AND REACTION TO IT

On March 17, 1890 the Wisconsin Supreme Court adjudged that devotional Bible-reading in public schools constituted sectarian instruction and made the school a place of worship; hence it was in violation of the Wisconsin Constitution.[43] The reaction of several of the Protestant churches in the state document the role that the Bible had in moral education in their views and hence are relevant to the thesis of this chapter.

The state's Baptists responded that the decision should lead to the establishment of denominational schools, where God and His holy word would be the "supreme and sole authority."[44] Several local Baptist associations expressed similar thoughts, since the Bible had been driven from the schools, erroneously labeled as a sectarian book.[45]

The Wisconsin Congregationalists saw the decision as weakening the moral fibre of the nation. They adopted the resolution of Professor J. J. Blaisdell of Beloit College, which expressed their stand on the ideal relationship between religion, government, and public education, which, if it were absent, could only result in the decay of civilization:

> 4.   That, as in the conception of our fathers, in which the Common School had its origin, the primary truths of religion were a fundamental element, so we hold the maintaining of that to be indispensable. Without it what the pupil learns ceases to have for him its true significance and relation to his life as a citizen and as a man, and morality has neither ground of authority nor directive principle. Without it the school will not preserve society from disregard of government and from falling sooner or later into fatal confusion. Inasmuch, then, as the principle for which we contend is recognized in the Constitution of the commonwealth, we require that the common and public schools, where the youth of the state are instructed, be not hindered from teaching them, in connection with the use of the Bible and otherwise, that they are beholden to a Divine Ruler of the Universe in the terms of Duty and ought to practice the Spirit, as exemplified and taught by Jesus Christ, of obedience toward Him and brotherhood toward all men.[46]

In a subsequent paper, Blaisdell pleaded that the Bible be returned to the public schools of the state for the safety of the republic:

The common school without religion is the Republic unsafe. Even for children trained in religious homes such training will not substitute for the training of the school-room. With the larger multitude of our children, who need it most, there is no home religious training, and without it in the school-room as parent of higher thought and of moral restraint and incentive, they go into the duties of citizenship a peril to the Republic.... But religion—the religion of the Bible—is provided for in the Constitution of our commonwealth as our birthright in the school-room, our birthright everywhere. The Constitution recognizes it as the common atmosphere of our civic life. To that birthright we make our claim.[47]

Presbyterian reaction was closely akin to that of the Congregationalist. The Presbyterian General Assembly of the United States declared its "unalterable devotion to the public school system as the most effective agency, next to the Church of God, in laying the foundations of popular intelligence, virtue and freedom in the United States."[48] That body proclaimed its loyalty to the Bible as the "Magna Carta of our best moral and religious influences" and regarded its expulsion from the public schools as a "deplorable and suicidal act."[49]

Wisconsin Presbyterians predicted dire calamities of social, moral, and intellectual nature to befall society shortly as a result of the Bible's expulsion from schools. They argued that the Court's decision tended to "weaken the schools as instruments of both intellectual and moral education," and was "fraught with most baleful consequences to society and the commonwealth." They called on "ministers, Sunday school teachers, and heads of families" to make "more widely known" the "inestimable service rendered to the cause of liberty, of civilization, of progress and of human welfare in general by the Christian Scriptures"?[50] A year later, in a report from a committee headed by the Rev. W.A. McAtee, Wisconsin's Presbyterians reiterated their loyalty to the public school system, but worried that it would become "defective" if moral training, "based upon fundamental religious convictions," as contained in the Bible, were excluded from the schools and sought the help of their fellow citizens to "aid us in deriving means for its revival" (McAtee, 1891, p. 16).

Madison's Presbyterians said the elimination of the Bible from schools gave the "Christian patriot cause for the gravest concern." The Bible, they contended, was the hub of the Christian religion, was not a sectarian book, but belonged to all Christians; it was "the central sun of the Christian system, not one of its planets; the one clear foundation of Christian truth, not one of its subordinate streams," The Court's decision was "out of keeping with our institutions, which are fundamentally Christian," put an "unseemly stigma upon the book to which we owe our liberties," and outlawed the "very Book from the schools" which that book "alone made free."[51] The Madison body then described the Bible's role in developing and maintaining the moral fibre of the school's students, as well as society's citizens:

> We cannot but regard the decision as greatly weakening our whole system of common schools. It impairs their efficiency as instruments of intellectual awakening and instruction by removing from them the greatest educational force and the most important body of literature known to mankind. It tends to a relaxation of discipline by silencing in the schools the only authoritative voice of moral obligation recognized in Christendom. And it sows broadcast the seeds of distrust in our common schools, in regard to their moral influence…. We regard the decision as having a dangerous tendency in the community at large as well as in the schools. The vast and grave social and political problems that are about and before us can only be successfully met by a people whose moral convictions are perpetually requickened and reinvigorated. This great work the Bible is alone equal to, and therefore, as citizens and patriots profoundly interested in our country's welfare, we deplore every action of our authorities which tends to lessen its influence.[52]

The Synod observed that the Bible-less schools were worthy of the words of Dante, "All hope abandon who enter here," nonetheless concluded its statements with the motto of "grand old John Wyckliffe, 'Nevertheless, I think the truth will conquer'."[53]

Other Wisconsin presbyteries added their voices in support of the Bible's moral role in schools and society. For instance, the Fond du Lac Presbytery declared that the "Bible is the source of our liberties and the true standard of moral authority." It is a "civilizing and educational force" and the "reading of the Bible in our public schools is an essential and necessary factor to the full, complete and healthy moral and educational development of the youth of our state and country."[54] The Welsh Presbyterian Synod resolved that "our government is founded on Christian civilization, which in turn rests on the Bible."[55]

The undisputed leading spokesperson for the Presbyterian Church in Wisconsin on the indispensability of the Bible in schools in particular and in society in general was the Rev. W. A. McAtee of Madison. In April of 1890 he wrote that when the Bible was driven out of New York City's public schools almost all moral instruction went with it, and as a result "tens of thousands of children are being reared in ignorance of the moral law and its requirements." The civil state, he argued, must for its own sake "teach reverence for God as the basis for morals" (McAtee, 1890a, p. 4). Thirty-six of seventy-one school commissioners in Wisconsin had reported that no instruction in morality was required in their schools. Parents were not up to the task, he averred, with the result that "thousands of our school children are not even taught to be clean, respectful, honest and truthful." This phenomenon was crucial, he maintained, because over a third of Wisconsin's population does not attend any Sunday school, so:

> we have a *generation of children coming forward to the responsibilities of self-government who have not been taught to reverence God, or love their fellow men, or at best, have had only slight and occasional instruction in these duties.* (McAtee, 1890a, p. 4)

This situation must be reversed, he held, and "nonsectarian" religion, must be returned to the public schools in the form of Bible-reading and the teaching of those "theistic principles which are common to all sects and distinctive to none, which *are indispensable for good character and good citizenship*" (p. 4). Three days later another letter from McAtee appeared in the pages of the *Journal*. This time McAtee argued on behalf of the nonsectarian religious function of the public schools, which in his eyes was "the law of the land." Religion, he wrote, *"is the only solid basis of morals, and that moral instruction not resting on this basis is only a building upon sand"* (p. 1).

McAtee's chief treatise about the Bible was entitled "Must the Bible Go?" In it he referred to the Bible as the "chief foe" of sectarianism, and asserted that:

> Keep the Bible away from the people, and they may be led almost at will by their religious guides. Put the Bible into their hands, let them read and interpret it for themselves, and ecclesiastical narrowness and intolerance will give way to breadth and liberality. (McAtee, 1890b, p. 14)

The Court's decision would have baleful consequences for Wisconsin's schools and society, because it would shut out:

> from any department of our civil life the salutary and vitalizing influence of religion itself. The whole people was religious not only, but Christian. It had a Christian history of more than a thousand years behind it. Christianity was a part of its very blood, and bone, and brain. It had settled these shores with a Christian motive. It had consecrated them to a Christian purpose. It had made Christianity ... part of the "fundamental law" of the land. All of its hopes for the permanence, prosperity and perpetuity of its work, rested on the firm basis of its religious faith. (McAtee, 1890b, p. 28)

Wisconsin now found itself to be the only "Godless commonwealth" in the nation, unable to receive the blessings of a free government that "can only be maintained by a firm adherence to justice, moderation, temperance, frugality, and virtue, and by frequent recurrence to fundamental principles." Its schools were now "*irreligious*," unsatisfactory, and incapable of forming the young in Christian virtue (McAtee, 1890b, p. 67).

Methodist clergy joined their Congregationalist and Presbyterian brethren in denouncing the legal mandate of separation for the Bible ftom the schools and likewise predicted deplorable results. The Rev. J. R. Creighton of Milwaukee blamed the "Romish hierarchy" for the debacle:

> Shall Bible America, at the beck of a foreign autocrat who has commanded that the system which lies at the basis of our nation's prosperity and moral elevation shall be separated and broken up ... ?[56]

Creighton was joined by the Rev. D. C. John of Racine, who said the government's ban on the Bible in schools would lead the pupils to think it was a corrupt book. He warned that nations that disrespected the word of God had come to ignominious ends.[57] The Rev. F. S. Stein of Milwaukee averred that it was the Christian origins of the nation that produced good citizens, which institutionalized the country's Christian character. The divorce of the Bible and its moral instruction from the public schools defeated the very purpose for which the schools had been founded:

> Our youth must be taught in public schools that the Ten Commandments are as important as the ten digits; that a lie is to be avoided as much as bad grammar; that dishonesty is to be guarded against as much as a wrong answer in arithmetic; that honesty and purity are as essential as history and physics. The Bible should therefore be the standard text on morality in every school room.[58]

The moral catastrophe which awaited Wisconsin sans the Bible in its schools was the theme of other Protestant spokesmen. A former president of the University of Wisconsin, John E. Bascom, proclaimed that the Bible was:

> the chief classic of the English language, the most wide-reaching and forceful historic record; it is incomparably superior to all other books in its intellectual productiveness, moral power and spiritual inspiration.[59]

The Protestant press exhibited similar sentiments. E. H. Merrell, President of Ripon College, wrote that "morality without religion" was impossible, and he foresaw legions of young Wisconsites graduating from the public schools morally bankrupt because they had been deprived of the character-building influence of the Bible (Merrell, 1890, p. 2), "Wisconsin," penned the Rev. John A. Dodds, "is well on the way toward the religion and morality of the Hottentots and of the French revolutionists." The decision that stripped the Bible from the schools was a "covenant with death and an agreement with hell."[60] An editorial in the Protestant publication, *The Advance*, described the decision as "at war with the good of our system of public schools." Two things to be "tabooed and banished and forever kept out of the public schools, are, the idea of God and any sense of honor and reverence to Almighty God."[61]

The future was bleak, indeed. Merrell declared that the "Secularized mind is not educated, and woe to the community when that form of ignorance becomes general," because while history has had its moral infidels, "there never has been, and there never will be, a 'moral infidel community'."[62] Dodds predicted the "wrath of Almighty God on the whole nation" unless the Bible was restored to the schools.[63]

CONCLUSION

Bible-reading had been a bastion of the Protestant position of moral education in the common schools from the onset. Indeed, it had been a staple of the schools since colonial times. The decision by the Supreme Court of Wisconsin that it constituted sectarian instruction and was therefore unconstitutional was not only the first of its kind but was also a harbinger of things to come. It presaged a like decision by the Supreme Court of the United States in 1963.[64] At the time of that decision, thirty-seven states permitted Bible-reading in the public schools; and more important perhaps, thirteen of those states mandated the practice (Boles, 1965, pp. 331-332). Bible-reading supporters remain; some of them maintain that moral and behavior problems in the nation's public schools at the onset of the third millennium are caused by the absence of the Bible, and they call for its return. In their view, God's word as expressed in the Scriptures is the only sure way for moral education to be effective in the education of the nation's young.

NOTES

1. Quoted in Welter (1962, p. 107).
2. Quoted in Dunn (1958, p. 222).
3. Ibid., p. 224.
4. Quoted in Dunn (1958, p. 260).
5. Quoted in Welter (1962, p. 106).
6. *Journal of the Senate of the First Legislature of the State of Wisconsin*, 1848. Madison: Phenodyne A. Bird, 1848, Appendix 2, p. 12.
7. Ibid., Appendix 7, p. 34..

8. *The Revised Statutes of the State of Wisconsin*, 1849. Southport, WI: C. Latham Sholes, 1849, pp. 404-405, 736, 541.

9. Ibid., p. 89.

10. Wisconsin Superintendents of Public Instruction. *Decisions in Appeals.* I, December 3, 1850, State Historical Society of Wisconsin, p. 94.

11. Ibid., August 28, 1851, p. 240.

12. Ibid., July 1851, pp. 226-227.

13. Ibid., February 21, 1852, pp. 287-288.

14. *Annual Report of the State Superintendent of Public Instruction for the State of Wisconsin*, 1853. Madison: David Atwood, 1854, p. 43.

15. Quoted in Fraser (2001, pp. 99-100).

16. Quoted in Kaestle (1983, p. 99).

17. Quoted in Dunn (1958, pp. 276-277,273).

18. Quoted in Tyack (1970, p. 227).

19. Quoted in Kaestle (1983, p. 99).

20. *Eleventh annual report on the condition and improvement of the common schools and educational interests of the State of Wisconsin for the year 1859.* Madison: James Ross, 1859, p. 34.

21. *Thirteenth annual report on the condition and improvement of the common schools and educational interests of the State of Wisconsin, for the year 1861.* Madison: Smith and Cullaton, 1861, p. 9.

22. *Fourteenth annual report on the condition and improvement of the common schools and educational interests of the State of Wisconsin, for the year 1862.* Madison: W. C. Roberts, 1862, p. 81.

23. *Fifteenth annual report of the superintendent of public instruction of the State of Wisconsin, for the year ending August 31, 1863.* Madison: William J. Park, 1863, p. 109.

24. Ibid., p. 102.

25. Wisconsin Superintendents of Public Instruction. *Decisions in Appeals.* II, February 18, 1860, State Historical Society of Wisconsin, p. 2.

26. "Religion in schools." *Wisconsin Journal of Education* (NS), I, 3 (September 1864), p. 80.

27. "Mr. McMynn's address." *Wisconsin Journal of Education* VI, 3 (September 1861), p. 78.

28. "Morals-Religion-The Bible," *Wisconsin Journal of Education* (NS), I, 2 (May 1865): 289-290.

29. *Spiller v. Inhabitants of Woburn.* 94 Mass. 127, in Bremner (1971, p. 1463).

30. Quoted in Michaelsen (1970, p. 32).

31. Quoted in Tyack (1970, p. 234).

32. "The Relation of the Church to the Common School," in the *Minutes of the Twenty Fourth Session of the Wisconsin Annual Conference of the Methodist Episcopal Church 1870.* Milwaukee: Index Printing Office, 1870, p. 29.

33. Ibid., p. 30.

34. Ibid., p. 31.

35. Quoted in Tyack (1970, pp. 230-231).

36. Quoted in Ibid., p. 223.

37. "Petition of Relators, State ex reI. Weiss and others, Appellants, vs. The District Board of School District No. Eight of the City of Edgerton, Respondent." *Wisconsin Reports.* 76 Wis. 177, pp. 179-180. Chicago: Callaghan and Co., 1890.

38. "Return of the District Board," Ibid., pp. 181-186.

39. Respondent's Brief. Brief of AA Jackson. State of Wisconsin. In Supreme Court." *The State of Wisconsin ex reI., Frederick Weiss, et al., Appellants, vs. The District Board of School District No. Eight of The City of Edgerton, Respondent.* Edgerton: F.W. Coon, 1890, pp. 24-29.

40. Ibid., p. 156.

41. Ibid., p. 171.

42. Ibid., p. 198.

43. William Penn Lyon, "Opinion," *Decision of the Supreme Court of the State of Wisconsin Relating to the Reading of the Bible in Public Schools.* Madison: Democrat Printing Company, 1890, pp. 12-222; Justice John B. Cassoday, "Opinion," Ibid., pp. 23-32.

44. *Minutes of the Wisconsin Baptist Anniversaries 1890.* Evansville, WI: R.M. Antes, 1890, p. 39.

45. *Minutes of the Central Wisconsin Baptist Association, at Its Thirty-Second Annual Meeting 1890.* Waupaca, WI: D.L. Stinchfield, 1890, p. 6; *Minutes of the Forty-Fifth Anniversary of the Walworth Baptist Association 1890.* Delavan, WI: W.G. Weeks, 1890, p. 5.

46. *Minutes of the Fiftieth Annual Meeting of the Congregational Convention of Wisconsin 1890.* Madison: Tracy, Gibbs and Co., 1890, p. 45.

47. J.J. Blaisdell, "The Edgerton Bible Decision," in *The Bible in the Public Schools 1890.* Binder's title. A bound pamphlet in the State Historical Society of Wisconsin, Madison, pp. 35-36.

48. *Minutes of the General Assembly of the Presbyterian Church in the United States of America 1890.* New Series, XIII. Philadelphia: Mac Calla and Co., 1890, p. 104.

49. Ibid.

50. *Minutes of the Synod of Wisconsin of the Presbyterian Church 1890.* Madison: Tracy, Gibbs and Co., 1890, pp. 13-14.

51. Madison Presbytery, *An Official Deliverance in Regard to the Late Decision of the Supreme Court of Wisconsin, concerning the Bible and Our Public Schools.* Janesville, WI: Wm F. Brown, Stated Clerk, 1890, pp. 1-3.

52. Ibid., p. 3.

53. Ibid., pp. 2-3.

54. Quoted in the *Milwaukee Sentinel,* April 11, 1890, p. 10.

55. *The Bennett Law.* A scrapbook in the Library of the State Historical Society of Wisconsin, Madison, dated June 15, 1890.

56. Rev. J.R. Creighton, quoted in *Milwaukee Sentinel,* April 14, 1890, p. 12.

57. Rev. D.C. John, quoted in *Milwaukee Sentinel,* April 21, 1890, p. 1.

58. Rev. F.S. Stein, quoted in *The Bennett Law,* a scrapbook in the Library of the State Historical Society of Wisconsin, dated April 3, 1890.

59. John E. Bascom, quoted in *Milwaukee Sentinel,* March 23, 1890, p. 12.

60. Rev. John A. Dodds, *Milwaukee Sentinel,* May 21, 1890, p. 4.

61.   "A Monstrous Judicial Decision: The Bible Unconstitutional," *The Advance*, March 7, 1890, p. 238.

62.   Merrell, "The Bible Outlawed from the Public Schools," p. 2.

63.   Dodds, *Milwaukee Sentinel,* May 21, 1890, p. 4.

64.   *School District of Abington Township* v. *Schempp.* 374 U.S. 203 (1963).

CHAPTER 9

McGUFFEY READERS

INTRODUCTION

Born in western Pennsylvania in 1800, William Holmes McGuffey grew up in frontier Ohio. He received his early education at home; by 1826 he was a professor of Ancient Languages at Miami University in Oxford, Ohio. The famous *McGuffey Readers* are named after him, though he authored but several of the first edition. The estimated sales of the various editions of the *Readers* reached 122,000,000 by 1920 (Krug, 1966, pp. 58-59).

Though the editions are usually lumped together, John Westerhoff points out that the only edition with which McGuffey himself was associated—the first—had a vastly different moral view than did the revisions, for example the 1879 revision that was the work of Henry Vail. McGuffey himself, Westerhoff contends, espoused the "prominent values of salvation, righteousness, and piety," which were entirely missing from Vail's edition. Vail's edition was compiled to "meet the needs of national unity and the dream of a 'melting pot' for the world's oppressed masses." Its lessons were "especially appropriate for a small-town, rural population that experienced stable, semi-extended family life, minimal mobility, and a simple life-style." The Calvinistic views of McGuffey, a Presbyterian minister, were altered and "severely secularized." Yet, Westerhoff argues that each new edition continued to "introduce students to the classics, to morality, and to a good character as understood by the emerging middle

Moral Education in America's Schools: The Continuing Challenge, 109–116
Copyright © 2005 by Information Age Publishing

class ... they strove to unify the nation around a common worldview and value system" (Westerhoff, 1978, p. 19).

The *Readers* had a stormy beginning. Charles Carpenter (1963) writes that "their ups and downs, claims of violation of copyrights, and the general difficulties of getting the readers accepted was in sharp contrast to the smooth sailing of the series in its later days" (pp. 81-82). Hugh Fullerton (1963) concludes that we are in McGuffey's debt, especially for the "deeper debt of unsconsciously absorbed ideals and moral and ethical standards" which are represented by the "name 'McGuffey'" (p. v). In Fullerton's view, "From 1836 until near the close of the century, he exerted the greatest influence, culturally, of any person in American history" (p. vi). The *Readers*, Dunn (1958) notes, "entered the field and assumed prominence, they effected a retardation of the process of elimination of the religious and moral elements from the school books of the United States" (p. 88). The *Readers* clearly merit inclusion in the treatment of moral/character education in America's schools.

THE MORAL VIRTUES

McGuffey, Benjamin Crawford maintains, emphasized the "values of industry, honesty and morality." He taught temperance in all things and all moral values constantly extolled that a person be interested in other people and ready to lend them a helping hand when needed. Religion as "a guide and necessity for life" was kept before the pupils "in a most wholesome and enlightened way" (Crawford, 1974, p. 86). The *Readers'* great achievement was described as the "complete integration of Christian and middle class ideals; and in that the respect the McGuffey Readers" were the "great textbook product of American middle class culture" (Mosier, 1947, p. 123). The *Readers* interwove the social and moral, the Christian and secular, virtues such as kindness, truthfulness, modesty, gentleness, thoughtfulness, control of temper, the love of magnanimity, and a general spirit of happiness and good will toward others (p. 151).

McGuffey's virtues had a close relationship with the temperance crusade; he condemned intemperance, gambling, and dishonesty. The social virtues were designed to make a "good Christian and a good citizen" and the *Readers* were to be admired, Mosier argues, for their "constancy and consistency of purpose, as well as for the charm of many of their stories and lessons" (Mosier, 1947, p. 152). Westerhoff (1978) holds that McGuffey warned "ominously of the dangers of drunkeness, luxury, self-pride, and deception and proclaimed handsome earthly reward for courage, honesty, and respect for others" (p. 25).

The long-lasting, widespread presence of the *Readers* in the common schools made ministers happy, because they reinforced the Protestant Christian climate of "children in tax-supported schools under the guidance of teachers of sound moral character, who daily led their charges in Bible-reading, prayers, and hymns common to all Protestant creeds" (Binder, 1974, p. 71). Lawrence Cremin (1980) writes of their "special genius" for the American context was to present American heroes as "exemplars of industriousness, honesty, and intelligence" and were assigned the stature of "Biblical heroes." George Washington, for instance, was compared to Moses. "The events of American history were portrayed as developments in a holy design, Columbus having been guided by the hand of Providence and the Revolution having been brought to a successful conclusion by the intervention of God" (p. 73). The school, fortified with moral agents like the *Readers*, was to be an "incubator of virtue," along with the Church (Tyack & Hansot, 1982, p. 21). McGuffey, called "*the* schoolmaster of the nation" by some (Westerhoff, 1978, p. 13), "probably did more to mold American thinking than any other single influence except the Bible" (Pringle & Pringle, 1955, p. 30). The *Readers* provide evidence to the nineteenth century belief that the "primary aim of elementary education was moral discipline" (Younker, 1963, p. 71).

McClellan attests that the nineteenth century textbook such as McGuffey's, which he termed the "Repository of truth," presented values a a "blend of traditional Protestant morality and nineteenth century conceptions of good citizenship," which taught the "love of country, love of God, duty to parents, the necessity to develop habits of thrift, honesty, and hard work in order to accumulate property, the certainty of progress [and] the perfection of the United States" (McClellan, 1999, p. 25). Mark Sullivan agrees: the *Readers* presented tastes that were "held in common, which constituted much of America's culture, its code of morals and conduct, its standards of propriety, … its 'horse-sense' axioms." McGuffey, he maintains, was sort of an "American Confucius"; his books were to the "average American, the storehouse of the fables, stories, mottoes, proverbs, adages, and aphorisms which constituted the largest body of ethical teaching he had, excepting the Bible, and the teaching of the Bible was overlapped by that of the readers" (Sullivan, 1932, pp. 22, 28).

SPECIFIC VIRTUES

McGuffey's *Readers* have been portrayed as emphasizing virtues that made America what it was, a free, democratic society that was the repository of God's choicest blessings. **Patriotism,** or **true Americanism,** received considerable attention, and will be the first to be discussed.

Reliance on McGuffey's books made social life dependable in the United States. Indeed, "unless the youth of America is grounded in moral truths so cogently taught" in the *Readers,* unless "traits of character" that the lessons highlighted be established in the young, unless the "deteriorating forces of society" be opposed by a strength greater than that of the "organized forces of crime, immorality, and disrespect for law and order, America may not expect to be exempt from the decadence which befell the great dynasties of history" (Minnich, 1936, p. 112). The country was described in the *Readers* as the "land of opportunity, where virtue is always rewarded with material success" (Perkinson, 1991, pp. 112-113). However, as McGuffey admonished a group of teachers from Ohio not to become enemies of their country by teaching the "crude notions and revolutionary principles of modern infidelity," the nation's privileged position would be upheld only if Christianity remained the religion of the country and the bulwark of its institutions (Curti, 1959, p. 19). McGuffey himself, openly admired by Henry Ford, was portrayed as "American as Uncle Sam" (Havighurst, 1957, p. 94.) During World War II McGuffey was represented as "what America fights for now; fair play, a hatred of despotism, a deep sense of democracy, a world of cooperation and kindliness" (Chamberlin, 1942, p. 324). Lewis Atherton maintains that the *Readers* preached that the United States was morally right in revolting against England, that the country had a "mission to show the world the way to a better society; that America had fought only for freedom; ... and that international conflicts pitted 'good' nations against 'bad' nations in contests of liberty against despotism" (Atherton, 1954, p. 107). In a textbook controversy in Twin Lakes, Wisconsin in the early 1960s, one parent, arguing for their adoption in the public schools in that jurisdiction proclaimed that "McGuffey teaches the basic morals of Americanism—honor your parents, honesty, love animals." Another supporter contended that had the *Readers* been used in mid-twentieth century schools, the defections by American military personnel who were prisoners of war would not have occurred in the Korean conflict.[1]

Honesty was regularly advocated. Students were exhorted by the Commandment, "Thou shalt not steal," and a host of lessons were directed to instill honesty (Minnich, 1936, pp. 90-91). **Obedience,** the Mosaic type, "Honor thy Father and thy Mother," was held up as a standard to follow. Obedience to one's father and mother, to teachers, and to the commandments of a personal God was called for. The penalties for disobedience were unavoidable, inescapable and proportional to the offense. **Kindness,** first of all in the family to one's parents was stressed. The Golden Rule and humanitarianism were held up as standards. Cruel children were swiftly and appropriately punished; kindness to impaired humans, such as the blind, and to animals was featured (Minnich, 1936, pp. 100-103; Mosier, 1947, pp. 132-135).

Minnich notes the prominence of **thrift** in McGuffey's panoply of virtues. "A penny saved is a penny earned," and the rhyme:

> He who would thrive
> Must rise at five.
> He who *has* thriven
> May *lie* till seven.

are cited by Minnich as prime examples of thrift's importance (Minnich, 1936, p. 104). Closely tied to thrift was **labor:** "THERE IS NO EXCELLENCE WITHOUT GREAT LABOR" was McGuffey's motto (pp. 105-106). Each of these virtues was taught through stories, as was the admonition to "keep busy," which would bring true happiness, for idleness would lead to the forgetting of the ways of God and falling into sin (Mosier, 1947, pp. 114-116). Abetted by **punctuality** and **persistence,** "honesty, integrity, truth, industry, thrift and hard labor" were vIrtues "more desired than gold" yet gold is the reward of such virtues. But this "gold" is to be used in accord with God's will who gives a "great deal of money to some persons, in order that they may assist those who are poor" (pp. 105-106).

Temperance occupies a rank of high standing, especially as it enables one to overcome the temptations of alcohol and gambling, several leading frontier vices (pp. 124-125). **Modesty** was closely akin to temperance. The *Readers* called for its inculcation in "thought, word, and action" on the part of adults so as to "produce the virtue of modesty in children" (p. 142). Mothers, in particular, were enjoined to instill modesty in their daughters, who as virtuous wives and mothers (women's highest calling), themselves would join the combat against the "appalling amount of moral laxity" that existed on the frontier (Atherton, 1954, pp. 85-95). Modesty called for special treatment. It was an "object of horror" if a young person didn't have this virtue (Mosier, 1947, pp. 140-141).

THE MIDDLE CLASS AND INDIVIDUALISM

The *Readers* insisted that "God Blesses the Industrious," as Mosier put it (1947, p. 100). The United States was particularly suited for the unlocking of God-given energies of humans through education, "moral and intellectual," which must be "chiefly," the responsibility of the individual. We are the "architects of our own future." As the father told his son in a story in the *Third Eclectic Reader* (1857, p. 211), it is "not *right* that the *diligent* should give up the fruit of their labor to feed the idle" (p. 101). Yet the *Readers* taught that "*God gives a great deal of money to some persons, in order that they may assist those who are poor*" (p. 106). Christian moralism was intertwined with the middle class, whose virtues were McGuffey's. For instance, wastefulness was almost as evil as unholiness (p. 114).

The early *Readers'* treatment of economic issues reflected Calvinist teaching that wealth was the outer symbol of inner salvation. Their stories justified the existence of economic inequalities as inevitable, and a part of the social order. Indeed, the primary purpose of government was the protection of property (Spring, 1997, p. 147). The *Readers* guaranteed the "assurance of material reward for virtue and overweening admiration for the self-made man" (Elson, 1964, p. 216). There were, however, obligations connected to wealth and privileged stats, as the *4th Eclectic Reader* intoned in 1878: "And if you do not improve the advantages you enjoy, you sin against your Maker" (p. 229). Nonetheless, these responsibilities notwithstanding, private property brought blessings to society because the rich were obliged to use their wealth through property to aid the unfortunate (Atherton, 1954, p. 80). Perhaps Mosier provides the best assessment of the bond between the *Readers* and middle class values: "The great achievement of the McGuffey Readers is the complete integration of Christian and middle class ideals; and in that respect, the McGuffey readers are the great textbook product of American middle class culture" (Mosier, 1947, p. 103).

A MATCH FOR THE TIMES

As Charles Carpenter (1963, p. 85) remarks, no other textbook bearing a single person's name approached the *Readers'* popularity. Donna Younker (1963) suggests that the *Readers* evidenced that the "primary aim of elementary education" of the nineteenth century was moral discipline (p. 71). Joel Spring (1997) contends that the *Readers* meshed well with the rising spirit of American capitalism, with its "numerous moral lessons designed to teach appropriate behavior in a developing industrial society with increasing concentration of wealth and expanding social divisions between the rich and the poor" (p. 145). Lewis Atherton (1954) argues that the *Readers* contained a "set of principles which remained unchallenged until the turn of the century" (p. 65). Writing in *Our Times*, Mark Sullivan maintains that the points of view and tastes put forth in the *Readers* constituted "much of America's culture, its code of morals and conduct, its standards of property, its honesty aphorisms, its 'horse-sense' axioms," to the extent that it was kind of an "American confession." The

Readers had the "largest body of ethical teaching" the nation had, "excepting the Bible and the teaching of the Bible was overlapped by that of the readers" (Sullivan, 1932, pp. 22-23). Their moral code and social teaching fit well with the spirit and rationale of the developing common school system in the second half of the nineteenth century, a system that served as the "bastion of Protestant morality, patriotic nationalism, and social order" (Binder, 1974, p. 72).

CONCLUSION

Mosier presents an assessment of the contributions of the McGuffey *Readers* to moral education when he writes that their "great achievement" is to be found in the "complete integration of Christian and middle class ideals; and in that respect, the McGuffey Readers are the great textbook product of American middle class culture." He claims that the *Readers* reflected "social and moral ideals as to defy distinction" as to whether they were "Christian or secular" (Mosier, 1947, pp. 123-124). Hugh Fullerton (1936) expounds on this idea, addressing McGuffey's influence in the process:

> McGuffey's religious, moral and ethical influence over millions of Americans, especially in the Middle West, is beyond computing, and it still remains the American standard. He taught rugged individualism, the dignity of labor, the basic virtues of thrift, honesty, and charity, and posited the punishment of doers of evil in a hundred examples. (pp. v-vi)

Fullerton avers that McGuffey's elementary lessons "dealt largely with problems of conduct" and constituted a "complete code of ethics, a manual of morals and manners." Their influence, he claims, "has never been equaled by any school text" (pp. vii-viii). Henry Vail concurs. He writes that:

> Thousands of men and women owe their wholesome views of life, as well as whatever success they may have attained to the wholesome maxims and precepts found on every page of these valuable books. The seed they scattered has yielded a million-fold. All honor to the name and memory of this excellent and useful man. (Vail, 1911, p. 71)

John Westerhoff quotes Fullerton on McGuffey's impact: "For seventy-five years his [McGuffey's] system and his books guided the minds of four-fifths of the school children of the nation in their taste for literature, in their morality, in their social development and next to the Bible in their religion." Westerhoff cites Ralph Rusk that McGuffey's influence may well have been "greater than that of any other wrier or statesman in the West," and concludes with the words of Robert Wood Lyon who viewed the *Readers* as "more than a textbook…. They were a portable school for the new priests of the republic," embodying a "vision of piety, justice and the commonwealth, a form of 'patriotic piety' which still has appeal" (Westerhoff, 1978, pp. 15-17).

Writing in 1955, Henry and Katherine Pringle allege that the *Readers* "probably did more to mold American thinking than any other single influence except the Bible" (p. 50). Perhaps it is best to end this treatment of the moral and character influence of the McGuffey *Readers* with a tribute from a relative of McGuffey, Alice McGuffey Ruggles. She maintained that the texts exemplified the "American ideals of work, education and character." They contained the *"moral"* lessons that "William saw as most important of all." The *Readers,* she concluded, were "suited to all tastes and all ages," and served to gather people around "as they had gathered about the Bible" (Ruggles, 1936, pp. 91-92).

NOTE

1.   "Back to McGuffey," *Time,* lxxvii, 17, October 20, 1961, p. 50.

CHAPTER 10

THE "AMERICANIZING" SECULAR SCHOOL

INTRODUCTION

The Civil War resulted in an expanded role of the federal government in the affairs of the nation. The War led to the industrial development of the North, which was accompanied by urbanization and immigration. It also contributed to a nationalizing trend that included the public schools. The public school was looked to as the instrument whereby national unity would be attained and maintained. A number of measures were enacted, including compulsory attendance laws, which were aimed at reaching this patriotic goal. The secular public school was increasingly seen as the vehicle for imparting moral education.

IN THE WAKE OF THE WAR

The Bible was to hold its place in what Robert Michaelsen (1970) has termed the "compound of evangelical Protestantism and Enlightenment Deism" that continued to be a "major component in the public school mix" (p. 257). Biblical principles still undergirded the moral nature of public schools, yet as the National Teachers Association declared in 1869, the "teaching of partisan or sectarian principles in our public schools is a violation of the fundamental principles of our American system of educa-

Moral Education in America's Schools: The Continuing Challenge, 117–125
Copyright © 2005 by Information Age Publishing
All rights of reproduction in any form reserved.

tion."[1] Protestants steadily united behind the common schools as the flood of immigrants, particularly Catholics, increased. As Warren Nord has stated: "Public schools became the cultural factories of Americanization, transforming the raw material of foreign culture into good American citizens."[2]

The national fervor that was tied to the patriotic, nationalistic function of the public school in the post-Civil War era was attested to by President Ulysses S. Grant. In an address to the Army of the Tennessee in Des Moines, Iowa in 1875, Grant urged the veterans to strengthen the union they had fought to preserve. To do that, he called on them to lend their efforts to the nation's institutions, which included "free thought, free speech, a free press, pure morals, unfettered to religious sentiments, and of equal rights and privileges to all men, irrespective of nationality, color or religion." Grant then turned his attention to education:

> Encourage free schools, and resolve that not one dollar appropriated for their support shall be appropriated to the support of any sectarian schools. Resolve that neither the State, nor nation, nor both combined, shall support institutions of learning other than those sufficient to afford every child growing up in the land the opportunity of a good common school education, unmixed with sectarian, pagan or atheistic dogmas. Leave the matter of religion to the family altar, the church and the private school, supported entirely by private contributors. Keep the Church and state forever separate. With these safeguards, I believe the battle which created the Army of the Tennessee will not have been fought in vain.[3]

Grant's speech was followed closely by a proposed amendment to the federal constitution by Senator James G. Blaine that echoed Grant's sentiments:

> No state shall make any law respecting an establishment of religion, or prohibiting the free exercise thereof; and no money raised by school taxation in any State, for the support of public schools, or derived from any fund thereof, nor any public lands devoted thereto, shall ever be under the control of any religious sect; nor shall any money so raised, or lands so devoted, be divided between religious sects or denominations. (Johnson, 1934, p. 21)

Blaine's proposal passed the House of Representatives by the whopping margin of 180 to 7, but failed to obtain the necessary two-thirds majority in the Senate where its margin was 28 to 16 (Johnson, 1934, p. 21). Blaine's proposed amendment reflected the mood of the nation at that time, a trend demonstrated by the 1876 Congress when it required any state henceforth admitted to the union to have a "system of public schools which shall be open to all the children of said State and free from sectarian control" (Butts, 1950, p. 144).

THE IDEOLOGY OF THE MORAL SECULAR SCHOOL:
WITH EMPHASIS ON WILLIAM T. HARRIS

As the nineteenth century progressed, the sentiments espoused by Grant and Blaine grew. The Protestant majority looked more and more to the allegedly nonsectarian common school as the lead agency (the sectarian Sunday school was second) in what William B. Kennedy (1966) has termed the "parallel institutions" strategy, designed to inculcate morality in the young (p. 27). The Reverend David H. Greer, an Episcopal clergyman who would become Bishop of New York, addressed the moral mission of the patriotic common school in an address to the Evangelical Alliance in 1889. Greer's words bear repeating:

> My point just now is this: that the public schools of this country being the creations of the state, which is itself secular, must be of a secular character, and that this secular character must not be tampered with or encroached upon by any religious body, Catholic or Protestant, on any ground or pretext whatsoever. They are for all creeds and for no creed, for Catholic, Protestant and agnostic. They are for all nationalities, native-born and foreign, for the Irish, German, and Italian, as well as for the American child, and their impartial, secular, and comprehensive character ... is the only one which can be in this country consistently and safely maintained.[4]

William Torrey Harris was an influential spokesman in this era for the basic moral mission of the secular public school. A public school leader who served as Superintendent of Schools in St. Louis and later as United States Commissioner of Education, Harris argued that these schools were far from being tainted with evil, as some advanced. Rather, he contended, the separation of religion and education was a manifestation of the separation between Church and state that had been decreed by the "Will of Providence" for the advancement of mankind (Harris, 1889, p. 582). Harris said the public schools' moral mission resided in their advancement of the virtues of punctuality, regularity, perseverance, earnestness, justice, truthfulness, and industry (Troen, 1975, p. 48). Neil McCluskey (1958) has summarized Harris' philosophy of moral or character education as follows:

1. All institutions in society are responsible for character education but each in its own way.
2. The school is the most effective agent for moral training through its atmosphere of discipline.
3. The development of moral habits in the school lays the groundwork for religious education in the Church.
4. The "celestial" or theological virtues of faith, hope, and charity are a part of the school's moral formation because these possess a secular base.

5. The Church alone because of its authoritarian methods and its sacred surroundings can teach religious truth.

6. Bible-reading has no proper place in the school because this is a religious exercise demanding authority and ceremonial.

7. Any general "nonsectarian" approach to religion in the common schools is only establishing one more sect.

8. The school must by the nature of things attend exclusively to secular learning; accordingly, the school must be *completely* secularized (p. 173).

The view that the secularization of the public schools fulfills the goal of the founders of the American government, who wished to separate religion from politics, became more popular. The public schools, without need of Church or Bible, were completely competent to teach morals sufficient to produce good citizens (Griffin, 1889, pp. 365-366), indeed, as an agent of the state that has the right of custody over the child, the public school is equipped to teach the morals of good citizenship, which is all that is required (Kendrick, 1889, p. 74).

The school question reached the floor of the 1889 meeting of the National Education Association (NEA) in Nashville. Following several speakers who represented the Catholic position on schooling, John Jay, and then Edwin Mead, spoke on behalf of the public schools. In his address Jay asserted that the public schools represented two outstanding features of the nation: first, that our common law is broadly Christian; and second, that as a result of the first point the law "affords the fullest scope for the liberty of conscience and freedom of worship by a complete separation of church and state." History shows, he contended, that these "combined and harmonious principles have secured peace, prosperity and strength by a popular government based upon the divine ethics of the Bible."[5] Mead argued that the Catholic Church, by coercing its members in matters such as school attendance, was denying them the rights of American citizenship. The parochial school, he maintained, "can never give anything else than a parochial education, whereas a public school, the conserver of democracy brings the divergent elements of American Society together."[6]

WISCONSIN: A CASE STUDY

Wisconsin presents an apt setting for scrutiny of the moral/character education role of the secular public school. It had a high percentage of recent immigrants, mainly Catholic and Lutheran, a compulsory school attendance law, and considerable concern that the Catholic and Lutheran immigrants of German descent were not preparing good citizens for the state and nation because of their adherence to old world ways, witnessed especially by their parochial schools and use of the German language. Additionally, the state had witnessed a fierce struggle over devotional Bible-reading in its public schools, a struggle that had culminated with a decision by its Supreme Court in 1890, the first of its kind in the nation, that said Bible-reading was sectarian instruction.

The Struggle over Compulsory Attendance Legislation

Republican Governor William Dempster Hoard, dissatisfied with the state's compulsory attendance law, addressed the Wisconsin legislature in 1889 on the subject of the vital importance of the common schools for full citizenship in the state. Hoard averred that the "child that is, the citizen that he is to be, has a right to demand of the state that it be provided ... with the ability to read and write the language of this country." He called for legislation to insure that such instruction would be guaranteed (Hoard, 1889, p. 18). A lay Methodist minister, Hoard had become convinced while on duty in Virginia during the Civil War that the lack of popular education accounted for what he believed was the immoral attitude of Virginians toward slavery (Rankin, 1925, p. 124). Religiously committed to a broad, tolerant version of Christianity, he had little use for organized ecclesiastical religion or for the "narrow creeds and the dogmas of man-made religion" (p. 210). Hoard felt strongly that use of the English language in school was the indispensable vehicle by which the country's traditions and heritage would be maintained, and a true American nationality, a loyal citizenship with religious underpinnings, could be forged (p. 123).

In the struggle over the compulsory attendance law, which required, among other points, that the subjects be taught in the English language for an institution to be recognized by the state as a school, Hoard argued that if the state could not compel the use of the English language then it had "no right" in any educational matters, and "thus the whole common school question becomes involved." For him, the struggle was "simply a contest between church and state, and all men who believe in 'rendering unto Caesar the things that are Caesar's and unto God the things that are God's' will take sides with the state."[7] Hoard went out of his way to commend those Catholics who taught in the public schools, who were, he said, supporters of "everything that is distinctly American. The state and the nation have no more faithful workers in behalf of American civilization than these teachers."[8]

Jesse B. Thayer held the office of state superintendent of schools at this time. Speaking before the NEA in 1890 Thayer held that "education which relates primarily to the rights, duties and needs of sovereign citizens must be entrusted to the state." To deny this, he maintained, "is to abrogate the principles upon which our civil government rests" (Thayer, 1890, p. 197). Thayer suspected that when the German clergy of both the Catholic and Lutheran faiths "unite in a political organization to secure the unconditional repeal of a compulsory law which has for its sole purpose instruction of all children of the state in the language and history of this their adopted country," he had the right to "suspect that there is something in the movement that is not exactly American, nor in harmony with the principles laid down by the fathers of this republic" (p. 196). All circumstances were "incidental and immaterial," he argued, "so long as the child received the education that qualifies him for the duties of citizenship" (p. 196).

The overwhelming sentiment on the part of the Protestant center (Baptists, Congregationalists, Methodists, and Presbyterians) supported the necessity of the English language requirement in Wisconsin's compulsory attendance law so as to instill the virtues of good citizenship. It was the Unitarians, though, who were most outspoken on the issue. The Reverend Joseph H. Crooker of the Unitarian Church in Madison spoke on "The Public Schools and The Catholics" in his sermon on Sunday, March 30, 1890. Popular education, secular and under the aegis of the civil state, was the only safeguard of liberty, he said. He termed the issue "critical" and it ultimately came to the point of "*Whether we shall maintain the modern state as a secular institution and its necessary function of secular education, or whether we shall surrender to the papacy and turn human progress back four centuries*" The stakes were huge; at stake was "civil liberty and modern civilization"; any surrender to the "deep-seated and far reaching" opposition to the system of secular education meant "the extinction of American liberty," *and any compromise that shall impair the efficiency and sovereignty of American citizenship means an eclipse of humanity*" (Crooker, 1890, p. 6).

William Dempster Hoard was soundly defeated in his bid for reelection to the office of Governor in November of 1890. The quarrel over education had made a major contribution to his defeat. Hoard recognized this, and claimed that the ecclesiastics, who sought their own power first, before that of the common good, would be a "menace to the progress of civilization and the perpetuity of our institutions."[9] The secular school was necessary in order for the young to develop a "clear intellectual understanding of the true and just proportions" of citizenship. The ecclesiastics, Hoard declared, had wisely directed their attack on education, because "This being a republic and the school house being the most potent influence, whereby men are emancipated from ecclesiastical control."[10] True citizenship, which depended on education in a secular context, was an essential ingredient to the existence of American liberty.

Bible-Reading in the Public Schools

In March of 1890 the Wisconsin Supreme Court unanimously ruled that devotional bible-reading in public schools constituted sectarian instruction and hence was in violation of the Wisconsin constitution. The decision outraged most Protestant churches in the state. The opinion of Justice Harlow S. Orton particularly enraged the Protestants. Orton, concurring with his colleagues, adjudged that the state was a secular entity; hence all of its institutions, including the common schools, must be divorced "from all possible connection or alliance with any and all religions, religious worship, religious establishments or modes of worship, and with everything of a religious character or pertaining to religion." The name "common schools" meant the schools were free to all children in the state but also that they were completely secular. The Bible, Orton held, was the "source of religious and sectarian strife" (1890, pp. 23-32). Orton's opinion was reflected in the thoughts of the Reverend Mr. G. E. Gordon, a Unitarian minister formerly of Milwaukee. Gordon claimed that American morality as embodied in the common schools was, and should be, based on secularism, and such was appropriate and effective for the common schools to impart:

> The exclusion of religious exercises, as such, and religious teaching, as such, from public school education, does not exclude morality. The morality that is embodied in our laws—a morality that requires honesty, chastity, cleanliness, industry, frugality, decency of speech, truthfulness etc. is just a morality based upon the very structure of civil society and would retain its hold upon human life if all theology was abolished. This morality can, and should, be taught by the schools of the state, because it is the foundation of the laws of the state. Those who say that such morality cannot be taught, except upon the authority of Bible or catechism, have not read the history of the rise and growth of human laws, nor do they kow anything of the foundations of moral sanctions.[11]

Gordon was joined in his position by the Reverend Joseph Crooker, a Unitarian clergyman from Madison. Crooker declare the nation was a "completely secular state," and so:

> as the secular state, which Wisconsin is by manifest destiny and by express declaration of its fundamental law, has, and can have, no religion, it follows

as a necessity that its schools can rightfully and lawfully have no religious instruction whatever.[12]

CONCLUSION

The elevated, almost sacred place the common school held in the latter part of the nineteenth century United States was attested to by many. One of those was Rasmus B. Anderson, a professor of Scandinavian languages at the University of Wisconsin, who put it this way: "Whoever directly or indirectly opposes the American common school is an enemy of education, of liberty, of progress. Opposition to the American common school is treason to our country."[13]

Ruth Miller Elson has documented the manner in which American textbooks of the nineteenth century reflected the moral tone of the common school. "The certainty of progress, the perfection of the United States," she wrote, was not to be questioned. The schoolbooks were "bent on persuading the child that his nation is superior to all others." The child was "expected to develop a fervent fath that the American example will inevitably and gloriously save Europe from its present state of corruption and decline." The books witnessed that "Whatever is good in ideas, behavior, and institutions" was identified "with the United States and its citizens" (Elson, 1964, pp. 339-342).

In fine, then, the secular common school of the latter part of the nineteenth century taught the sovereignty of God, was morally elevating, was a form of a common religion that would unite all Americans, that would fully develop the character of all the young so they could carry out their duties of citizenship, which were of the highest priority, was the vehicle to express the will of the people, was the sole way in which the state educated to promote the common good, and was, more than any other institution, capable of transforming the young into morally good, responsible citizens. "The secularization of education," which this common school represented, was, as Ellwood P. Cubberley (1919) put it, "an unavoidable incident connected with the coming to self-consciousness and self-government of a great people" (p. 173).

NOTES

1. Quoted in Nord (1995, p. 72).
2. Ibid., p. 75.
3. "The President's Speech at Des Moines," *Catholic World*, 22, 130, January, 1876, p. 17.

4. Quoted in Anson Phelps Stokes, *Church and State in the United States.* II. New York: Harper Brothers, 1950, 687.

5. John Jay, "Public and Parochial Schools," *National Education Association Journal of Proceedings and Addresses.* Session of the Year 1889, held at Nashville, Tennessee. Topeka: Kansas Publishing House, Clifford C. Baker, 1889, p. 161.

6. Edwin H. Mead, "Has the Parochial School Proper Place in America?," *National Education Association Journal of Proceedings and Addresses.* Session of the Year 1889, held at Nashville, Tennessee. Topeka: Kansas Publishing House, Clifford C. Baker, 1889, p. 145.

7. *Milwaukee Sentinel*, April 6, 1890, p. 11.

8. Ibid.

9. Quoted in William F. Whyte, "The Bennett Law Campaign," *Wisconsin Magazine of History* X, 4 (June 1927): 388-389.

10. William Dempster Hoard, "The Farmer as Citizen," in the Hoard Papers, in the Archives of the Library of the State Historical Society of Wisconsin, Madison.

11. *Milwaukee Sentinel*, March 23, 1890, p. 12.

12. *Milwaukee Sentinel*, June 30, 1890, p. 4.

13. Quoted in Michaelsen, *Piety in the Public School*, p. 119.

CHAPTER 11

A SPECIAL CASE—
THE FREEDMEN

INTRODUCTION

Due to the institution of slavery, the freedmen constitute a special case in the consideration of the moral/character education in American schools. Due to its importance and to the limitations of space, this chapter will focus on the state of Virginia in the years immediately following the end of Reconstruction. It will be divided into two sections. The first will treat the initial years of common schooling, with emphasis on the work of Virginia's first State Superintendent of Public Instruction, William Henry Ruffner. The second will deal with the institution set up to prepare teachers for the separate (by race) schools for African Americans, Hampton Institute.

THE COMMON SCHOOL

James Anderson, in his excellent book, *The Education of Blacks in the South, 1860-1935*, points out that the freedmen had played a central role in establishing the idea of universal public education in the southern states during Reconstruction (Anderson, 1988, p. 19). As the states of the former confederacy reentered the Union, however, whites regained control of political power in those states and African Americans were excluded from

Moral Education in America's Schools: The Continuing Challenge, 127–140
Copyright © 2005 by Information Age Publishing
All rights of reproduction in any form reserved.

any meaningful participation in decision-making. That happened in Virginia, as the freedmen demonstrated "extraordinary eagerness" for the "advantages of schools," both by the schools they had established themselves and by their participation in the schools maintained by the Freedmen's Bureau (Anderson, 1988; Alderson, 1952, p. 57). The Constitution of 1869, which replaced the more "radical" version of 1868 (the so-called "Underwood Constitution"), was approved and Virginia was readmitted to the Union in 1870 (V. Dabney, 1971, pp. 369-373).

The Superintendency of William Henry Ruffner

Ruffner was elected state Superintendent by the legislature, was directed to produce a plan for the organization of public schools in Virginia, the plan was approved by the legislature, and Virginia had its state school system in 1870. There were a number of challenges to Ruffner's plan, which surfaced almost immediately. The first was a challenge to the civil state's right to educate; the second, germane to our purposes, was the race question.

Ruffner had been an opponent of slavery. He believed in the "power of common school education" to elevate the African American race (Ruffner, 1880, p. 3). He characterized the African Americans in Virginia as "an enigma, yet part of my work." He believed the African American race "craves education," and "wants to do right … and is the most amicable of races"; their civilization was "progressing"; and, finally, "as a class they are in character weak and ignorant—and hence to that extent a dangerous element in society…." The only way of "making them safe members of society" was by educating them (p. 10). No supporter of those who advocated integration of the races in the public schools, he advocated separate schools by race. He defended his so-called "middle of the road" position, and claimed that to deny African Americans an education, as some white traditionalists were recommending, would "lash into fury all the passions of war."[1] Freedmen made up nearly one-half of the population of the state, and the 1870 census indicated that 207,000 of them were totally illiterate (C.W. Dabney, 1936, p. 132). This, despite the efforts of the schools established by African Americans themselves and by those run by the Freedmen's Bureau, the latter having taught an estimated "50,000 young freedmen" to read and write (Alderson, 1952, p. 90).

Opposition

The success of the African American-run schools and of those operated by the Bureau was viewed by some white Virginians with alarm. Robert

Lewis Dabney of the Union Theological seminary in Richmond (a fellow Presbyterian minister), Bennett Puryear of Richmond College, and J. William Jones, a Baptist minister who wrote under the *nom de plume* "Civis" were Ruffner's foremost opponents.[2] All three opposed public schooling in general and the schooling of African Americans in particular. "Civis," who identified himself as a "friend of the Negro, but a friend to him in his proper place of subordination," inveighed against the schooling of blacks in a series of articles that were replete with racist assumptions and endorsements of inequality, all of which were said to be the work of the Almighty:

> The line of demarcation between the races is not accidental or the result of outward surroundings; it has been fixed by the finger of God.... The law of nature, which is always the law of God, is inequality, not equality; diversity, not uniformity; and the happiness of the whole animal kingdom is best subserved by this arrangement.... *The whites and negroes cannot live together as equals*. Why cannot this be done? Our modern reformers ask. I answer: because God, for wise reasons not difficult to be understood, has made it impossible. It is forbidden by a law of nature.[3]

Mixed schooling was particularly reprehensible, "Civis" contended, because it would lead to "corruption of blood" and would "constitute a crime against decency and morals ... against God and nature."[4]

Ruffner had running battles with these three especially, and with others who thought like them, throughout his superintendency. He encouraged his fellow white southerners to educate the freedmen "with a view to elevate their character, and to adapt them to the successful discharge of the new duties imposed upon them by their changed condition." He urged the local school superintendents to join in his efforts and compared their undertaking to a religious crusade.[5]

Ruffner incurred the disfavor of those who advocated mixed race schools. He joined Barnas Sears of the Peabody Fund and leading white southerners who opposed the federal civil rights bills of 1874 and 1875 that would have mandated "mixed schools." He reasoned that the implementation of such a clause would deal a death blow to public education in the South (C.W. Dabney, 1936, p. 153ff.).

It was the charges of his long-time friend and colleague, Robert Lewis Dabney, however, which stung him deeply. Dabney was a forceful and committed opponent to public schools and especially to those operated for blacks. Expenditures for these schools were even more deplorable at a time when Virginia could not pay its debts. He averred that many whites were keeping their children home to work so they could pay to give "a pretended education to the brats of the black paupers" who "loaf and steal," and that the freedmen's low character, ignorance, low morals, dependent nature, and lack of ambition could not be cured by education. He regarded as "utterly deceptive, farcical and dishonest" the position that blacks deserved an education, thereby to become decent citizens (R.L. Dabney, 1876, p. 251ff.). Educated African Americans would become surly and insolent, disinterested in their true calling that was manual labor. A greater danger was miscegenation, which he argued was the real goal of the state school board. This would lead to the mingling of the blood "which consecrated the battle fields of the Confederacy, with this sordid, alien taint." The practice would eventually spread to the Yankees in the North, he predicted, and would spread across and "putrify" the entire nation (p. 257ff.).

Like "Civis," Dabney's attack on black education led him into a rejection of all public schooling, which belonged by divine right to the parents. The civil state was usurping this fundamental family right in establishing tax-supported public schools.

Ruffner Responds

Ruffner countered the objections of all three of his major critics. He expressed the belief that education would "foster among the Negroes a pride of race which would have a purifying and stimulating power and will gradually overcome that contemptible ambition to associate with white people, which has been instilled into their minds by the blundering policy of the Northern people and the federal government."[6] He outlined the benefits of African American education, citing improved efficiency in labor, responsible citizenship, and reduction of crime and pauperism. He denied that African Americans were intellectually inferior, declaring that "It is utterly denied that there is any such difference between the two races in susceptibility of improvement, as to justify us in making the Negro an exception to the general conclusion of mankind in respect to the value of universal education" (Ruffner, 1871b, p. 108ff.). In this statement he was reflecting a long held belief that he had first publicly uttered in a sermon delivered in 1852 when he said "No one ... can assign any limit to the improvement which may be effected under suitable culture; and there can be no reasonable doubt that the Negro has abundant capacity for all the ordinary affairs of human life, including self-government, and may attain to as high a degree of civilization as any other race" (Ruffner, 1852, pp. 8, 48).

Yet, as noted above, he opposed mixed race schools, and advanced a moral reason for his position, viz., African Americans as a class "move on a far lower moral plane than whites." Given that observable gap in manners and morals between the two races, he thought it understandable that southern whites would "refuse to associate their children with [African Americans] in the intimate relations of a school." Thus, to mix the races in school would be "vain and foolish ... base and malicious." Any attempt to force integrated public schools would lead to their destruction (Ruffner, 1874, p. 88ff.).

Conclusion

Ruffner remained a champion of universal public education, for African Americans and whites, which led some to call him a "Negrophile" (Fraser, 1970, p. 363). He held that African Americans have a "*moral* claim" on society and that it would be unwise and unjust to exclude them from the "pale of our Christian sympathies." He believed that African Americans were "improvable under culture" and there were the same redemptive reasons for educating blacks as for educating whites: members of both races could "be made more intelligent, more moral, more industrious, and more skillful."[7]

HAMPTON NORMAL AND AGRICULTURAL INSTITUTE

Hampton began operation in 1868 with twenty students. Initially it was supported by money from the Freedmen's Bureau and "Northern friends" of its founder and first principal, Samuel Chapman Armstrong, and on land donated by the American Missionary Association (AMA), an abolitionist wing of the Congregational Church.[8] Staffed at the beginning in the main by "Christian ladies from the North," Hampton was to "prepare youth of the south, without distinction of color, for the work of organizing and instructing schools in the southern States."[9] James Anderson points out that it was founded and maintained as a normal school; approximately 84 percent of the 723 graduates from Hampton's first twenty classes became teachers. Further, no trade certificates were awarded to graduates until 1895 (Anderson, 1988, p. 34).

Hampton's Philosophy of Moral Education

Hampton's original philosophy can most accurately be described as a blend of manual labor, which would instill discipline in the students, and which in turn would lead to self-control with the result of forming a moral person. Based on a pan-Protestant interpretation of the Christian religion, it was accompanied by some specific racial and social views.

Labor was initially required for all students for the "purpose of discipline and instruction."[10] Hampton was to prepare its students for a life of usefulness, which was necessary because they came from an environment that was bereft of "right home influences."[11] Boarders were preferred to day students, and Hampton was to fill a role in the South parallel to that of Harvard and Yale in the North.[12] Armstrong described the basic moral task of Hampton as follows:

> Such a school should strive quite as much to be a center of moral as of intellectual light, for deficiency of moral force and of self-respect are the chief misfortunes of the race. The tone of their society is low, the law of marriage and chastity is scarcely understood, it is vitally necessary that their course of instruction should aim to enlighten their conscience and elevate their religious sentiments.[13]

The benefits of labor would be manifold. Most critically, the high standards of discipline generated would weed out the unworthy through a "perfectly fair and firm administration," and would result in the "production of skilled, persevering teachers, of wise leaders, of peacemakers rather than noisy and dangerous demagogues."[14] African Americans could not supply the kind of leadership required for this system, so whites were necessary to provide it. The right kind of leadership would avoid the pitfall of "superficially educated leaders" who had the "most unlimited influence among the colored people." The white leaders would enable Hampton to be free from the phenomenon of the "blind leading the blind," and the "spread of the belief that political rights are obtained by political warfare than by advancement in knowledge and in ability to take care of themselves."[15] By combining work with study, Armstrong contended, Hampton's graduates would steer clear of the "false standards of ordinary schools" and assert the superiority of character over scholarship.[16] So armed, Hampton's graduates would be in a position to teach others the habits of living and labor, of general deportment, and the "right ideas of life and duty," which composed the "important lessons of life." Hampton's fundamental charge then, as its leader saw it, was "to civilize; class instruction is not all of it."[17]

Hampton's Racial Views

Armstrong had definite views about the participation of African Americans in political life: they should not participate actively in politics, Armstrong, a self-proclaimed "friend of the Negro race," maintained. This would constitute appropriate Reconstruction. African Americans were "not capable of self-government," he claimed (Anderson, 1988, p. 17).

They should refrain from taking part in political life because they were culturally and morally deficient, and hence unfit to hold office or to vote in a "civilized" society. What they needed was moral, not mental, development so that one day they could be politically enfranchised. The African American lacked the ability to "see the point of life clearly, he lacks foresight, judgment and hard sense." The critical problem for the African American race was "not one of brains, but of right instincts, of morals and hard work." The freedmen had "low ideas of honor, and morality, and want of foresight and energy." The African American race, he argued, was mentally capable but morally feeble. The African American had "three centuries of general demoralization, and behind that, paganism." This historical legacy, Armstrong averred, deprived the African American race of the moral wisdom and foresight necessary for responsible political activity. The white race, on the other hand, had so developed over the course of history, "in moral strength, in guiding instincts, in power to 'sense things' in the genius for this or that."[18]

These overall racial views explain the racial philosophy that undergirded the educational operation of Hampton Institute. The low status of African Americans explained their dependence on direction and guidance from whites, and of an education fitting to their low status. They were, he opined, in a period of "pupilage and docility," which required regular oversight, including having bathing mandated, their meals presided over, personal attire inspected, and rooms visited daily.[19] The system Armstrong developed at Hampton was to "be at once constructive of mental and moral worth, and destructive of the vices characteristic of the slave." What were those vices? They were "improvidence, low ideas of honor and morality, and a general lack of directive energy, judgment and foresight."[20] The former slaves' "deficiencies of character" were, for Armstrong, "worse for him and for the world than his ignorance." His aim was to send out teachers for the African American schools who had "moral strength as well as mental culture."[21]

Hampton was to educate "in the original and broadest sense of the word—to draw out a complete manhood." A curriculum was drawn up that made "allies" of the "needle, the broom, and the wash-tub, the awl, the plane and the plow," of the "globe, the black board and the textbook."[22] The "moral and intellectual" aspects of education were to be combined. The freed women were in desperate need of this arrangement, both for themselves and for their men. "Her average state is one of pitiable destitution of whatever should adorn and elevate her sex," Armstrong wrote.[23]

Armstrong took special pride in the "disciplinary features" of Hampton. To become a "strong and worthy man," the freedman was in need of "much external force, mental and moral, especially upon the plastic natures with whom we deal." The work upon the heart was "the most important of our work," which called for the teaching of the "vital precepts of the Christian faith, and of striving to awaken a genuine enthusiasm for the higher life."[24]

In 1872 Armstrong addressed the education of black teachers at Hampton, teachers who would labor in the racially separated schools in Virginia. The normal school should prepare them so that they:

> should strive quite as much to be a center of moral as of intellectual light, for deficiency of moral force and of self-respect are the chief misfortunes of the race. The tone of their society is low; the law of marriage and chastity is scarcely understood. It is vitally necessary that their course of Instruction should aim to enlighten their consciences and elevate their religious sentiments.[25]

Unless such a program was put in place, Armstrong warned, the teacher graduates of Hampton might join in the "dangerous social and political combinations" that were being advanced by the race's "superficially educated leaders." The race's "plastic character" puts them completely under their leaders' dominance, he held. Properly prepared teacher would combat this danger.[26]

Armstrong's views of African Americans were widely held by influential white Virginians. For instance, the "Report of the Committee of Visitors" to Hampton following their visit to the institution in 1873 contained the following:

> The colored race is not overrated, either morally or intellectually. On the contrary, their characteristic infirmities are distinctly recognized, and diligently combated. Consequently, the immediate neighbors of the institution, and the white people of Virginia generally, as they come to understand the matter, are more friendly from year to year ... and the negroes admit they will have themselves only to blame, if they go to the wall.[27]

Armstrong never deviated from his opinion of African Americans who, he said, were in a period of "pupilage and docility."[28] Those who opposed Hampton's mission of preparing "not only teachers but civilizers" refused to recognize the mental capacity of the African Americans that Armstrong maintained was "considerably below that of the average white youth."[29] The opposition to Hampton's programs for its students by some African American politicians and newspaper editors was countered by the "commendation of intelligent southern men of every class," which was fitting because Hampton had recognized the "deficiency of character" that was the major drawback of the ex-slave.[30] As a consequence of replacing "pure schooling" with the union of experience and work he claimed that "there has been a progress in southern sentiment in respect to the negro, readily apparent only to those who can look behind the front presented by politicians and periodicals."[31]

Armstrong continued this theme of moral flaw in the 1880s. For instance, in his *1880* "Report" he remarked that while the lower class African Americans were "passionately responsive to certain doctrines of Christianity," they did "not take kindly to its morality." The only antidote for this moral deficiency was "moral" work, not political action. Overall, the African American student had a weak "mental digestion," and it would take "generations" before they could reach the level of the whites. The most formidable obstacle to their progress remained a deficiency in "moral strength," which stemmed from "inherited tendencies ... like mill stones about their necks dragging them down."[32]

The Work of Hampton's Teacher Graduates

The overarching goal of Hampton Institute was to prepare "a body of colored teachers, ... thoroughly trained, not only in the requisite knowledge and best methods of teaching, but also in all that pertained to right living, including habits of intelligent labor."[33] Subsequently, Armstrong attested to the importance of teacher education in society in general and as Hampton's mission in particular when he described the teacher as a "great power in society," always in the background, but a source of "influence" nonetheless. "Hence," he wrote, "a nobly endowed institution for training teachers becomes a strong pillar to the state; and, if properly surveyed, it will command respect for itself and its course among men of all opinions."[34] He alluded to the potential impact of an African American teacher in a racially segregated school in his appeal for funds that year: "Can you make better use of seventy dollars a year, than by giving education to a colored student here who shall become a teacher? Can you, in any better way, fulfill your duty to the ignorant and unfortunate?"[35]

In his 1872 *Report*, Armstrong mentioned that twenty graduates of Hampton had already taught more than one year in either Virginia or North Carolina, and that twenty-three more would soon join them. He argued that their work proved that Hampton's mission was a success.[36] Approximately a decade later he claimed that Hampton's graduates had instructed about 30,000 students.[37] While he regularly gave glowing reports on their accomplishments, he also uttered a warning on the challenges to their moral mission they would encounter in the midst of an immoral environment:

> The work of our graduates as teachers has commended itself to many of the best men of the South, and promoted a better public opinion upon Negro

education. The ability of colored youth to acquire any degree of knowledge can no longer be doubted. The question now is whether they will hold out against the sensuality and corruption in the midst of which they will labor. The moral tone of Negro society is appallingly low. The race needs enlightened consciences and pure religious sentiments. It is the aim of this institution to send out educators of high moral purpose, who will stand for principle rather than personal advancement and oppose the rising tide of corruption, created by bad living and political combinations, the radical idea of which is to get a living by something else than hard work.[38]

Armstrong frequently cited communications from local superintendents of schools that spoke to the worth of Hampton's teacher-graduates, and of the magnitude of the obstacles they faced in carrying out their mission. For instance, in 1872 Major W. W. Ballard of Roanoke County, one of a number of former Confederate officers who served as superintendents of schools in that era, praised two Hampton graduates who were teachers in the Roanoke district "I am gratified that ... those from your institute realize the low state of morals existing among the colored people, and look upon the position they hold as so many levers to elevate from their deplorable state, those who are placed under their instruction."[39]

Hampton's reputation among white civic and educational leaders as a producer of good teachers added to the demand of their services, Armstrong wrote, especially since so "much of the work now done in colored schools is worthless" due to the lack of properly trained teachers.[40] The teacher's role in these schools was broader than mere instruction, Armstrong penned. They were "not only routine teachers, but civilizers," they were far from being "mere pedagogues."[41] Virginia needed 1,000 more like them,[42] and "nearly every graduate conducts a Sunday school and many of them are useful as evangelists," he wrote.[43] The "little army of Hampton's graduates," he commented with satisfaction in 1878, was "becoming a power."[44]

The Institute's graduates constituted another source of the proof of the value of their work. Their letters, deemed "encouraging" by Armstrong, told of their work, their gratitude to their alma mater, their low wages, the challenges that temperance posed to their people, the ignorance of those people, and their assessment of the incompetence of the African American clergy.[45] It was, one alumnus teacher wrote, "the principles instilled in me while at Hampton" that he would never forget and that would keep him steadfast in his work.[46]

There was an occasional reference in Hampton's official documents to opposition to the Hampton rationale. Armstrong had referred to the necessity of, "weeding out" students who had a bad attitude. In 1877 he complained of prejudice against the Hampton work ethic by African

Americans from the "larger cities," lamenting that "Eight years ago over one-half of our boys were good plowmen; now a good plowman is an exception." He also noted complaints about the curriculum "in some colored circles," viz., the absence of the classics.[47] He observed that "it is hard to impress" even some of Hampton's students "with the value of ordinary good sense and the moderate worth of mere mental acquirement in the struggle of life."[48]

It was the influence of "preachers, politicians, and editors of their own race" that Armstrong singled out as the cause of unrest among Hampton's graduates and students. These trouble-makers, he wrote, "resent the introduction of intelligent ideas into religion and the regulations of life, They could easily be conciliated by instituting Latin for labor. The colored people at large and their leading men, as a whole, are, however, most appreciative and give the school and its graduates the heartiest support. But negro opposition is no novelty."[49] Nonetheless, it was the model he had forged at Hampton, he averred, that held the solitary hope for African Americans, not only in the South, but in the entire nation, who, he said:

> seek education less universally, but with a better idea of what it is. It is not the "Open Sesame" they once deemed it was. Freedom is disillusioned. "Salvation by hard work," is an understood thing.... The freedmen are working into more settled and pleasant relations with their neighbors. Although rum, demagogues and other evil influences within and without are pushing them down, yet I believe with long-continued and wise effort, and by infinite patience and care, that "the fate of the Negro, the romance of American history" may become a bright record.[50]

The Night School

James Anderson (1988) wrote that the "heart" of Hampton's manual labor programs was put in place in 1879 when Armstrong established the night school with Booker T. Washington as its principal (p. 54). Students in this school were required to work ten hours per day, six days per week, eleven months per year for two years. Two years of night school work were equal to one year of the normal school course. In their final two years of normal school the students had to study four days and work two each week (pp. 54-55). The night school embodied Hampton's social philosophy because it gave the staff ample time to observe the students' character, work habits and political attitudes, presenting them with the opportunity to "weed out" students with undesirable attitudes before admitting them into the regular normal school (p. 55).

The night school became more critical to Hampton's operation as the nineteenth century progressed, because the day school enrollment declined significantly with the passage of time. By 1893, for instance, 305 of Hampton's total enrolment of 541 were in the night school. Night school students were "chiefly farm laborers, domestic servants, and mill hands" (p. 55).

It is important to note that the students' industrial training was not technical; it involved a low level of trade training, and was extremely limited (p. 59). In 1887 the students protested this kind of training, to no avail. Armstrong, meanwhile, wrote that at Hampton there "was no begging except for more work" (pp. 60-61).

CONCLUSION

In *The Education of Blacks in the South, 1860-1935,* Anderson is critical of what he terms the "Hampton Model." He argues that "Armstrong represented a social class, ideology and world outlook that was fundamentally different from and opposed to the interests of the freedmen." He refers to what took place at Hampton in 1868 and thereafter as "a conjuncture of educational pedagogy and social ideology of different origins and character" than what the ex-slaves sought (Anderson, 1988, p. 83). Anderson also observes that Hampton's crucial importance in teacher education—it was the leader of its kind—has been obscured by the "Traditional emphasis on its trade and technical aspects; its primary mission, though, was to prepare teachers for the segregated primary schools of the South" (p. 83). This task was to be accomplished through the combination of work and Christianity, mixed with specific racial views that were permeated with a specific sociopolitical view.

Looking back, it is clear that in its first several decades Hampton Institute reflected and influenced the prevailing view of African Americans on the part of the ruling white class, i.e., that they were of an inferior class, in dire need of "civilizing" moral action by whites. The curriculum of Hampton was constructed with the position that wedded labor and practical study, with the expected results of self-discipline, self-control, moral growth, and to a controlled extent, economic self-sufficiency of its graduates. It would then be the solemn duty of these graduates to bring about these same attitudes in the children of the African American, segregated schools in the South. Hampton's teacher education program was aimed at having African Americans be an economic asset to the South. to instill in them the appropriate moral/character education for their class, and through them the children they were to teach, and to teach them to accept their political and economic subordination to whites (as a moral imperative) in a white-dominated southern society of that and subsequent eras.[51]

ACKNOWLEDGMENT

Many of the citations in this chapter were made possible through the courtesy of Hampton University Archives.

NOTES

1. "Dr. Dabney Emotional." (The Public School System.) 1st Series. William Henry Ruffner Papers, Historical Foundation, Montreat North Carolina.
2. Hunt, T.C. & Wagoner, Jr., J.L. (1988, p. 1). The attribution of "Civis" to Jones is from Fraser (1970).
3. Civis (J. William Jones). "The public school in its relation to the Negro." Reprint from *The Southern Planter and Farmer* (1877), pp. 4, 8f., 16, in William Henry Ruffner papers, Historical Foundation, Montreat, North Carolina.
4. Civis, "The Public School in its Relation to the Negro," *The Southern Planter and Farmer, II* (January 1876), pp. 8-14.
5. Ruffner, *The Educational Journal of Virginia* 2 (February, March, May, 1871), pp. 155f., 191 [272], [280] (December 1870), p. 72ff.
6. Ruffner, in C.W. Dabney (1936, p. 160).
7. Ruffner, "The Public Free School System." Reprint of articles in the *Richmond Dispatch and Enquirer,* April and May, 1876, p. 9, in the Ruffner Papers.
8. *Report upon the Hampton Normal and Agricultural Institute.* Hampton: July 1869, p. 4; *Catalogue of the Hampton Normal and Agricultural Institute, for the Academic Year* 1871-1872. Hampton: Printed at the Normal School, 1872, pp. 3-4.
9. *Catalogue,* 1871-1872, p. 5; *Report,* 1869, p. 3.
10. *Catalogue,* 1871-1872, p. 16.
11. "Report of the Principal." *Reports of the Officers of the Hampton Normal and Agricultural Institute, Hampton, Virginia, for the Academical and Fiscal Year, ending June 30,1878.* Hampton: Normal School Steam Press, 1878, p. 20.
12. Ibid., p. 21.
13. Ibid.
14. Ibid., p. 23.
15. Ibid., p. 28.
16. "Report of the Principal." *Reports of the Hampton Normal and Agricultural Institute, for the Fiscal Year, ending June 30,* 1876. Hampton: Normal School Steam Press, 1876, p. 7.
17. "Report of the Principal." *Reports of the Hampton Normal and Agricultural Institute, for the Fiscal Year, ending June 30,1875.* Hampton: Normal School Steam Press, 1875, p. 8.

18. Quoted in Anderson (1988, p. 39).

19. "Report of the Principal," *Reports*, 1876, p. 9; "Report of the Principal," *Reports*, 1875, p. 8.

20. "Report of the Principal," *Catalogue, 1870-1871*, quoted in Bremner (1970, p. 1193).

21. Ibid., pp. 1193-1194.

22. Ibid., p. 1194.

23. Ibid., p. 1195.

24. Ibid., p. 1196.

25. "The Training of Negro Teachers at Hampton, 1871-1872," *Catalogue, 1871-1872*, quoted in Bremner, Ibid., p. 1197.

26. Ibid.

27. "Report of the Committee of Visitors to Hampton Institute (1873)," in Sol Cohen, ed., *Education in the United States: A Documentary History.* 3. New York: Random House, 1974, p. 1654.

28. "Report of the Principal," *Reports*, 1876, p. 9.

29. "Report of the Principal," *Reports*, 1876, p. 3.

30. "Report of the Principal, " *Reports*, 1878, p. 11.

31. Ibid., p. 14.

32. "Report of the Principal," *Reports of the Hampton Normal and Agricultural Institute, for the Fiscal Year, ending June 30, 1880*. Hampton: Normal School Steam Press, 1880, p. 10.

33. *Report upon the Hampton Normal and Agricultural Institute*, 1869, p.3.

34. *Catalogue of the Hampton Normal and Agricultural Institute, for the Academic Year 1871-1872*, p. 20.

35. Ibid., p. 24.

36. Ibid., p. 22.

37. "Report of the Principal," *Reports*, 1879, pp.9-10.

38. "Report of the Principal," *Reports*, 1872, p. 27.

39. "Report of the Principal," *Catalogue*, 1873, pp. 27-28.

40. "Report of the Principal," *Reports*, 1877, p. 5.

41. "Report of the Principal," *Reports*, 1878, pp. 10-11.

42. "Report of the Principal," *Reports*, 1875, p. 9.

43. "Report of the Principal," *Reports*, 1874, p. 6.

44. "Report of the Principal," *Reports*, 1878. p. 9.

45. Eunice C. Dixon, "Report on Graduates," *Reports*, 1882, p. 10.

46. Miss A. E. Cleveland, "Report on Graduates," *Reports*, 1882, p. 6.

47. "Report of the Principal," *Reports*, 1877, p. 5.

48. Ibid., p. 6.

49. "Report of the Principal," *Reports*, 1878. p. 9.

50. Ibid., p. 14.

51. See Anderson (1988, pp. 33-78), for his overall interpretation of the Hampton Model.

CHAPTER 12

THE EARLY TWENTIETH CENTURY—THE "CITIZENSHIP" FOCUS

INTRODUCTION

Chapter 10 dealt with moral education under the influence of the post-Civil War period, termed the "Americanizing" public school. That "Americanizing" trend continued and intensified in the early years of the twentieth century, heavily influenced by immigration. More than 18 million immigrants entered the country between 1891 and 1920, with approximately 11.5 million hailing from southern and eastern Europe (Butts & Cremin, 1953, p. 308), the latter regarded as "undesirable" by American nativists.[1] The public high school grew rapidly during this period, rising from an enrollment of 80,000 in 1870 to 7,000,000 in 1940, a ninety fold increase compared with a threefold increase in the total population (Michaelsen, 1970, p. 137).

The school, elementary and high, was exhorted to accept its leadership responsibility in the training of the young, For instance, Ellwood P. Cubberley, a leading public school advocate of the time, penned in 1909 that schools needed to address the "evils and shortcomings of democracy" that immigration had brought to America, especially in corrupt city government. The public schools would counteract those problems by instilling "fundamental moral and economic principles" in the "masses." The

Moral Education in America's Schools: The Continuing Challenge, 141–149
Copyright © 2005 by Information Age Publishing
All rights of reproduction in any form reserved.

schools were to teach a knowledge of values and how to "utilize leisure time" (Cubberley, 1909, p. 65). One speaker at the National Education Association (NEA) convention in 1916 declared that a "revolution" was needed in moral training in the public schools, teachers were exhorted to "establish moral and social standards for our time," and they "must help to influence public opinion as to the necessity for positive moral education" (Fahey, 1916, pp. 638-639). "Our work," another speaker at that meeting that year stated, was to "make men and women, and character-building is the fundamental, the all-important part of this work" (Carmart, 1916, p. 1011). No longer formally religious, the school's "curriculum, daily life and goal could be called religious" (Michaelsen, 1970, p. 136). The public school became the primary institution of American democracy, as Michaelsen points out, and the "cradle and bulwark of its liberties." It became a "prime article of American faith to 'believe in' the public school" (p. 137).

THE SCHOOL RESPONDS TO THE CHALLENGE

Michaelsen cites the "Syllabus on Ethics" that was adopted by the New York City public schools as an instance of the school's shouldering its duty in this area. The document stressed the centrality of "moral education" in the schools, work to be accomplished "not only in formal instruction and training" but also "in the general atmosphere and spirit of the class room and of the school" (Michaelsen, 1970, pp. 138-139). Relying on the personality of the teacher, it involved factors such as the cultivation of a "sense of reverence" that was "vital to morality" and the development of a feeling of "social membership," an attitude of "loyal membership" in the family, community, and nation (p. 139).

The increasing importance assigned to the moral role of the public school at this time, due in part to what the *Cardinal Principles Report* would assert later was the declining influence of home and church,[2] was due to what E. B. Andrews contended in 1901 was "one of the splendid new tasks which the school of the twentieth century is to undertake and achieve."[3] Six years later the NEA created a Committee on Moral Instruction in the Schools that regularly affirmed the importance of its topic until it was replaced by the Committee on Training for Citizenship.[4] Also, in 1907 David Snedden asserted that the reform school was the model for the emerging high school to emulate, because it was concerned not only with the intellectual but also with the vocational, social, and moral development of its charges (Church & Sedlak, 1976, p. 312).

Moral Education on the NEA Agenda

The NEA's committee on teaching morals in the public schools issued a tentative report in 1911 that is instructive as to what role public education leaders saw for the school in the field of moral training. Arguing that the nineteenth century was the "marvel of the ages" in technological development, the committee averred that out of this era came "new moral problems of great importance." What was needed was a "course of study for use in the public schools."[5] The committee called attention to developments that documented a national concern for moral education, such as the recently started Character Development League in New York City, and the identification of moral instruction in public schools as one of the aims of the Religious Education Association. It alleged that to have "strong and beautiful characters in adult life, certain elemental virtues must be inculcated in children and youth." It went on to spell out those virtues, which formed the "very basis of character," namely "obedience, kindness, honor, truthfulness, cleanliness, cheerfulness, honesty, respect for self and for others, helpfulness, industry, economy, power of initiative, justice, usefulness, patriotism, courage, self-control, prudence, benevolence, system, neatness, politeness, fortitude, heroism, perseverance, sympathy, conservation to duty, unselfishness, comradeship, patience, temperance, hopefulness, determination, and fidelity."[6] Pupils, the committee maintained, "should not only have some idea of the meaning of these virtues but they should be trained in the practice of them until they become fixed habits." To that end the committee presented a tentative course, lest moral training be "left to chance," and neglected, which, it claimed, happens "frequently." The school should be organized so that students have opportunities for "moral training daily."[7]

Committee members expressed their views on the subject. M. G. Brumbaugh, Superintendent of Schools in Philadelphia opined that the "secularization of the school" does not make it other than an "essentially spiritual and moral force." "Character and conduct," he contended, are as "essential a product of the public school as is knowledge" (Brumbaugh, 1911).

It was John L. Carr, Superintendent of Schools in Bayonne, New Jersey, who presented the assembled NEA members with the principles that supported moral growth. These were:

1. Direct the fundamental instincts of children into proper channels.
2. Allow harmful impulses, instincts, and interests to die for lack of stimulus, or from repression, or by substituting better ones for them.

3. Cultivate desirable emotions such as joy, and sympathy and repress evil emotions such as anger, hatred, and envy.

4. Exercise in any virtue or desirable trait of character is necessary for its development.

5. Habits are largely acquired by imitation and suggestion.

6. Noble ideals are a potent inspiration in the formation of character.

7. A clean, healthy, well-developed, well-nourished body under good control is a powerful aid to moral development.

8. Knowledge of what things are helpful and what are harmful is important.

9. Strong, positive, abiding interest in things worth while is one of the effective means of developing moral character.

10. Training for efficiency wards off many temptations as well as leads to the development of much that is good (Carr, 1911, pp. 351-353).

Carr then proceeded to present suggestions for implementation of the moral education program through Kindergarten and Primary Grades (K-4), Intermediate and Grammar Grades (5-8), and High School Grades (9-12), with a description of the latter as "no other period of the child's school life is as important as the high school period" (pp. 353-366).

Under the heading of "Means of Moral Training Afforded by the Public School" the committee cited the "influence of environment," which included buildings, classrooms and the like. The "moral" atmosphere of the school and "proper school spirit" were evidence of the "moral influence of the school environment." Free play, friendships, games and all organizations made up the "social life of the school." Student participation in school government and the many virtues identified by the committee above (see note 5) constituted the "discipline and routine work of the school." Knowledge, which combats ignorance, which is the "greatest cause of human misery," was to be found in the "course of study." Above all was the "personality of the teacher," which was the "most important of all school agencies" in developing students' moral character (Carr, 1911, pp. 367-376).

Clifford W. Barnes, Executive Chairman of the International Committee on Moral Training, based in Chicago, addressed the relationship of moral and religious training in the public schools. Barnes argued that in teaching morals the teacher should acknowledge the religious basis on which morality rests. She should show how religion played a part in the development of a person's character and the "winning of success," but should avoid all dogma. Barnes called on the schools to provide worship once a day as the "universal practice" nationally. School personnel should provide an atmosphere as the "medium" for the introduction of religion. It was the task of the teacher, through his or her personality, to bring religion to the aid of morality. Barnes summarized this section of his remarks with the statement that "moral training should be increasingly emphasized in our system of education" (Barnes, 1911a, pp. 397-400).

Barnes, like so many other educators of that time, saw the nation on the brink of a better day. He stated: "Unless the signs all fail us, we are nearing the dawn of a new era which bids fair to form a better setting to the song of the Herald Angels than any which has gone before." The "most significant" of all the signs was the "earnest effort being made by schools as an agency for the development of character." A widespread cry, emanating from all quarters, "far and near," was "being raised to make the school a greater safeguard of the nation's virtue, to increase its efficiency as an agency for moral training and the development of character...." (Barnes, 1911b, pp. 400-402).

The NEA continued to serve as a forum for the expression of views on public schools and moral/character education throughout the second decade of the twentieth century. For instance, in 1912 James B. Davis spoke of the role of guidance in developing ethical character. Guidance, he maintained, truly means the "better understanding of one's own character; it means an awakening of the moral consciousness that will lead the pupil to emulate the character of the good and great who have gone before; it means the conception of oneself as a social being ... and from this viewpoint, the appreciation of one's duty and obligation toward his business associates, toward his neighbors, and toward the law." Guidance, in this sense, would be the "means of raising the standard of moral efficiency in the coming generation" (Davis, 1916, p. 713). Davis called on the senior year of English in the high school to develop "Social Ethics" in the students by asking questions such as "Why should I, the professional or business man, be interested in the public schools, the slums, the settlement houses, the church, the Y.W.C.A., or other fields of social service? What do I owe to the community in which I live? How can I improve the moral conditions in my neighborhood?" (p. 716).

The Importance of Athletics and Self-Government

Athletics were looked to as a source for building moral character. C. S. Hicks of the Massachusetts Agricultural College described athletics in high schools and colleges as a "laboratory where many of the good and bad traits of character are acquired," hence its importance in the "moral training of the student" (Hicks, 1912, p. 1147). At that same meeting another spokesman called athletics in schools an "essential moral factor":

> Moral education to most people means the presentation to boys and girls by teaching and preaching the precepts and maxims of a moral or ethical or religious code of conduct, the exhortation to act in accordance with such a code, and the leading of an exemplary life by the teacher and preacher. This is good as far as it goes. In most cases, it fails at the point of application— the practice of moral and ethical principles in the real life of the boys and girls.

Continuing, he averred that the child's "real life" is one that "he lives out with his fellows." In that life he is "free to pick and choose, to determine for himself what he will or will not do." It is through "associations and relationships" formed in free situations that "fundamental virtues or vices get their grip upon mind and heart." Athletics, he stated, "provides for an expression of youthful instinct and interest that is vital to the development of character. It is an essential factor in any scheme of moral education" (Ehler, 1912, pp. 1150-1151).

Other extracurricular activities were viewed as potential assets to the moral development of youth. One of these was participation in self-government. Henry Neumann, Leader of the Brooklyn Society of Ethical Culture in Brooklyn, New York told the NEA delegates in 1913 that students would learn the values of self-government by electing their own officials. The country's "greatest opportunity is to liberate character— democratic character," he asserted (Neumann, 1913, pp. 41-45).

The Cardinal Principles Report

The Cardinal Principles, formally known as the Commission of the Reorganization of Secondary Education (CRSE), emerged at the summer meeting of the NEA in 1913 (Krug, 1969, p. 300). The recommendations of the Cardinal Principles report spring not only from the temper of the times in which they were written and from the backgrounds of its members, but also from the charge given the committee. Responding to the task of formulating a comprehensive reorganization of secondary education in the nation, the group set forth seven objectives toward which all efforts in secondary education were to be directed and by which the curriculum would be evaluated. These objectives were: health, command of fundamental processes, worthy home membership, vocation, citizenship, worthy use of leisure, and ethical character.[8] These goals were stated in terms of the effect schooling had on students, rather than as processes by which students master subject matter. It seems the committee believed that the current need of society determined what secondary education should be.

"Ethical character" was the seventh and last aim. The committee maintained that it was "paramount" among the objectives of a secondary school in a democracy.[9] Ways in which ethical character could be developed, the committee held, included "wise selection of content and methods of instruction" throughout the curriculum, the "social contacts" pupils had with each other and with their teachers, the "opportunities afforded by the organization and administration of the school" in order that students might develop a "sense of personal responsibility and initiative," and most of all, the "spirit of service and the principles of true democracy which should permeate the entire school."[10] "Specific consideration" should be given to the "moral values" to be obtained, which included the possibility of a distinct course in "moral instruction."[11]

"Citizenship" was another critical goal in the Cardinal Principles. The "assignment of projects and problems" to students for "cooperative solution" was cited as a means to develop "attitudes and habits important in a democracy" in order that all pupils develop a "sense of collective responsibility."[12] The "democratic organization and administration of the school itself" was described as "indispensable" in achieving the goal of citizenship. All subjects were to contribute to this aim, but the "social studies geography, history, civics, and economics" were to have this goal as their dominant aim.[13]

The authors of the Cardinal Principles looked to the "unifying function" of the comprehensive, citizenship-directed nature of the high school. With the diversification in religion, race, and vocational groups that existed in the country the school was the "one agency that may be controlled definitely and consciously by our democracy for the purpose of unifying its pupils." It was up to the secondary school to play the "important part" in this process because the elementary school, with its "immature pupils," could not alone develop the "common knowledge, common ideals, and common interests essential to American democracy."[14]

Citizenship was so crucial in the eyes of this Report that its members called for the creation of a new position in the high school, that of "Citizenship Director." Her/his tasks were to determine whether the students were "developing initiative and the sense of personal responsibility."[15] Suggestions to the director to fulfill her/his tasks included the "school paper, debating society, and general school exercises."[16]

The Report concluded with the affirmation *of* the committee that it was the "firm belief" *of* its members that "secondary education in the United States must aim at nothing less than complete and worthy living for all youth."[17]

Reaction to the Report

The Report was generally well received in the educational community (Krug, 1969, p. 394). In February, 1919, the National Association of Secondary School Principals "heartily" endorsed the seven objectives.[18] Its Curriculum Committee asked "Can each subject in the present curriculum be justified on the ground that it contributes definitely and vitally to some or all of these seven ends? If it does not, is the proper remedy reform from within or elimination?[19] For instance, Latin, as currently taught, could not be justified as a school subject, but the Committee hoped it could be reformed and thereby "justify itself."[20]

Principal F. R. Willard of the high school in Watertown, Massachusetts enthusiastically supported the report. He averred that "It will be seen at a glance that these seven main objectives take care of the whole man, body, soul, and mind."[21] Relating the seven objectives to the major social questions of the day, Willard wrote:

> If democracy is to prevail over bolshevism and all other forms of revolution it must chiefly be by means of a system of education inculcating in the minds of youth the cardinal principles governing various kinds of controls—bodily, mental, social, economic, political, esthetic, and moral.[22]

Willard's thinking involved implications of the Report for social classes. The "classes," he declared, had always understood objectives as morality and power to think (or at least thought they did), but the "masses" never did: "The seven objectives under discussion are of the sort that the masses can comprehend, because they deal with the stuff life is made up of."[23]

CONCLUSION

Michaelsen has observed that the "decisive formula' in the early years of the twentieth century was that the "common school brings common experience which precipitates a common faith which is essential to the common welfare. (Michaelsen, 1970, p. 156). The public school, elementary and secondary, was the indispensable agency for developing good citizenship in American democratic society, interpreted as moral or ethical behavior. The "common faith" was indeed a "nativistically conceived and religiously buttressed nationalism;"[24] it was the foundation of moral/character education in the early twentieth century.

NOTES

1. See, for instance, Ellwood P. Cubberley, *Public Education in the United States.* Boston: Houghton Mifflin Company, 1919, p. 338.

2.   National Education Association, *Cardinal Principles of Secondary Education.* Washington, DC: Government Printing Office, 1918, pp. 7-8.

3.   Quoted in Michaelsen (1970, p. 139).

4.   Ibid.

5.   National Council of Education, "Tentative Report of the Committee on a System of Teaching Morals in the Public Schools," *Journal of Proceedings and Addresses of the National Education Association of the United States.* Winona, MN: The Association, 1911, pp. 343-344.

6.   Ibid., pp. 344-345.

7.   Ibid., p. 345.

8.   National Education Association, *Cardinal Principles of Secondary Education.* Washington, DC: Government Printing Office, 1918, pp. 10-11.

9.   Ibid., p. 9.

10.   Ibid.

11.   Ibid., p. 10.

12.   Ibid., p. 8.

13.   Ibid.

14.   Ibid., p. 14.

15.   Ibid., p. 18.

16.   Ibid.

17.   Ibid., p. 21.

18.   Ibid.

19.   Ibid.

20.   Ibid.

21.   Quoted in Ibid., p. 395.

22.   Quoted in Ibid.

23.   Quoted in Ibid.

24.   Ibid., p. 159.

CHAPTER 13

THE IMPACT OF JOHN DEWEY ON MORAL EDUCATION IN SCHOOLS

INTRODUCTION

As we have seen in previous chapters, concern for moral education is not really a new approach in American education. Historically, we know that teachers have a long tradition of incorporating concern for the social good and well-being of students through a wide variety of curriculum enrichment programs. For example, in the formative stages of many American institutions of higher education, it was expected that both professors and students would be actively engaged in projects that would help improve their neighboring communities, as well as efforts extended beyond close geographic boundaries.[1]

Educators recognize that American education has had, over centuries of history and tradition, a number of purposes including transmission of cultural heritage, the training of professionals, moral education and the generation of new knowledge through research. For example, the history of Spellman College, beginning in 1881, is replete with stories of students being sent to neighboring communities to teach a range of skills from hygiene to literacy.[2] These projects were incorporated as part of their formal coursework, and represent some of our earliest and best practices in an historical tracing of implicit moral education curriculum.

Moral Education in America's Schools: The Continuing Challenge, 151–159
Copyright © 2005 by Information Age Publishing
All rights of reproduction in any form reserved.

At the core of such pedagogical methods is the assumption that formal educational processes (passive learning and teaching in the classroom) can be significantly enriched by non-schooling experiences, and vice versa. Many educators are stating unequivocally that foremost among their goals is that of giving young adults the skills and breadth of knowledge to think deeply about the structures of the society, and to appropriate values which must govern their personal and professional lives.

BIOGRAPHICAL SKETCH

In the first half of the twentieth century, John Dewey reigned as the most eminent American philosopher of education. John Dewey was born on October 20, 1859, the third of four sons born to Archibald Sprague Dewey and Lucina Artemesia Rich of Burlington, Vermont. He attended public schools in Burlington, and entered the University of Vermont in 1875. His close contact at the university with his philosophy teacher, H.A.P. Torrey, influenced Dewey to ultimately pursue his doctorate of philosophy at John Hopkins University. While at John Hopkins, Dewey's philosophical development was largely influenced by George Morris, a German-trained Hegelian philosopher, and G. Stanley Hall, one of the most prominent American experimental psychologists at the time.[3]

After obtaining his doctorate in 1884, Dewey accepted a teaching post at the University of Michigan, where he stayed for ten years. While at Michigan, Dewey collaborated with James H. Tufts, with whom he would later write *Ethics* (1908; rev. ed. 1932). In 1894, Dewey left Michigan to teach at the University of Chicago. It was during his years at Chicago that Dewey's Hegelian idealism yielded to an experiential based theory of education, which would soon come to be most closely associated with pragmatism. He introduced this interest in a series of four essays entitled collectively "Thought and its Subject-Matter," and directed an experimental Laboratory School at the university, where he practiced his ideas of experiential education.[4]

The experience in the laboratory school provided the material for his first major work on education, *The School and Society* (1899). However, Dewey had several disagreements with the administration regarding the Laboratory School, and he subsequently resigned from the university in 1904 to accept a post at Columbia University. Dewey spent the rest of his professional life at Columbia, in the Department of Philosophy. However, his interest in moral education did not diminish at Columbia, and he quickly became involved with work at Teachers College. During his first decade at Columbia, Dewey published what would become two of his most famous works: *How We Think* (1910; rev. ed. 1933), which articulated his theory of knowledge and its application to education, and *Democracy and Education* (1916).

Dewey frequently contributed to popular magazines such as *The New Republic* and *Nation,* and he became increasingly more involved in a variety of political causes, including women's suffrage and the unionization of teachers. He was often invited to speak on behalf of these political causes, and his retirement in 1930 from teaching did not diminish his interest in active citizenry.[5] Dewey continued to remain a vital force, working throughout his retirement, until his death in 1952, at the age of ninety-two.

DEWEY'S "NATURALISTIC" VIEW OF MORAL EDUCATION

Dewey's approach to moral education reaffirms his belief that as moral thinkers we are not just passive spectators of the world we come to judge. We are involved participants, or as Shakespeare observed, we are actors on the stage of the world. Dewey's ethical theory recognized that students learn through a variety of educational environments, and that their unique and individual perspectives can contribute greatly to the learning and teaching environment in the classroom. As early as 1899, Dewey commented in *School and Society*:

> Plato somewhere speaks of the slave as one who in his actions does not express his own ideas, but those of some other man. It is our social problem now, even more urgent than in the time of Plato, that method, purpose, understanding, shall exist in the consciousness of the one who does the work, that his activity shall have meaning to himself.[6]

It was one of Dewey's complaints that traditional models of education made the student an entity separate from the lessons, thus erecting barriers between subject and object that could not easily be overcome. By setting educational objectives firmly within the natural world, Dewey's theory of naturalistic moral education attempted to avoid many of the traditional problems of both empirical and rational epistemology.[7] In presenting such an argument, it is important to recognize the epistemological framework which drove Dewey's propositions; i.e., the understanding that all practical knowledge is (in some way) the product of social construction.

In *Human Nature and Conduct* and *Art as Experience,* Dewey suggests that the truest goals of education (indeed, of human social life) should be threefold: first, we should seek to harmonize our experiences both as individuals and as members of society; secondly, as educators we must seek to "release from tedium" learning experience by injecting "variety and creative expression" into the curriculum.[8] The third of Dewey's stated goals concerned the meaningfulness of experience as a "deeper" conveyer of knowledge. When we seek to answer these challenges, we are attending to "the central issue of ethical concern" both as educators and as individuals. In the second quarter of the century John Dewey developed a rather unique educational philosophy that made use of both rational and empirical principles.

Culbertson (1982) notes that "While he [Dewey] accepted the positivist view that science is centered in experience rather than in metaphysical speculation, he rejected the idea that the study of ideals falls outside scientific inquiry" (p. 11). In *The Sources of a Science of Education* (1929) Dewey explained "The final reality of educational science is not found in books, nor in experimental laboratories nor in the class-rooms where it is taught but in the minds of those engaged in directing educational activities" (p. 32). Dewey's work would shape scholarship in education for several decades, before being challenged in the next quarter century by the movement known as logical positivism.

Turning to his work in naturalistic epistemology, we find that Dewey sets himself against any philosophy that would pose an impassable gulf between action and the good, subject and object, self and non-self, experience and nature. In fact, we may infer that Dewey (1929) thought the conceptualization of education as either socially minded or intellectually minded created a very counter-productive polemic. He suggested that "There is no kind of inquiry which has a monopoly of the honorable title of knowledge."[9]

An epistemological corollary of this naturalistic vision in moral education would be to relinquish the quest for certainty. With this caveat, all our moral judgments are understood to be hypothetical and constantly changing in light of our experiences. The cognitive abilities of the human species, including its capacity for sophisticated science, are to be understood as abilities developed through the evolutionary process. Dewey comments further in this regard:

> Until the instincts of construction and production are systematically laid hold of in the years of childhood and youth, until they are trained in social directions, enriched by historical interpretation, controlled and illuminated by scientific methods, we certainly are in no position even to locate the source of our economic evils, much less to deal with them effectively.[10]

The importance of Dewey's theories of naturalistic epistemology and experiential education is critical in helping us understand the justification for moral education curriculum. He understood that education is ultimately social, communal, interactive and reciprocal. This means that attention must be given to the interaction between the students and teacher in each educational experience, as well as the temporal connections between past and present experiences.

THE FAILURE OF RATIONALIST AND EMPIRICIST MODELS

Dewey strongly believed that any plausible conceptualization of moral education would necessarily need to call for additional development of a model in which the dimensions of theory and practice, and of individual and society, are joined in curriculum development. For these reasons, Dewey was critical of both rationalism and empiricism as those two philosophical frameworks were strictly understood. The implications of those conceptual frameworks created an unpalatable dichotomy for understanding moral agency: either human experience is not a part of the world of nature at all (as in Descartes' rationalism) or else a Humean arch-empiricism must reign.

But neither of those perspectives can do justice to all the variety of experiences that we value and hold dear as meaningful, and which we presume are therefore capable of some degree of moral judgment. For example, a strictly empirical understanding of human intelligence is limited to an elucidation of electrical brain-state activity, which would preclude the exploration of our potential to make rational moral decisions. In fact, Dewey seems to carry on a continuous dialectical debate with empiricism as it is traditionally conceived:

> Empiricism is conceived of as tied up to what has been, or is, "given." But experience in its vital form is experimental, an effort to change the given; it is characterized by projection, by reaching forward into the unknown; connection with a future as its salient trait. The empirical tradition is committed to particularism. Connections and continuities are supposed to be foreign to experience, to be by-products of dubious validity.[11]

Like William James, he believes that pragmatism is a valuable middle ground between the extremes of empiricism and rationalism, incorporating what is best in both. The main problem with these traditional rival epistemological views, he believes, is that each operates with an impoverished notion of what experience is. Dewey's point here seems to be that experience and knowledge are a matter of interactions between knower and the known, and neither is left at the end exactly as it was at the beginning. What counts as intelligent intervention, according to Dewey, is a matter of method. And a method is legitimate if it succeeds in transforming confused situations into clear ones:

The function of reflective thought is to transform a situation in which there is experienced obscurity, doubt, conflict, disturbance of some sort, into a situation that is clear, coherent, settled, harmonious...."[12]

The same is true of our values, Dewey believes. Here, too, no certainty is possible, but it does not follow that all values are equally valuable, or that they are all on a par, or that whatever an individual happens to like is therefore worthy of value. Some views about value are superior to others, and we can improve our opinions about morals and values without demanding absolute certainty.

Dewey thinks that intelligence can be as effective in the realms of value and morality as it is in science. Because the basic cognitive situation is the problem situation, and because hypotheses are created to resolve such situations satisfactorily, the concepts involved in hypotheses are necessarily related to our concerns and interests. Ideas, concepts, and terms, then, are intellectual tools we use as long as they serve our purposes and discard when they no longer accomplish that task. They are to be construed as instruments for solving problems.

As an example of such instrumentation, we may cite the role of physicists and chemists in creating concepts that serve the purposes of these sciences: explanation, prediction, and control. But Dewey would suggest that these concepts no more reveal what the world really is than any other sort of concept does. They too are merely instruments serving certain purposes, and there is nothing prior or more basic about them that should cast a disparaging shadow on concepts which serve other purposes. According to Dewey, many philosophers have been misled in thinking that only empirical science actually reveals the true nature of reality:

"Science" was set apart; its findings were supposed to have a privileged relation to the real. In fact the painter may know colors as well as the meteorologist; the statesman, educator and dramatist may know human nature as truly as the professional psychologist; the farmer may know soils and plants as truly as the botanist and mineralogist. For the criterion of knowledge lies in the method used to secure consequences and not in metaphysical conceptions of the nature of the real.[13]

Dewey's insight suggests that the empiricist's commitment to objectivity has, paradoxically, shunted the very qualities which are manifest in experience away from the realm of knowledge. The empirical conception of knowledge rejected all analyses of experience that included the subjective report of the person having the experience. The rather bizarre conclusion then becomes that only knowledge which is completely devoid of the subject's perspective can "really" be a "truthful" account.

Perhaps the apparent conundrum of this view is more obvious to us now in virtue of our growing familiarity with Dewey's philosophy of moral education, which regards the subjective perspective as essential to the evaluation of what is known. With regard to the conditions constitutive of knowledge, this view of moral decision-making parallels very closely Dewey's theory of naturalistic epistemology.

IMPLICATION OF DEWEY'S THEORY FOR EDUCATIONAL PRACTICE

Today, Dewey would probably advise that in order for our students to cope with and be able to manage their futures, they must develop the skills and processes of social inquiry gained through experience, and they must be able to ask really tough questions. But none of this will be achieved unless the educational leaders of today accept their responsibility to encourage and support the development of critical and reflective thinking. For many educators, nurturing citizens who will be full participants in the democratic process is a primary impetus for their commitment to a moral education curriculum. Dewey championed this sentiment in 1899, in his widely popular *School and Society*:

> What the best and wisest parent wants for his own child, that must the community want for all of its children. Any other ideal for our schools is narrow and unlovely; acted upon, it destroys our democracy.[14]

Echoing Dewey's concern to promote democratic educational values, Engle and Ochoa (1988) called for a "new citizenship" that emerges from grassroots community efforts and is active and participatory. They suggest, as did Dewey, that only an "engaged citizenry" can illicit the profound changes needed to keep democracy alive and viable as a working form of government. This assessment suggests, in part, what the citizen of the future will have to do to be productive, effective, and able to function within an ever changing society.

Educational leaders must also reach out to work more closely with the communities of which they are a part, and to connect students in our schools with the broader communities in which they live and will eventually work. As Dewey concludes in his 1899 introductory chapter, *The School and Social Progress*, "Knowledge is no longer an immobile solid; it has been liquefied. It is actively moving in all the currents of society itself" (Dewey, 1916, p. 40).

CONCLUSION

Dewey's approach to moral education in *Democracy and Education* empha-sized an eclectic synthesis of Rousseau and Plato's educational philoso-phies. He criticized Rousseau's idealization of the individual, but also challenged Plato's view as exclusively favoring the interests of society. This eclecticism points to Dewey's perception of the individual as one who is essentially situated within a social context. He believed that moral educa-tion must reflect the individual's purpose of gaining full citizenship within the community, while still maintaining the individual rights associated with democracy. Dewey understood the importance of experience and cooperation, as echoed again: "Upon the ethical side, the tragic weakness of the present school is that it endeavors to prepare future members of the social order in a medium in which the conditions of the social spirit are eminently wanting.... The mere absorption of facts and truths is so exclusively individual an affair that it tends very naturally to pass into self-ishness.... So thoroughly is this the prevalent atmosphere that for one child to help another in his task has become a school crime" (p. 29).

Dewey was the most influential advocate of the progressive movement in education, which was quite popular and broadly integrated into the practices of American public schools. However, progressive education was very sharply diminished during the Cold War, as the dominant concern in education became focused on the creation of stronger mathematics and science curriculums. Dewey has more recently experienced a renewed interest, particularly among constructivist and postmodern philosophers like Richard Rorty and Jürgen Habermmas. However, that discussion must be left to another time.

NOTES

1. That expectation continues through the pedagogical method of service learning; cf. *PraxisI: A Faculty Casebook on Community Service Learning*, 1993, ed. Joseph Galura & Jeffrey Howard, OCSL Press.

2. Maryland was the first state to require service learning credits for high school graduation. The Project for Public and Community Service credits the Campus Compact Initiative (1995) for fostering moral education through peer mentoring in the Maryland public high schools.

3. The influence of his early training in psychology would become increas-ingly more obvious in Dewey's pedagogical writings, especially in *My Peda-gogical Creed*, which was originally published by E. L. Kellogg & Co. in 1897.

4. While at the University of Chicago, Dewey was greatly influenced by his association with Jane Addams, who created Hull House as an outreach for Chicago's marginalized immigrants. Dewey served on the Hull House

Board of Trustees for many years, and met regularly with Addams to discuss pedagogical issues. See especially Marilyn Fischer's *On Addams*, Wadsworth Philosophers Series, 2004.

5. It is interesting to note that despite Bertrand Russell's strong criticisms of Dewey's educational philosophy, Dewey actively defended Russell against a conservative faction who wanted Russell dismissed from his post as Chair at the College of New York in 1940.

6. John Dewey, "School and Society" in *The Later Works: 1925-1953*, ed. Jo Ann Boydston. Carbondale: Southern Illinois University Press, 1981-90.

7. In an address to the National Herbart Society in 1897, Dewey commented "The much and commonly lamented separation in the schools between intellectual and moral training ... is simply one expression of failure to conceive and construct the school as a social institution, having social life and value within itself." (as cited in *John Dewey on Education: Selected Writings*, edited by Reginald D. Archambault).

8. See especially the introduction to *Human Nature and Conduct*, published by Henry Holt, 1922.

9. Elsewhere in *Sources of a Science Education* (p.197) he comments: One might even go as far as to say that there are as many kinds of valid knowledge as there are conclusions wherein distinctive operations have been employed to solve the problems set by antecedently experienced situations.

10. *School and Society*, p. 39.

11. Ibid. p. 23.

12. Ibid., p. 100.

13. Ibid., p. 221.

14. Ibid., p. 19.

CHAPTER 14

THE EDUCATIONAL POLICIES COMMISSION

INTRODUCTION

The General Education Board offer of $250,000 for five years to develop long range policies for education was accepted by the National Education Association (NEA) and the Department of Superintendence in December of 1935 and the Educational Policies Commission (EPC) was born (Ortenzio, 1977, p. 5). The newly-formed group held its first meeting in June, 1936, and sought "agreed-upon bodies of common sense on the social role of the schools" (Krug, 1972, pp. 252, 249). The EPC was to span the depression, World War II, The Cold War, and the early years of the War on Poverty before its demise in 1968. Educationally, it witnessed the rise of movements such as the Civilian Conservation Corps (CCC), the National Youth Administration (NYA), wartime curricular reforms, Life Adjustment in the wake of the war, the National Defense Education Act in the aftermath of Sputnik, and the Elementary and Secondary Education Act of 1965.

Intended to be "representative of the full scope of public education in this country,"[1] it was also viewed as an "amplification and interpretation of the seven aims" of the Cardinal Principles of 1918 (Krug, 1972, p. 253). Lawrence Cremin observes that the EPC was one of the groups that tried, and failed, to reorient the CCC to educational aims (Cremin, 1961, p. 322). Throughout its three decade history the EPC preached the mes-

Moral Education in America's Schools: The Continuing Challenge, 161–171
Copyright © 2005 by Information Age Publishing
All rights of reproduction in any form reserved.

sage that American democracy relied on moral and spiritual values, and that the public school was the foremost agent in their inculcation in the young.

MEMBERSHIP

The EPC was dominated over the years by members of the NEA, the American Association of School Administrators (AASA), and the Department of Superintendence. In the mid-1940s it was comprised of the presidents of Cornell and Harvard universities, United States Commissioner of Education John Studebaker and his predecessor George Zook, and what Lawrence Cremin has described as "leading pedagogical lights," George Stoddard, George Strayer, and Pearl Wanamaker (Cremin, 1961, p. 329). Later, influential persons such as James Bryant Conant and Dwight Eisenhower were numbered in its ranks. Eisenhower, for instance, consistently contended that "democracy is a political expression of a religion" (Ortenzio, 1977, p. 221).

EPC's positions on moral and spiritual values were expressed in a series of publications that marked its history, especially in the first two decades of its existence. It is from these documents that one learns of the emphasis on moral education of this potent policy organization.

THE EPC IN THE DEPRESSION AND PRE-WAR YEARS

In its first year of existence the EPC confronted what it termed *Some Current Problems in American Education*. Among these were the identification of appropriate "Objectives." Eleventh in its list was the question: "should religious sanctions be involved in the character objectives of the public schools?"[2] Two years later, in *The Purposes of Education in American Democracy*, the EPC again took up the matter of educational policy objectives. These objectives depend, the group asserted, on a "Scale of Values," which determines "what is good and what is bad, what is true and what is false." Objectives were "essentially, a statement of preferences, choices, values." In individual and social living people make judgments that "are based, in the last analysis, on moral standards or ideals."[3] Ethical judgments were primary, and control the application of other standards. For instance, a purpose of the school is frequently described as "worthy home membership." What is *"worthy* home membership?" Schools are instructed to "develop *good* citizens." What is a *"good* citizen?" Science, the EPC proclaimed, can help determine what the facts are, but it has "no answer to the question whether existing conditions *ought* to be changed or perpetuated." It is "ethics alone" that "lifts a finger to the things that ought to be."[4]

In 1940, as the war intensified and United States involvement in it drew nearer, the EPC published *Education and the Defense of American Democracy*. Education, it argued, had to play a "central role" in the defense of our democratic way of life. This required an "understanding of the nature and goals of democracy." Schools were to foster this understanding by identifying the nature of democracy and the goals to which it aspires.[5] Specifically, education should portray the American dream of a "nation with liberty, justice and opportunity for all." It should "promote understanding of the civil liberties and the political institutions through which the democratic ideal finds expression." It is able to "confirm that faith in the worth and improvability of each individual which is the basic tenet of democracy." "Slogans, rituals, and appeals to emotion are not enough," the EPC declared. What was needed was "Knowledge, reflection, and the master teacher, experience, are essential to moral defense."[6]

Continuing, the EPC averred that schools should play a leading role in the development of all its citizens of:

> deep and abiding loyalties to the central values of democracy—to the conception of the dignity and worth of the individual; to the principle of human equality and brotherhood; to the processes of free inquiry, discussion, criticism, and group decision; to the canons of personal integrity, honesty, and fairness; to the idea of the obligation and nobility of labor; to a concern for the good of the community.[7]

Children need to be taught to "love these values, to struggle to make them prevail in the world, to live, and if need be, to die for them." Properly presented by schools, the "appeal of American democracy" is potentially "far more powerful than that of any dictatorship," it is a "vital function" of schools to "develop a strong motivation to work for the achievement of national goals and to make whatever sacrifices are necessary for their attainment."[8] Moral defense of American democracy requires maintenance of conditions conducive to national unity, and here the teacher, "above all others, should stand as an example of the responsible use of civil liberties."[9] The "call of the hour" is for "unity of aims and cooperative action." In this process, the EPC thundered, "the schools of America are ready and determined to play their part."[10]

"What are the Loyalties of Free Men?" the EPC asked in 1941.[11] Answering its own question the Commission replied: "*First, the free man is loyal to himself as a human being of dignity and worth.*" It was the school's obligation to instill this sense, the "first and most fundamental obligation of all democratic education," in each student, in the process striving to "a rouse in each individual a profound sense of self-respect and personal integrity."[12] The second loyalty was defined as the *"free man is loyal to the principle of equality and brotherhood."* It fell to the school never to discriminate against any person, to create a "sense of responsibility for correcting" any violations of equality and brotherhood.[13]

The free man is *"loyal to the process of untrammeled discussion, criticism, and group decision,"* which is the third criterion. He/she is committed to the Bill of Rights and opposed to the "suppression of liberties," which would bring about the end of a society of free men.[14] *"Fourth, the free man is loyal to the ideals of honesty, fair-mindedness, and scientific spirit in the conduct of the democratic process."* Under this tenet the school should refuse to tolerate any violations of these qualities and "strive to cultivate in the young a deep and general hostility toward such violations.[15]

Loyalty to the *"ideal of respect for and appreciation of talent, training, character, and excellence in all fields of socially useful behavior"* made up the fifth characteristic. Schools should "impress upon the young" the need to recognize and place "in posts of public concern and responsibility persons of the highest talent, training, and virtue."[16] *"Sixth, the free man is loyal to the idea of the obligation and the right to work."*[17] Schools should not tolerate loafing, shifting responsibility to others, but rather express a "sense of gratitude" to those who work, especially in the field of hard labor.[18]

Loyalty to the *"idea of the supremacy of the common good"* constituted the seventh characteristic of the free man. In light of this mark the schools should do all they can to "moderate the egotistical tendencies and strengthen the social and cooperative impulses of the rising generation."[19] The eighth and final mark of the free man in this EPC document was that the *"free man is loyal to the obligations to be socially informed and intelligent."* The role of teachers was crucial here. They must "command the respect, evoke the enthusiasm, and even enlist the affection of the pupil."[20]

THE EPC IN THE MID-FORTIES

Cremin contends that the belief that the advent of good progressive education had come about in the mid-1940s, as witnessed most clearly in a "series of pronouncements" issued by the EPC, viz., *Education for All American Youth* (1944), *Educational Services for Young Children* (1945), and *Education for All American Children* (1948). He goes on to write that the message of these three volumes is clear: "Americans must organize a comprehensive public school system concerned with all young people from the age of three through twenty… " (Cremin, 1961, p. 329),

The first of the above-named documents, *Education for All American Youth* claimed that a person with good character "consistently respects the rights of other persons and seeks their welfare as well as his own." It was not possible to "put a finger" on a few spots in a school's program and say, "This is our program of character education." The school's teachers should agree as to what is "*good* character." Teachers should help students become "sensitive to ethical issues" of which they have heretofore been unaware, cooperating with the home and church along the way, in order for the greatest moral good to occur.[21]

Issued a year after the war ended in 1946, *Policies for Education in American Democracy* focused its attention on "THE OBJECTIVES OF CIVIC RESPONSIBILITY."[22] These objectives called for the "educated citizen" to: "be sensitive to the disposition of human circumstances"; to "correct unsatisfactory conditions"; to "understand social structure and social processes"; to have a "defense against propaganda"; to "respect honest differences of opinion"; to have a "regard for the nation's resources"; to "measure scientific advance by its contribution to the general welfare"; to be a "cooperating member of the world community"; to "respect the law"; to be "economically literate"; to "accept his civic duties"; and to act upon an "unswerving loyalty to democratic ideals."[23]

Turning specifically to schools in 1948 the EPC averred that the first requirement for a good school was that it "rest on values that are good." The second precept was that it "be efficient in promoting the good values."[24] The Commission recognized that the "purpose and program of any school depend upon some judgment regarding what is good or bad in the conduct of human affairs." It defined education as a "program of social action toward goals that are based on a scale of values."[25] The "controlling" value in the United States, the EPC declared, could be best summed up in one word, "democracy." Citizens in a democracy "exhibit a concern for the general welfare, a feeling of kinship with others, a respect for the laws and social institutions which protect our rights and the rights of others."[26] It was the school's responsibility to instill this value of democracy in the children, The Commission reminded educators that value statements are useless "unless they influence the curriculum and hence the experience which the child has in the school."[27]

THE EARLY FIFTIES

The final episode of EPC's involvement in moral education that we will consider took place in the early 1950s. In 1952 the Commission stated that among the purposes of the school was the aim of helping young people grow in "insight into ethical values and principles."[28] There were two documents, however, one jointly authored by the National Congress of Parents and Teachers, which deserve the lion's share of attention.

Moral and Spiritual Values in the Public Schools (1951)

In 1951, the EPC (James Bryant Conant and Dwight Eisenhower were members at the time) published a report entitled *Moral and Spiritual Values in the Public Schools*. At the outset the Commission defined their terms: "By moral and spiritual values we mean those values which, when applied in human behavior, exalt and refine life and bring it into accord with the standards of conduct that are approved in our democratic culture." The American people expect their schools to teach "moral and spiritual values," the Commission declared, and the schools have accepted that challenge.[29] The public schools were the appropriate agency to teach these values in a democracy; should the United States "maintain a separate system of religious schools, the common public school system as we know it, with its indispensable contribution to unity and common loyalties, would disappear from the American scene." The Commission "accepted as an established premise that the vast majority of American youth should and will continue to attend the public schools," whence they derive "brotherhood, democracy, and equality."[30]

The public schools would teach religion as "consistent with the American concept of freedom of religion," which "must be based. not on the inculcation of any religious creed, but rather on decent respect for all religious opinions." The permssible brand of religion taught must be derived from the "moral and spiritual values which are shared by the members of all religious beliefs."[31] Education "uninspired by moral and spiritual values is directionless," unable to infuse the values of good citizenship "in terms of intelligent loyalty to moral and spiritual values, as they apply to political processes and civic issues."[32]

There were three options available to the public schools. First, give up the effort to teach values; second, return to the past by ignoring the industrial revolution; and third, the only viable alternative, was to equip students with the "insight and will to live by moral and spiritual values."[33] The Commission then identified the values it said the American people were agreed on, values that the public schools were to teach:

1. Human personality—the basic value;
2. Moral responsibility;
3. Institutions as the servants of man;
4. Common counsel and voluntary cooperation;

5. Devotion to truth;
6. Respect for excellence;
7. Moral equality, using the same moral standards to judge every-one;
8. Brotherhood;
9. The pursuit of happiness;
10. Spiritual enrichment.[34]

These values are interrelated, according to the commission. While all of the school's resources should be used to teach them, the most effective way of inculcating them is through "experience and example."[35]

The commission believed that moral and spiritual values can be actively promoted in the public schools by:

1. Defining as goals the accepted moral and spiritual values in our society;
2. Encouraging and helping the individual teacher;
3. Giving attention to moral and spiritual values in teacher education;
4. Teaching these moral and spiritual values at every opportunity;
5. Utilizing all of the school's resources;
6. Devoting sufficient time and staff to personal relationships;
7. Assuming an attitude of friendly sympathy toward the religious beliefs and practices of students;
8. Promoting religious tolerance actively;
9. Teaching about religion as an important part of our culture.

The above suggestions should be welcomed by all in a democracy, the commission declared: "No practice suggested here should offend any person who seeks to advance the moral and spiritual values in our society."[36]

In its concluding statement to this crucial utterance on the way to teach moral and spiritual values, the EPC summed up its position in stating, "Thus, the public schools will continue to be indispensable in the total process of developing moral and spiritual values. They can and should increase their effectiveness in this respect. Their role is one that no other institution can play as well."[37]

Moral and Spiritual Education in Home, School, and Community

The EPC concluded its 1951 publication *Moral and Spiritual Values in the Public Schools* with the plea that the public schools needed "partners" in the task of imparting moral and spiritual values to children.[38] Help was not long in coming. In 1953 the National Congress of Parents and Teachers (PTA) published, in cooperation with the EPC, *Moral and Spiritual Education in Home, School, and Community.*[39] Referring to the 1951 EPC volume in its "Foreword," the PTA noted that it had developed "Action Programs for Better Homes, Better Schools, Better Communities" in 1952, with the first point of this program being "Emphasize moral and spiritual values to build an America worthy of its heritage of faith in God and of freedom."[40] Local PTA groups were urged to "emphasize moral and spiritual values" through various PT A programs in behalf of the "welfare of children and young people."[41] "Recent changes in American life" such as the weakening of family life, the advent of military service, and the onset of "impersonal relationships" had created "unusual hazards to healthy moral and spiritual growth" in the nation's youth.[42] The nation's world leadership position depended not only on production capacity but also "on our firm belief in the worth of the individual, in the concept of institutions as the servants of men, in the brotherhood of man, and in the right of all men to seek spiritual fulfillment."[43] The young, the PTA declared, need more help "in learning how to get along with others and in finding a purpose in life."[44] Quoting the 1951 EPC document, the PTA averred that "a system of moral and spiritual values is indispensable to group living," and that nothing "can produce a good and secure society if personal integrity, honesty, and self-discipline is lacking."[45]

Again quoting the above-mentioned EPC document, the PTA defined moral and spiritual values as "those values which, when applied to human behavior, exalt and refine life and bring it into accord with the standards that are approved in our democratic culture."[46] These moral and spiritual values were identified as "1. Human personality—the basic value; 2. Moral responsibility; 3. Institutions as the servants of man; 4. Common consent; 5. Devotion to truth; 6. Respect for excellence; 7. Moral equality; 8. Brotherhood; 9. Pursuit of happiness; 10. Spiritual enrichment."[47]

Directing their attention to the role of the schools, the PTA asserted that "Every activity, every remark of the teacher, every relationship of teachers with students, every subject, even the school building itself is teaching young people values of some kind. This is true whether or not there is a conscious effort on the part of the school administration and the teachers to teach moral and spiritual values."[48] Responding to the question, "HOW CAN THE SCHOOL TEACH VALUES?," the PTA took yet another lesson from the 1951 EPC publication. It listed the menu as:

1. Demonstrate respect for the individual child, his needs, and his abilities.
2. Provide situations in which moral decisions occur.

3. Provide the example of teachers and school staff.

4. Provide aesthetic experience.

5. Provide knowledge of the contributions, the struggles, and the ideals of men of every age and land.

6. Provide training in seeking the truth.

7. Provide experience in democratic group experience.

8. Teach about religion.

9. Provide guidance.

10. Develop skills for meeting family, vocational, and civic responsibilities.[49]

Local PT A groups were exhorted to address such questions as "What does your school do to teach moral and spiritual values? Are school activities coordinated in such a way that aids character development? What prevents the teachers in your school from doing a better job?[50] Under the heading of "Summing Up," the PTA contended that "perhaps at no time in our history" had there been such a need for a "sturdy morality and a firm spiritual strength ... been so great."[51] It was the task of the school, in union with the home and community, to commit themselves lest "children grow up morally and spiritually illiterate."[52]

CONCLUSION

The EPC's days came to a close in 1968, the victim of the desire to have *ad hoc*, rather than a standing, policy committee, on the part of national educational organizations (Ortenzio, 1977, p. 316). Throughout its lifetime the commission had endeavored to emphasize the essential nature of democratic moral and spiritual values included in the charge of America's public schools. Perhaps no better description to utilize as a conclusion of its work can be had than to quote from its 1951 document: "there must be no question whatever as to the willingness of the school to subordinate all other considerations to those which concern moral and spiritual standards."[53]

NOTES

1. National Education Association, *A National Organization for Education: Educational Policies Commission*. Washington, DC: National Education Association, 1937, p. 3.

2. Educational Policies Commission, *Some Current Problems in American Education*. Washington, DC: National Education Association, 1936, p. 4.
3. Educational Policies Commission, *The Purpose of Education in American Democracy*. Washington, DC: National Education Association, 1938, pp. 1-2.
4. Ibid., pp. 4-6.
5. Educational Policies Commission, *Education and the Defense of Democracy*. Washington, DC: National Education Association, 1940, pp. 7-12.
6. Ibid., pp. 12-13.
7. Ibid., p. 13.
8. Ibid., pp. 13-15.
9. Ibid., pp. 17-18.
10. Ibid., p. 22.
11. Educational Policies Commission, *The Education of Free Men in American Democracy*. Washington, DC: National Education Association, 1941, p. 55.
12. Ibid., p. 56.
13. Ibid., p. 57.
14. Ibid., p. 58.
15. Ibid., p. 59.
16. Ibid.
17. Ibid., p. 60.
18. Ibid., p. 61.
19. Ibid., p. 62.
20. Ibid.
21. Educational Policies Commission, *Education for All American Youth*. Washington, DC: National Education Association, 1944, pp. 143-146.
22. Educational Policies Commission, Policies for Education in American Democracy. Washington, DC: National Education Association, 1946, p. 240.
23. Ibid.
24. Educational Policies Commission, *Education for All American Children*. Washington, DC: National Education Association, 1948, p. 1.
25. Ibid., p. 2.
26. Ibid., pp. 2-3.
27. Ibid., p. 114.
28. Educational Policies Commission, *Education for All American Youth: A Further Look*. Washington, DC: National Education Association, 1952, p. 239.
29. Educational Policies Commission, *Moral and Spiritual Values in the Public Schools*. Washington, DC: National Education association, 1951, p. 3.
30. Ibid., p. 5.
31. Ibid.
32. Ibid., pp. 6-7.
33. Ibid., pp. 12-13.
34. Ibid., pp. 15-29.
35. Ibid., p. 60.

36. Ibid., p. 80.
37. Ibid., p. 100.
38. Ibid.
39. National Congress of Parents and Teachers, in Cooperation with the Educational Policies Commission, *Moral and Spiritual Education in Home, School, and Community*. Chicago: National Congress of Parents and Teachers, 1953.
40. Ibid., p. iii.
41. Ibid., p. 1.
42. Ibid., p. 2.
43. Ibid.
44. Ibid., p. 3.
45. Ibid., p. 5.
46. Ibid.
47. Ibid., p. 6.
48. Ibid., p. 14.
49. Ibid., p. 15.
50. Ibid., p. 16.
51. Ibid., p. 26.
52. Ibid.
53. Educational Policies Commission, *Moral and Spiritual Values in the Public Schools*, p. 54.

CHAPTER 15

KOHLBERG'S STAGES OF MORAL DEVELOPMENT

INTRODUCTION

Lawrence Kohlberg was born in 1927 in Bronxville, New York (Peters, 1981). After his high school graduation from the Andover Academy in Massachusetts, Kohlberg chose to put his academic pursuits on hold in order to assist in the transport of European war refugees trying to resettle in Israel. He enrolled in the University of Chicago in 1948, and earned an undergraduate degree in only one year by testing out of many course requirements. His graduate studies in psychology were also completed in Chicago, and his doctoral dissertation reflected the strong influence of Piaget on his own moral developmental theory (Crain, 1985, pp. 118-136). Kohlberg taught at the University of Chicago from 1962-1968, and then moved to Harvard University, where he remained until his death in 1987. Kohlberg was influenced by Piaget's stage theory of moral development in children.

According to Piaget, children undergo significant changes in moral reasoning abilities around the ages of ten or eleven (Piaget, 1981). As an example of this difference in moral reasoning, Piaget cites the reaction of a younger child who hears a story about one boy who accidentally breaks fifteen cups when trying to help his mother and another boy who breaks one cup while stealing cookies. When asked which boy behaved badly, the young child responds that the first boy was bad because he broke more

Moral Education in America's Schools: The Continuing Challenge, 173–179

cups (Piaget, 1965). Piaget points to this example to demonstrate the extent to which younger children (pre ten through twelve years) will be inclined to consider the accumulation of consequences as the determinant factor for moral worth. However, older children (post ten and older) will be inclined to judge moral worth as a function of intentions rather than consequences.

KOHLBERG'S METHOD OF RESEARCH

Kohlberg's stages of moral development are hierarchically integrated, which he explains as a movement from one stage to another without loss of insights gained at earlier stages. In other words, one does not simply reject the more naïve conclusions from previous stages, but rather is able to connect those conclusions to more critical scrutiny and broader conceptions of moral action (Berkowitz & Gibbs, 1985, pp. 197-218). One of Kohlberg's earliest research projects involved interviews with ten, thirteen, and sixteen year old boys who were given hypothetical moral dilemmas such as the following scenario: In Europe, a woman was near death from a special kind of cancer. There was one drug that the doctors thought might save her. It was a form of radium that a druggist in the same town had recently discovered. The drug was expensive to make, but the druggist was charging ten times what the drug cost him to make. He paid $200 for the radium and charged $2,000 for a small dose of the drug. The sick woman's husband, Heinz, went to everyone he knew to borrow the money, but he could only get together about $1,000 which is half of what it cost. He told the druggist that his wife was dying and asked him to sell it cheaper or let him pay later. But the druggist said: "No, I discovered the drug and I'm going to make money from it." So Heinz got desperate and broke into the man's store to steal the drug for his wife. Should the husband have done that? (Berkowitz, 1985).

The point of these interviews was to understand how the boys justified their responses to these questions; i.e., Kohlberg was interested in assessing the level of moral reasoning skills demonstrated by the subjects. For example, after presenting the children with this hypothetical moral dilemma, the interviewers would ask if Mr. Heinz was entitled to the medicine, or if Mr. Heinz violated the rights of the drugstore owner. The children were asked to explain their response in order to better understand their stage of moral development. After classifying the various responses into stages, Kohlberg solicited independent raters to classify samples of these responses to see if others would score his stage criteria in a similar way (Benninga, 1991, pp. 3-20). This procedure of interrater reliability did find agreements to be high, confirming for Kohlberg that these responses represented distinct stages of moral development.

THE PRECONVENTIONAL LEVEL OF MORAL DEVELOPMENT (LEVEL I)

Piaget's work had found that changes in moral reasoning skills coincided with the age that a child begins to enter the general stage of formal operations. Building upon Piaget's findings, Kohlberg found changes that extended beyond those observed by Piaget. Kohlberg's theory of moral development involves six stages of moral skills orientation, which he attributes to three distinct levels of cognitive development.[1] The first of these levels Kohlberg labeled Preconventional insofar as actions are guided primarily by concern for the consequences of those actions. The Preconventional Level (Level I) of moral development includes the first two stages of moral skills orientation; in stage one, children are inclined to act based primarily on their perceptions of degrees of punishment or other negative consequences.

In this first stage, obedience to rules will simply reflect some deference to authority, particularly when the authority figure is perceived as physically forceful. In response to the Heinz dilemma, children at this first stage of development usually say that Mr. Heinz should not have stolen the drug because "It's against the law," or "It's bad to steal" (Gibbs, 1991, pp. 183-222). When asked to explain their response further, the elaboration offered is in terms of the consequences of Heinz' actions; e.g., they typically would explain that stealing is bad "because you'll get punished" (pp. 183-222). Although most children at this first stage did think Heinz was wrong to steal the medicine, Kohlberg noted that a child could support the action and still be at this initial stage of reasoning. For example, a child might say, "Heinz can steal it because he asked first and it's not like he stole something big; he won't get punished" (Rest, 1979). In this example, the child has approved of Heinz's action, but the moral reasoning is still elementary because the concern is primarily focused on what authorities permit and punish.

In the second stage of the Preconventional Level, children exhibit an egocentric preoccupation with satisfying their own needs. At this stage, the child begins to understand evaluative labels of "right" and "wrong" behaviors, but is still motivated to heed such labels only as this will benefit their naïvely egocentric interests. At this stage children begin to recognize a multiplicity of viewpoints with respect to the hypothetical Heinz Dilemma. "Mr. Heinz might think it's right to take the drug, but the druggist would not." One child suggested that Heinz could steal the drug if he wanted to help his wife, but that "he doesn't have to if he wants to marry someone younger and prettier" (Kohlberg & Mayer, 1972, pp. 449-496). Another child said Heinz could steal provided he and his wife had children, because he would need her "to look after the children" (Kohlberg, 1979, pp. 31-53).

Even at this second stage of moral development, the children are still reasoning from the preconventional perspective of consequences and benefits. They rest their moral judgments about Mr. Heinz based on what they perceive to be his self-interests. Kohlberg explains that this first level of moral reasoning is "preconventional" insofar as children are not yet responding as members of society. Rather, they see moral answers mostly in terms of what those persons in positions of authority say they must do.

THE CONVENTIONAL LEVEL OF
MORAL DEVELOPMENT (LEVEL II)

The second level of moral development, the Conventional Level, reflects a child's growing concern for approval from others, and an increased interest in maintaining social order. In stage three of the Conventional Level, children begin to self-identify as "good girl" or "good boy" based on their perception of meeting the expectations of others with whom they identify. At this stage, the children begin to see Heinz's motives as good, and judged the druggist's motives to be bad. They saw the druggist as selfish, greedy, and "only interested in himself, not another life" (Gibbs, 1991, pp. 183-222).

The children at stage three often responded that it was the druggist who should be put in jail because of his lack of concern for Mrs. Heinz. The following response from one thirteen year old boy is representative of this assessment: "It was really the druggist's fault, he was unfair, trying to overcharge and letting someone die. Heinz loved his wife and wanted to save her. I think anyone would. I don't think they would put him in jail. The judge would look at all sides, and see that the druggist was charging too much" (Berkowitz, 1985, pp. 197-218). We see that at this stage children believe that we should meet some set of moral criteria that matches the expectations of society by behaving in "good" ways.

When pressed to elaborate, children at stage three defined good behavior as having good motives and interpersonal feelings such as love, trust, and concern for others. They would usually argue that Mr. Heinz was right to steal the drug because "He was a good man for wanting to save her," and "His intentions were good, that of saving the life of someone he loves" (Gibbs, 1991, pp. 36-42). When asked what Heinz should do if he did not love his wife, they responded that he should steal the drug because "I don't think any husband should sit back and watch his wife die" (Kohlberg & Mayer, 1972, pp. 449-496). According to Kohlberg, these stage three responses are "conventional" because they have the expectation that these judgments would be shared by the entire community, and that anyone would be right to do what Heinz did.

This need to please and seek approval will eventually yield to Kohlberg's fourth stage, in which the child becomes increasingly motivated to act from a sense of duty and respect for social convention. The need to please still remains a strong influence at this fourth stage of moral development; however, actions may now be oriented more towards the child's perception of "doing the right thing" even if it should conflict with the popular choice of the group (Hoffman, 1991, pp. 275-301). In this last stage of the Conventional Level, we begin to see the emergence of moral reasoning that attaches strong value to the maintenance of social order and respect for authority. Although the responses at stage four are similar to those of younger children in stage one (both judged Heinz's actions to be wrong) Kohlberg explains that the moral reasoning behind these responses is very different. Children in stage one cannot elaborate on their responses without demonstrating their primary concern for consequences. By contrast, in stage four, the subjects are able to explain their understanding of laws as being necessary for society as a whole. According to Kohlberg, it is this universal perspective that advances the child's moral reasoning skills to such a higher level.

THE POSTCONVENTIONAL LEVEL OF MORAL DEVELOPMENT (LEVEL III)

Kohlberg's last level of moral development is the Postconventional level. In this final level of development, regard for the rules of social order is initially defined in terms of a legalistic or contractual orientation. In response to the Heinz dilemma, children in stage five do not generally approve of breaking laws because laws are "social contracts" that we must honor or change through the democratic process. Thus, in stage five, the standards of right and wrong behavior are reflected primarily through legal and institutionalized rules that have prior interest in protecting and supporting the social structure.

However, in this stage, children also begin to view the wife's right to live as an intrinsic moral right that should be protected by society. Thus, one respondent strongly defended Heinz's action on these grounds: It is the husband's duty to save his wife. The fact that her life is in danger transcends every other standard you might use to judge his action. Life is more important than property (Kohlberg, 1979, pp. 31-53). Children in this stage of development begin to reflect on the essential elements of a good society, and they make moral judgments based on these considerations regarding the nature of a good society. In stage five, children typically reason that property has little value without respect for life. Kohlberg refers to this viewpoint as the "prior-to-society" perspective because the moral agent is evaluating a response "outside" the situation of his or her own community, although still exhibiting concern for society "as a whole" (Kohlberg & Candee, 1984).

In stage six, this preoccupation with conformity to the law will yield to standards of right action that are increasingly more indicative of autonomous judgments guided by internal processes of rational thought and personal reflection. In the Heinz dilemma, this would require each person to consider the implications of their actions on others. Such a perspective must be completely impartial, assuming a viewpoint similar to John Rawls' "veil of ignorance" (Rawls, 1971). In Rawls' theory of justice, we each must act as if we did not know which role we may occupy in society. Thus, if the druggist reasoned in this way, he should have recognized that life is more important than property because he would be able to understand that, if he were in Heinz's place, he would not want others to value private property over his own wife's life. This "just and fair" solution is based on the principle of impartiality, in which everyone deserves full and equal respect.

In this final stage of moral development, one's individual principles of moral conscience would presumably yield judgments based on the principle of universality. Like Immanuel Kant, Kohlberg believes that the highest order of moral reasoning is that stage at which one chooses to act in a way that reflects a universal principle of action. The similarities between Kohlberg's final level of post-conventional morality and Kant's categorical imperative are striking. The statement of Kant's categorical imperative suggests that the most rational moral judgment must be based on one's intention to always act in such a manner as would be acceptable for everyone everywhere. Kant also emphasized the necessity for an autonomous will, which freely chooses based on one's sense of obligation to perform moral actions that are capable of being universalized. Kohlberg implicitly reiterates Kant's point regarding the significance of the "good will" and he attributes the ability to act morally at this highest stage of development to the internalization of universal ideals, such as respect for others as persons with intrinsic worth.

CONCLUSION

Kohlberg continued his research on moral development, and in his later writing, introduced a strategy which he calls the "Just Community" approach to moral education. In this approach, Kohlberg and some of his colleagues created a democratic class for high school students that encouraged the students to understand themselves as members of a community rather than as individuals loosely connected by one classroom experience (Hoffman, 1987). Influenced by Piaget who found two stages of moral development in children, Kohlberg has suggested six stages, ranging from early childhood and continuing throughout our lifespan. For Kohlberg, reaching the highest level of moral reasoning requires a postconventional level of moral thinking that demands reflective and autonomous scrutiny of moral options.

Kohlberg's theory of moral development does have its critics. For example, some have argued that Kohlberg's stages are not sensitive to cultural variance (Raths, Harmin, & Simon, 1966). Another criticism is that Kohlberg's theory suffers from gender biases, a view that has been most carefully articulated by Carol Gilligan, who was a research assistant to Kohlberg (Gilligan, 1982). Gilligan suggests that Kohlberg's stages are based on a male conception of morality which, she argues, neglects to appreciate the "different voice" in a female conception of morality. Whatever questions might remain concerning the efficacy of Kohlberg's theory, his influence has nonetheless been tremendous in developmental psychology. The implications of Kohlberg's stages of moral development for educational practice remain critical points for discussion, not only for early childhood programs but for adolescent programs as well. There is certainly much room to explore further the connections between Kantian ethical frameworks and Kohlberg's postconventional level of moral development.

NOTE

1. Although he would later drop the sixth stage of development, we will include that stage in our discussion here since it represents the ultimate level of moral development for Kohlberg. His later revision omits the sixth stage because he reconsiders the likelihood of reaching that advanced stage of moral development. However, it is only at the sixth stage that we see the similarities emerge between Kohlberg and Kant's ethical theories.

CHAPTER 16

THE VALUES CLARIFICATION MOVEMENT

INTRODUCTION

Values clarification is a contemporary theory of moral education based predominately on the work of Raths, Harmin, and Simon (1978), Simon and Kirschenbaum (1973), and Simon, Howe, and Kirschenbaum (1972). Since the initial publication of *Values Clarification* by Sidney Simon, Leland Howe, and Howard Kirschenbaum in 1972, more than 400,000 teachers have been trained in the methods of this educational movement in moral education.[1] Described as a pedagogical method that would purportedly clarify ethical behavior for students, the authors suggested that teachers should encourage students to make fully autonomous ethical decisions based on personal choice and analysis of particular situations that presented themselves as moral dilemmas.

Because our value systems impact all of our conscious decisions and actions in our lives, it is important to understand the basis for our values, and to align them with our behavior. Values clarification in moral education programs can be viewed as any process an individual chooses that will help him or her better articulate and clarify the values that he or she believes are important. This methodology relies heavily on the assumptions of humanistic psychology, particularly the view that valuation involves a process of self-actualization, and the potential to freely act upon one's choices.[2] One of the primary stated aims of the values clarifi-

Moral Education in America's Schools: The Continuing Challenge, 181–188

cation approach is to help students use emotional awareness to reflect upon personally held beliefs and to clarify such beliefs vis-à-vis their own personal value systems.

HISTORICAL BACKGROUND FOR THE VALUES CLARIFICATION APPROACH

The seeds of this values clarification model were planted by John Dewey, who, as we discussed in Chapter 13, was convinced that education must be relevant to the child's experiences "so that ... his creativity and autonomy will be cultivated rather than stifled."[3]

You will recall that Dewey described moral education as a process of deliberation called "valuation" in which students critically analyze the merits of a variety of behavioral responses to certain ethical dilemmas. Dewey's method of valuation was more fully developed by one of his students at Columbia University, Louis E. Raths, who wrote extensively about the level of individual engagement necessary for autonomous decision-making regarding moral judgments (Raths et al., 1978; Simon, 1972; Simon & Kirschenbaum, 1973).

In 1957, the Soviet Union's successful launch of Sputnik prompted an unparalleled curriculum revision program in American education. Revitalized attention to mathematics and scientific methodology made empirical verification of information the standard by which to judge all knowledge claims. The new science curriculum promoted the accumulation of data and data analysis based on the strictest definition of verifiability.[4] The movement known as logical positivism supported the view that non-empirical knowledge claims should also be subjected to this strict scientific scrutiny, and claims to moral judgment processes thus became suspect. For example, a microscopic investigation in a laboratory environment could easily lead one to discover how many layers of tissue lay between a frog's veins and skin, but no similar process existed for discerning the moral rightness or wrongness of any action.

This tension between moral valuation and moral judgments was further exasperated by the logical positivists' claim that all moral language was simply reflective of emotional responses and personal matters of taste.[5] Thus, my moral judgment that slavery is wrong could be translated as "I personally find slavery disagreeable" and as such would have no significant bearing on the "true" accumulation of empirically verifiable knowledge.

The impact of such devaluation of moral education was felt with devastating results in American public schools, where moral education virtually vanished from the curriculum until the 1970s. When values clarification theory was introduced in 1972, its almost instant rise to popularity could be explained by its strong similarity to the logical positivists' evaluation of moral values.[6] Like that earlier philosophical position, the values clarification theorists also seemed to suggest that objective morality was a non-empirical relic of our prescience stages of human development. Therefore, the benefits of engaging in any dialogue involving moral language could only be understood in terms of individual choices and tolerance for all perspectives (since none could be empirically confirmed or denied). It is into this cultural milieu that the values clarification movement would soon flourish.[7]

UNDERSTANDING THE
VALUES CLARIFICATION METHODOLOGY

The values clarification approach to moral education emphasized the role of teachers as facilitators of discussion. As facilitators, teachers were not to suggest their own personal values, nor suggest shared societal values as moral options for their students.[8] Teachers were instead guided to help students clarify their own personal values by following a seven step valuing process. This sevenfold process describing the guidelines of the values clarification approach was formulated by Simon et al. (1972): choosing from alternatives, choosing freely, prizing one's choice, affirming one's choice, acting upon one's choice, considering the consequences of acting, and acting consistently over time (Simon et al., 1972). These seven processes can be further described as follows:

1. *Prizing and Cherishing*:   Students are encouraged to clarify their values through exercises in which they rank or compare items or opinions based on their own personal preference.

2. *Publicly Affirming*:   Students are asked to state their opinions in class group discussions and in written exercises such as diaries or personal journals. Sentence prompting is a popular strategy used for helping students discover their own attitudes, which (presumably) they might not otherwise explicitly know.

3. *Choosing From Alternatives*:   In this process, students are provided relevant information in order to make informed decisions regarding their personal values clarification project. This stage usually requires review of what could be considered as pros and cons for a particular value adoption; e.g., what happens during an abortion procedure? What are the medical risks of abortion as compared to childbirth?

4. *Choosing After Consideration of Consequences:* After the information has been reviewed and considered, students are to choose their own values based on the information they received in class and their own emotional responses and feelings about that information.

5. *Choosing Freely:* At this stage of the values clarification process, students are encouraged to choose their values without regard for anything other than their own autonomous decision-making skills. The purpose of this stage is to safeguard against dogmatic and non-reflective adoption of values to which the student may not personally subscribe.

6. *Acting:* Students are encouraged to demonstrate their beliefs through their actions. For example, if they claim to value concern for the homeless, they might decide to act upon that value by starting a clothing drive or legislative letter writing campaign.

7. *Acting with a Pattern, Consistency and Repetition:* In this final stage of the values clarification process, students come to realize that their actions should reflect their values with consistency and repetition (Simon et al., 1972).

REVIEW OF VALUES CLARIFICATION STRATEGIES

The values clarification method suggests that personal values may best be adopted (or rejected) only after an examination of the individual's whole life.[9] To this end, students might be asked to draw a diagram or conceptual map of what they believe to be their unique achievements in their life, including their goals for the future. Another strategy that is often used in the classroom is a survival game scenario in which students are asked to rank the moral importance of ten persons who are soliciting admittance to a bomb shelter (Simon & Wendkos-Olds, 1976). The authors suggest that moral values are subjective to the individual, and that teachers should guide their students to make independent, autonomous decisions based on their individual preferences and desires.

For example, students are encouraged to reflect on the significance of values in their own lives, and then assess and prioritize such values based on the utilitarian benefit they have attached to that significance. Thus, a value does not become *valuable* until it is autonomously chosen by an individual based on his/her assessment of the usefulness of the value.[10] Viewed in this light, values are construed as having no intrinsic worth in and of themselves. Practices used in the values clarification method most commonly include small group discussions, hypothetical scenarios posing some moral dilemma, rank order scaling exercises for prioritizing personal values, and personal journals or diaries.[11]

Like Kohlberg's cognitive moral development approach, values clarification assumes that the valuing process is internal to each person; but unlike the developmental approaches it does not suggest some universally accepted set of core values.[12] Instead, there are three primary areas of foci, which are described as prizing one's beliefs and behaviors, choosing one's beliefs and behaviors, and acting on one's beliefs. The values clarification method teaches that behavior is not morally good or evil, but is rather well chosen or foolish actions that will vary based on considerations of time, place, and other relevant circumstances.

According to this method of moral education, a choice is good, healthy, or wise if its outcome is pleasing to the individual after consideration of the seven fold criteria, and a choice is bad, unhealthy, or unwise if it fails to meet these criteria. The values clarification approach was revisited in 1996 by Raths, Simon, and Harmin and was rearticulated as full value discussion, with "full value" being defined as "[a value] which is truly and entirely held by a person."[13] Answering yes to all seven of the following questions defines a full value:

1. Was the value chosen freely?

2. Was the value chosen from alternatives?

3. Was the value chosen after considerations of the consequences of this value?

4. Do you cherish the value? In other words, does the value make you happy?

5. Are you willing to publicly affirm that this is a value to hold?

6. Are you acting on the value?

7. Do you display this value repeatedly and consistently?[14]

It is interesting to note the obvious similarities between the seven processes of the values clarification method and these seven questions offered to identify a full value. The 1996 version would appear to be virtually identical to the 1972 publication, despite rather heavy criticism from public stakeholders in American education curriculums.

OBJECTIONS TO THE
VALUES CLARIFICATION METHODOLOGY

The initial popularity of this process approach in teaching moral education was its strong appeal to neutrality and the non-judgmental analysis of hypothetical moral dilemmas. Tolerance for different perspectives is considered to be deeply valued in our pluralistic and individualistic society, and the values clarification method appealed to those who viewed "traditional" moral education as overly dogmatic and insensitive to the expression of different moral values.[15] However, it is often difficult to discern the difference between values clarification programs and the advocacy of ethical relativism. This resemblance between values clarification theory and ethical relativism poses itself as an especially contentious problem for educators since ethical relativism is dismissed by most ethicists as a philosophically bankrupt theory.[16]

Both secular and theistic moral philosophers have found ethical relativism to be problematic for several reasons. First, the idea that any value system can itself be value neutral is logically contradictory. If we mean to suggest that all values should be opened to equal perusal and discernment for plausibility, then that same expression of equal consideration must also be applied to this value. In other words, if I autonomously choose to reject such value neutrality and opt instead for a traditional value system, then ethical relativism would require acceptance of my choice (since it posits that all values are equally plausible). This is not just a semantic disagreement; indeed, the difficulty with supposed positions of value neutrality has been replete in the history of ethical studies.[17]

A second objection to the values clarification theory relies on a critical consideration of the consequences of complete value neutrality. For example, by promoting the acceptance of all values as equally appropriate, the values clarification method yields the rather bizarre (and unintended) consequence of requiring the acceptance of practices that we would otherwise find to be morally reprehensible, like slavery, ethnic cleansing, and apartheid. Clearly, this logical consequence was not the authors' intention, particularly since they felt that one of the strongest positive characteristics of their methodology was the promotion of tolerance for a diversity of values.

However, we see that a careful analysis of value neutrality actually leads to a (contradictory) conclusion, viz., the recognition that we ought not to be equally tolerant of *all* values, and that some values are in fact more desirable than others. Unfortunately, the values clarification agenda explicitly denies this consequence by explicitly declining to criticize or devalue any particular moral value. Therefore, to remain consistent with the agenda of values clarification, the teacher is not supposed to criticize any moral practice nor express belief in a true discernment between right and wrong moral action. Was Hitler as good as Gandhi? The values clarification method would seem to suggest that there is no legitimate answer to that question.

CONCLUSION

The fact that we value pluralism in our society does not preclude the likelihood that there are certain core values that are relatively common to most of us. For example, we would most likely agree to the promotion of certain basic values, like fairness, honesty, and common courtesy. We understand that a classroom without these values would potentially yield chaos; there could be no admonishment for cheating, or interrupting a fellow student, or jeering at a peer's stutter, or taking all of the pencils that were intended for everyone to share, or name-calling, bullying, taunting, and harassing. What these behaviors all have in common is a lack of regard for the values of honesty, fairness, and common courtesy.

In our post-Columbine educational landscape, it is surely evident that we need to agree on the inclusion of some such core set of values in American curriculum development. Although some form of the values clarification methodology was adopted by the majority of American public schools during the 1970s and 1980s, the movement has been strongly criticized for its relativistic moral framework. Consequently, the promotion of values clarification programs has diminished since the early 1990s, and has been replaced by an interest in *character education* that would presumably reflect core values shared by citizens in a democratic pluralistic society. The character education movement popularized in the last decade (1990s to present) is the topic of our next chapter.

NOTES

1. That number may be much higher now, since values clarification programs are continuing to grow in American public schools; see Purpel (1991, p. 311).

2. Humanistic psychology was most strongly influenced by the theories of Gordon Allport in the fifties; Abraham Maslow and Carl Rogers in decades of the sixties and seventies.

3. Dewey (1939). Although Dewey would not agree that all values are equally palatable; indeed, he repeatedly expressed confidence in democratic values that he took to be transcultural in nature (see his *Human Nature and Conduct*, 1922, and *Theory of Moral Life*, 1908/1960).

4. See Wynne's (1989, pp. 19-36) comments on these curriculum changes.

5. This view was so predominant in 1940s American philosophic circles that some universities diminished courses in ethics. See Adler (1996).

6. See Bloom (1987) for an interesting account of logical positivism. Bloom was not referring explicitly to values clarification programs in his criticism, but the similarities can be seen. See also Beauchamp (1982).

7. While most contemporary philosophy has rejected/reversed favor for logical positivism, it has still remained a strong influence in K-12 education.

See Solomon, Schaps, Watson, and Battistich (1992). (See website for the text at http://www.quasar.ualberta.ca/ddc/incl/solomon.htm).

8. This might also be traced to the influence of Paulo Freire's *Pedagogy of the Oppressed* (1970/1993); see also Superka (1976) and Huitt (1994, pp. 33-44).

9. Interestingly, Aristotle also made a similar point in his Nicomachean Ethics, "but we must add "in a complete life" for one swallow does not make a spring" (as cited in Christensen, 1999, p. 366).

10. In *The Closing of the American Mind* (1987) Alan Bloom attributes this subjective evaluation of values to Friedrich Nietzsche, who proclaimed that it is the human will that attaches moral worth to actions and defines good and evil.

11. These and other strategies have also proven useful for some programs that otherwise discount the values clarification methodology; see Coles (1986).

12. The educational literature on K-12 moral education programs is replete with confusion vis-à-vis Kohlberg's interest in universal values. Although Kohlberg did favor autonomous, rational decision-making, he did not agree with values clarification authors that all values are subjective in nature. For Kohlberg, the process of moral discovery may be individual, but the values discovered are critically reflective only when they represent more than one's self interest. See also Gailbraith and Jones (1975, pp. 16-22).

13. The (old) values clarification movement has been retooled in this 1996 version, perhaps to make it more palatable to earlier critics; however, the changes are so minimal as to seem disingenuous. See also Goldman (1996, p. 136).

14. Ibid.

15. This point remains a legitimate concern for K-12 educators, and is repeatedly reflected in Dewey's work on moral education, as well as Paulo Freire's. See Kohn (1990, 1991, pp. 496-506).

16. Not the least of these was Plato's objection to the PreSocratic philosopher Protagoras' claim that all truth is relative. (See Plato's *Theatetus* for this discussion.)

17. For an excellent discussion on this point see Rachels (1989, p. 40). For a philosophical defense of objective moral values, see Lewis (1947, pp. 95-121; 1984).

CHAPTER 17

THE CHARACTER EDUCATION MOVEMENT

INTRODUCTION

As we have seen previously, some form of moral education curriculum has been part of virtually every school in America, although such curriculum was severely curtailed during the period from 1940-1960 (McClellan, 1992). Many have noted that by 1950 formal character education programs were conspicuously absent from American schools (Houston, 1998, p. 6). The influence of logical positivism was strong during this twenty year period, and would continue to influence subsequent attempts to reintroduce some moral education curriculum. Because of the radical distinction between the so-called objective facts of science and the subjective values of individual judgments, logical positivists considered moral education to be situational and relative at best. It was into this arena that Lawrence Kohlberg's cognitive development approach and subsequently the values clarification movement were both introduced to American public school education during the 1960s and 1970s, respectively. While both of these programs seem to have had some impact on student thinking, neither the values clarification nor the cognitive moral development approach has demonstrated significant impact on student behavior (Leming, 1993, pp. 63-71).

Frustrated by the lack of success in these moral education approaches, and supported by a strong public agenda to reintroduce so-called tradi-

Moral Education in America's Schools: The Continuing Challenge, 189–197
Copyright © 2005 by Information Age Publishing

tional character education into the public schools, the decades of 1980-1990 saw a resurgence of interest in "core virtues" and character education programs that would support the same. The 1994 Gallup Poll of the Public's Attitudes toward the Public Schools, conducted by Phi Delta Kappa, indicated a strong and growing public support for character education programs, and a majority of those polled favored stand-alone courses on habit formation of values and appropriate ethical behavior in the public schools (Elam, Rose, & Gallup, 1994, pp. 41-64). An even more interesting finding of the 1994 Gallup Poll was that over 90% of the respondents approved the teaching of core moral values, and two thirds of those surveyed also valued instruction about world religions (pp. 41-64). Given the violent and uncivil cultural milieu of our country during these decades, we should not be surprised by this growing public support for character education programs in our public schools. As concerns about crime, delinquency, drug and alcohol abuse, and juvenile gang violence have grown, so has our interest in finding character education programs that work. We will turn now to some of those programs, looking first at the approach developed by Thomas Lickona, and then consider other national character education programs.

THOMAS LICKONA: A FOCUS ON CORE VALUES

A leading developmental psychologist, Thomas Lickona is one of today's strongest supporters of the new character education movement. Lickona suggests that the current crisis of our youth culture is the result of several factors, such as a decline of the family and disturbing trends in mass media programs. While it was once true that the family served as the main moral authority for children, the family structure has been undermined in American youth culture by media images and advertising that denigrate core values such as respect and responsibility, or what Thomas Lickona calls "the fourth and fifth R's" (Lickona, 1991). In *Educating for Character* (1991), Lickona conveys a sense of urgency for character education curricula, and argues that schools must initiate programs to develop character that make use of all aspects of a student's school experience (Lickona, 1991). Faced with the overwhelming popularity of destructive media images in youth culture, Lickona suggests that schools must mandate conscientious character education curricula that will help to guide young people toward more appropriate behaviors and morally sound choices. He argues that good moral conduct and decision making will not be learned if it is not taught. This sounds remarkably like Aristotle, who argued that we are born morally neutral, waiting to be marked by the impression of good or bad experiences and habits.[1] Offsetting the negative impact of inappropriate mass media images is an enormous challenge, one that Lickona suggests may only be met by the combined efforts of families, religious institutions, and (most particularly) schools.

In his more recent *Character Matters* (2004) Lickona further suggests that our schools must play a central role in developing character education programs that offer healthy alternatives to media images that promote risky behaviors such as drinking, fighting, and sexual promiscuity (Lickona, 2004). Lickona's plea is reiterated by Mary Pipher, whose expose of adolescent girls' behavior, *Reviving Ophelia*, served to remind us all of the power of adolescent peer pressure (Pipher, 1994). Pipher argues convincingly that American teenagers seem to believe that normal adult experiences include binge spending, binge drinking, and binge sexual activities (p. 82).

Most educators who choose to implement character education programs attempt to focus on core values that are universally accepted by all cultures. For example, Gibbs and Earley (1994) identify these core values as compassion, courage, courtesy, fairness, honesty, kindness, loyalty, perseverance, respect, and responsibility (Fishkin, 1984). The operative definition of values in this context might best be described as standards of behavior that are accepted by a group or an individual, and which contribute to the overall well-being of the group as well as serving the best interests of the individual. Thomas Lickona emphasizes that effective character education must help children to first understand these core values, and then adopt them as their own, as would be evidenced through their actions in their personal lives.

Lickona (1993) suggests that core values are those which promote human rights and affirm our human dignity (pp. 6-11). Analogous to Immanuel Kant's categorical imperative, Lickona's understanding of core values meets the standard test of being capable of being universalized.[2] In other words, a core value would necessarily be one which we would want others to hold as well; it must be universally applicable for everyone everywhere in order to be truly reversible in an ethical sense. Seen in this light, core values not only justify our civic responsibilities in a democracy, but they would also be recognized by rational persons in other cultures as well.

Likona (1991) also differentiates between moral values such as honesty and responsibility, and non-moral values such as one's preference for vanilla over strawberry ice cream. Moral values are those which are obligatory in the sense that we must act upon them even if we would prefer to shrug the responsibility. In contrast, non-moral values carry no such obligation to act because they simply express our own personal tastes and interests. We turn now to a brief description of six character education programs that are currently in use in our schools.

MODELS OF CHARACTER EDUCATION PROGRAMS IN SCHOOLS

There are several models of character education programs currently available for school adoption. The first of these we will consider is The Center for the Advancement of Ethics and Character (CAEC).[3] The CAEC mission statement notes the organization's commitment to providing educators with the resources necessary to foster the development of strong character and good judgment in students. CAEC also has a website that offers many character education resources for teachers, administrators, students, parents, and scholars/researchers.

The second character education program that we found is The Center for the 4th & 5th Rs which is obviously tailored after Thomas Lickona's model for the promotion of respect and responsibility as core values.[4] The Center describes character education as "essential to the task of building a moral society and developing schools which are civil and caring communities." It serves as a regional, state, and national resource in character education.

The third program is also modeled after Lickona's, and is currently the largest character education program in the country, called CHARACTER COUNTS![5] This coalition boasts the most comprehensive program for K-12 education, and is currently used in over 2000 schools and youth groups nationally. The CHARACTER COUNTS! Coalition was founded in 1993 with 27 organizations. Today, more than 450 national, regional and local organizations are members; hundreds of youth groups are learning about the Six Pillars of Character—trustworthiness, respect, responsibility, fairness, caring and citizenship. The third week in October was designated by Congress as National CHARACTER COUNTS! Week, to focus the nation's attention on the importance of teaching, enforcing, advocating and modeling good character.[6]

The fourth model is the Character Education Partnership (CEP), which is a nonpartisan coalition of organizations and individuals who are committed to developing moral character and civic virtue.[7] Their mission statement declares this commitment as "one means of creating a more compassionate and responsible society."[8] Members of the CEP also share the belief that core values such as respect, responsibility, and honesty should be modeled in our schools. The CEP defines character education as "the long-term process of helping young people develop good character, i.e., knowing, caring about, and acting on core ethical values such as fairness, honesty, compassion, responsibility, and respect for self and others."[9] CEP has developed 11 Principles of Effective Character Education to serve as a guide for educators and communities:

1. Character education promotes core ethical values as the basis of good character.

2. "Character" must be comprehensively defined to include thinking, feeling and behavior.

3. Effective character education requires an intentional, proactive and comprehensive approach that promotes the core values in all phases of school life.

4. The school must be a caring community.

5. To develop character, students need opportunities for moral action.

6. Effective character education includes a meaningful and challenging academic curriculum that respects all learners and helps them succeed.

7. Character education should strive to develop students' intrinsic motivation.

8. The school staff must become a learning and moral community in which all share responsibility for character education and attempt to adhere to the same core values that guide the education of students.

9. Character education requires moral leadership from both staff and students.

10. The school must recruit parents and community members as full partners in the character building effort.

11. Evaluation of character education should assess the character of the school, the school staff's functioning as character educators and the extent to which students manifest good character.[10]

A fifth program is the Development Studies Center, a non-profit organization founded in 1980 to "foster children's intellectual, social, and ethical development."[11] One of the Center's primary stated goals is to support educators in creating caring communities of learners in schools. The center describes a caring community of learners as "a place where adults and children practice such core values as kindness, respect for others, and responsibility, and where children learn important subject matter and develop their intellectual capacity."[12] The sixth program is the International Center for Character Education, which defines its purpose to "enable school personnel, parents, teacher educators, faith community members, youth providers, and concerned individuals to come together to study, discuss, learn, practice, reflect, and write on issues, programs, problems and promises regarding the character education of children and youth."[13]

This brief description of these six programs does not represent an exhaustive list of options available to schools, but it does indicate some of the trends that have been influential in local, regional, and national character education programs over the last decade.

CONCLUSION

The character education movement promotes the teaching of core values that can be taught directly through various course curricula. Core values are embedded in many academic programs through the formal curriculum, especially in literature, social studies, and social science classes. Most of the character education programs promote a strong emphasis on student accountability and hold students to high levels regarding academic achievement. In most schools that have adopted a character education program, service learning is also a major source for delivery of core values instruction for most middle school and high school students.[14] Service learning provides students with an opportunity not only to incorporate values into their own character framework, but also to act on those values in socially responsible and meaningful ways. Schools that actively engage students in community and civic service projects may also use those experiences as the source of discussions in the classroom regarding civic and social responsibility in a democratic society.[15]

A variety of interdisciplinary and co-curricular activities are also employed in the promotion of character education in public schools. For example, school organizations and club activities such as drama, sports, and student government also provide a myriad of opportunities for students to make important decisions about core values. Many of these programs have strong character education components as an integral part of the students' experience, and are designed to encourage students to practice values such as initiative, diligence, loyalty, tact, generosity, altruism, and courage (Wynne, 1989, p. 25).

A review of the research on character education programs is yielding some interesting findings regarding shared characteristics of schools that report successes (Leming, 1993, pp. 63-71). In schools that report positive developments for students with respect to character education, there are common expectations among students, administrators, teachers and staff. For example, students are encouraged to be active rather than passive members of policy and rules committees that set standards for school behavior. Because the students in these schools have contributed to setting the policy standards, they tend to accept responsibility for meeting those standards (and/or dealing with the consequences of non-compliance). According to Leming (1993) this research suggests that discipline, when established by the students themselves, is a strong component of character education programs (pp. 63-71).

Although most of the values that may be considered to be universal are well rooted in world religions, there are some religious groups that object to teaching these core values without their explicit identification with a divine source. Such groups (mostly fundamentalists) accuse schools of teaching secular humanism by their omission to identify God as the source of core values (Page, 1995, p. 22). Although the Constitution itself contains no language regarding religion, the First Amendment, approved in 1791 as part of the ten amendments known as the Bill of Rights, contains a clause that deals with the issue of what the government is and is not allowed to do regarding religion: "Congress shall make no law respecting an establishment of religion or prohibiting the free exercise thereof" (Kreisbach, 2002).

Ironically, teachers and administrators have occasionally met resistance from parent organizations that would otherwise support character education, but worry that educators are promoting a secular humanist education with their teaching of core values. Given that the Supreme Court's interpretation of the establishment clause of the First Amendment prevents public schools from directly teaching religious values, the charge of secular humanism levied by religious groups against public educators may seem, on the surface, to be unwarranted. However, religious groups are concerned to preserve both tenets of the establishment clause in the First Amendment, and rightly point out that while schools are careful not to "establish religion" in the classroom, they have not been vigilant in preserving the students' right to freely exercise their religious values.

This dilemma poses itself as almost intractable in the public school domain, particularly when character education curricula materials are reviewed by teachers, administrators and school boards. For example, the idea of a core set of moral values has traditionally been strongly associated with the religious teachings of Judeo-Christianity. Religious parents (and educators) see no good reason to diminish that association, although they also recognize the need to present multiple representations of the core values. Their complaint arises when schools insist on representing such core values as completely devoid of association with any religious tradition. This complaint is legitimized when we consider that intentionally severing the discussion of core values from religion is historically inaccurate; i.e., the analysis of core values as having been created exclusively by humans misrepresents the richness and historical influence of the role of religion in articulating such values.

Goble and Brooks (1983) make the case that character education can be separated from religious values without conflicting with religious tenets. Public school educators are required by law to separate church and state, but they may still teach certain core values that are accepted by both secular and religious teachings. For example, Goble and Brooks point to Confucianism as a moral philosophy that does not conflict with Catholic moral philosophy, despite its non-religious roots.[16] Although Catholic moral teaching does not separate religion from moral values, it is possible nonetheless to find many of the same (Catholic) core moral values in other moral philosophies, such as the example of Confucianism, which also promotes core values like filial piety and strong moral character. Therefore, it is, at least in principle, possible to separate our discussions about core values from the desire to promote particular religious values as espoused by faith. Such a compromise may be our best hope in order not to leave our public school educators in a precarious dilemma with respect to the promotion of character education curriculum. In the meantime, we need to promote dialogue about the meaning of right and wrong, of the ethical values that are good as opposed to evil, and continue to discuss what constitutes a set of core values that can be accepted by both religious and non-religious members of our community. Until we begin to have these conversations in earnest, we will continue to be plagued by the diminished engagement in civic service and an increasing lack of responsible social behaviors.

NOTES

1. The notion of a "tabula rasa" or blank slate is most often associated with Aristotle's discussion in the Nicomachean Ethics about the source of our virtuous behaviors.

2. Kant's categorical imperative is that we must always act in such a way that the maxim of our action can be willed to be universalized (i.e., made applicable to everyone).

3. Further information regarding CSE is available through the American Academy of Pediatrics (2002) at http://www.aap.org/advocacv/childhealthmonth/media. htm.

4. Further information regarding the Center for 4th & 5th Rs is available through the New Mexico Media Literacy Project at http://www.nmmlv.orf!.

5. Further information regarding the CHARACTER COUNTS! Coalition is available at Character Counts Coalition, 400 Admiralty Way, Suite 1001, Marina del Rey, Calif. 90292-6610; (310) 306-1868 at www.charactercounts.org.

6. For more information regarding National CHARACTER COUNTS Week see the Aspen Declaration on Character Education. (1992) at http://www.charactercounts.or;/asll..en.htm.

7. Further information regarding CEP is available at the Character Education Partnership, 91816th St. NW, Ste. 501, Washington, DC 20006; Web site: http://www.character.org.

8. Ibid.
9. Ibid.
10. Ibid.
11. Further information regarding the Development Studies Center is available through the New Mexico Media Literacy Project at: http://www.nmmlv.org.
12. Ibid.
13. Further information regarding the International Center for Character Education is available through the New Mexico Media Literacy Project at: http://www.nmmlv.org.
14. Further information regarding service learning programs can be obtained through Learn and Serve America, http://nationalservice.org/Learnlindex.htmL National Schools of Character, (202) 296-7743, ext. 12 or email geninfo@character.org
15. Quest International, P.O. Box 4850, Newark, Ohio 43058-4850 www.democracv. org/Links.html has a list of links to organizations and resources in character education, service learning, education for democratic citizenship, and school reform.
16. Ibid. also see Michael Ebert (1994) who emphasizes that religious parents are concerned about school undermining the established moral belief system of their children.

REFERENCES

Adler, M. J. (1996). *The time of our lives*. New York: Fordham University Press.

Agnew, D.L. et al. (Eds.). (1960). *Dictionary of Wisconsin biography*. Madison: State Historical Society of Wisconsin.

Alderson, W.T. (1952, January). The Freedmen's Bureau and Negro Education in Virginia. *The North Carolina Historical Review, XXIX*(1).

Anderson, J. (1988). *The education of Blacks in the south, 1860-1935*. Chapel Hill: The University of North Carolina Press.

Atherton, L. (1954). *Main street on the middle border*. Bloomington: Indiana University Press.

Baast, P.A. (1888, February). Our Catholic schools. *Catholic World, XLVI*(275).

Bailyn, B. (1960). *Education in the forming of American society*. Chapel Hill: The University of North Carolina Press.

Barnard, H. (1971). What Connecticut would be with good schools. In R. Welter (Ed.), *Writings on American popular education: The nineteenth century*. Indianapolis, IN: The Bobbs-Merrill Co.

Barnes, C.W. (1911a). Relation of moral and religious training. *Journal of Proceedings and Addresses of the National Education Association of the United States*. Winona, MN: The Association.

Barnes, C.W. (1911b). Status of moral training in the public schools. *Journal of Proceedings and Addresses of the National Education Association of the United States*. Winona, MN: The Association.

Beauchamp, T.L. (1982). *Philosophical ethics: An introduction to moral philosophy*. New York: McGraw-Hill.

Bell, S. (1930). *The church, the state, and education in Virginia*. Philadelphia: The Science Press Company.

Bennett, J.R. (1889). *Opinion in the case of Weiss, et al. Vs. the School Board of Edgerton*. Edgerton, WI: F. W. Coon.

Benninga, J.S. (1991). Moral and character education in elementary school: An introduction. In J.S. Benninga (Ed.), *Moral, character, and civic education in the elementary school*. New York: Teachers College Press.

Berkowitz, M.W. (1985). The role of discussion in moral education. In M.W. Berkowitz & F. Oser (Eds.), *Moral education: Theory and application*. Hillsdale, NJ: L. Erlbaum.

Berkowitz, M.W., & Gibbs, J.C. (1983). Measuring the developmental features of moral discussion. *Merrill-Palmer Quarterly, 29*.

Biechler, J.A. (1958). *Kilian C. Flasch, Second Bishop of LaCrosse*. Unpublished master's thesis, St. Paul Seminary, St. Paul, MN.

Billington, R.A. (1938). *The Protestant crusade 1800-1860: The origins of American nativism*. New York: The Macmillan Company.

Binder, F.M. (1974). *The age of the common school, 1830-1865*. New York: John Wiley and Sons.

Bloom, A. (1987). *The closing of the American mind*. New York: Simon and Schuster.

Board. (1839). *Second annual report of the State Board of Education, covering the year 1838*. Boston: Dutton and Wentworth, State Printers.

Board. (1844). *Seventh annual report of the State Board of Education, covering the year 1843*. Boston: Dutton and Wentworth, State Printers.

Board. (1845). *Eighth annual report of the State Board of Education, covering the year 1844*. Boston: Dutton and Wentworth, State Printers.

Boles, D.E. (1965). *The Bible, religion, and the public schools* (3rd ed.). Ames: Iowa State University Press.

Boorstin, D.J. (1958). *The Americans: The colonial experience*. New York: Vintage Books.

Borrowman, M.L. (1965). Liberal education and the preparation of teachers. In M.L. Borrowman (Ed.), *Teacher education in America: A documentary history*. New York: Teachers College Press.

Bourne, W.O. (1971). *History of the Public School Society of the City of New York*. New York: Amo Press and *The New York Times*.

Bremer, F.J. (1976). *The Puritan experiment*. New York: St. Martin's Press.

Bremmer, R.H. (Ed.). (1970). *Children and youth in America. A documentary history, Vol. I: 1620-1865*. Cambridge, MA: Harvard University Press.

Bremner, R.H. (Ed.). (1971). *Children and youth in America: A documentary history, Vol. II: 1866-1932*. Cambridge, MA: Harvard University Press.

Brumbaugh, M.G. (1911).Moral education: The problem stated. *Journal of Proceedings and Addresses of the National Education Association of the United States*. Winona, MN: The Association.

Buetow, H.A. (1970). *Of singular benefit: The story of Catholic education in the United States*. New York: Macmillan.

Bums, J.A. (1912). *The growth and development of the Catholic school system in the United States*. New York: Benziger Brothers.

Burns, J.A., & Kohlbrenner, B.J. (1937). *A history of Catholic education in the United States*. New York: Benziger Brothers.

Butts, R.F. (1950). *The American tradition in religion and education*. Boston: The Beacon Press.

Butts, R.F., & Cremin, L.A. (1953). *A history of education in American culture.* New York: Holt, Rinehart and Winston.

Calhoun, D. (Ed.). (1969). *The educating of Americans: A documentary history.* Boston: Houghton-Mifflin.

Carmart, A.M. (1916). Manners and morals—Our problems. *National Education Association Journal of Addresses and Proceedings 1916.* Ann Arbor, MI: The Association.

Carpenter, C. (1963). *History of American schoolbooks.* Philadelphia: University of Pennsylvania Press.

Carr, J.W. (1911). Moral education through the agency of the public school. *Journal of Proceedings and Addresses of the National Education Association of the United States.* Winona, MN: The Association.

Chamberlin, J. (1942, March 21). McGuffey and his Readers. *School and Society, 55*(1421).

Christensen, K.R. (1999). *Philosophy and choice.* New York: Mayfield.

Church, R.L., & Sedlak, M.W. (1976). *Education in the United States: An interpretive history.* New York: The Free Press.

Clinton, D. (1971). To the parents and guardians of the children belonging to the schools under the care of the New York Free-School Society. In W.O. Bourne, *History of the Public School Society of the City of New York.* New York: Amo Press and *The New York Times.*

Cohen, S. (Ed.). (1970). *Education in the United States: A documentary history* (Vol. 3). New York: Random House.

Cohen, S. (Ed.). (1974a). *Education in the United States: A documentary history* (Vol. 1). New York: Random House.

Cohen, S. (Ed.). (1974b). *Education in the United States: A documentary history* (Vol. 2). New York: Random House.

Cohen, S.S. (1974). *A history of colonial education, 1607-1776.* New York: John Wiley and Sons.

Coles, R. (1986). *The moral life of children.* Boston: Houghton-Mifflin.

Commager, H.S. (1958). Schoolmaster to America. In H.S. Commager (Ed.), *Noah Webster's American spelling book.* New York: Teachers College Press.

Conway, J. (1884, October). The rights and duties of the church in regard to education. *The American Catholic Quarterly Review, IX*(36).

Crain, W.C. (1985). *Theories of development.* New York: Prentice-Hall.

Crawford, B.F. (1974). *The life of William Homes McGuffey.* Delaware, OH: Carnegie Church Press.

Cremin, L.A. (1959). Horace Mann's legacy. In L.A. Cremin (Ed.), *The republic and the school.* New York: Teachers College Press.

Cremin, L.A. (1970). *American education: The colonial experience 1607-1783.* New York: Harper and Row.

Cremin, L.A. (1980). *American education: The national experience, 1783-1876.* New York: Harper and Row.

Cremin, L.A. (1961). *The transformation of the school: Progressivism in American education 1876-1957.* New York: Heritage Books.

Crenshaw, O. (1983, Fall). *General Lee's College* (Vol. I). Unpublished typescript, reproduced and bound by Cyrus Hall McCormick Library, Washington and Lee University.

Crooker, Rev. J.H. (1890). *The public school and the Catholics*. Madison: H. A. Taylor, Printer and Stereotyper.

Cubberley, E.P. (1909). *Changing conceptions of education*. Boston: Houghton-Mifflin.

Cubberley, E.P. (1919). *Public education in the United States*. Boston: Houghton-Mifflin.

Cubberley, E.P. (Ed.). (1920). *Readings in the history of education*. Boston: Houghton Mifflin.

Culbertson, W.C. (1982). The four year reliability of a test of learning problems. *Journal of Experimental Education, 50*.

Curti, M. (1959). *The social ideas of American educators*. Totowa, NJ: Littlefield, Adams and Co.

Dabney, C.W. (1969). *Universal education in the south* (Vol. 1). New York: Arno Press and *The New York Times*.

Dabney, R.L. (1876, April). The Negro and the common schools, *The Southern Planter and Farmer, XXVII*, 251ff.

Dabney, V. (1971). *Virginia: The new dominion*. Garden City, NY: Doubleday.

Davis, J.B. (1916). Vocational and moral guidance through English composition in the high school. *Journal of Proceedings and Addresses of the National Education Association of the United States 1916*. Ann Arbor, MI: The Association.

Dewey, J. (1916). *Democracy and education: An introduction to the philosophy of education*. New York: Macmillan.

Dewey, J. (1939). *Theory of evaluation* (International encyclopedia of unified science, Vol II). Chicago: University of Chicago.

Dreisbach, D.L. (2002). *Thomas Jefferson and the wall of separation between church and state*. New York: New York University Press.

Downs, R.B. (1977). *Henry Barnard*. Boston: Twayne Publishers.

Draper, L.C. (1858). Moral and religious instruction in public schools. In the *Sixth annual report on the condition and improvement of the common schools and educational interests of the State of Wisconsin for the year 1858*. Madison: Atwood and Rublee.

Dunn, W.K. (1958). *What happened to religious education? The decline of religious teaching in the public elementary school, 1776-1861*. Baltimore, MD: The Johns Hopkins Press.

Dwight, T. (1888, July). The attack on freedom of education in Massachusetts. *The American Catholic Quarterly Review XIII*(51).

Ehler, G.W (1912). Athletics: An essential moral factor. *Journal of Proceedings and Addresses of the National Education Association of the United States 1912*. Ann Arbor, MI: The Association.

Elam, S.M., Rose, L.C., & Gallup, A.M. (1994, September). The 26th annual Phi Delta Kappa/Gallup poll of the public's attitudes toward the public schools. *Phi Delta Kappan, 76*(1), 41-64.

Ellsbree, W.S. (1939). *The American teacher: Evolution of a profession in a democracy*. Westport, CT: Greenwood Press.

Elson, R.M. (1964). *Guardians of tradition: American schoolbooks of the nineteenth century.* Lincoln: University of Nebraska Press.

Fahey, S.H. (1916). Moral education: What the school can do. *National Education Association Journal of Addresses and Proceedings 1916.* Ann Arbor, MI: The Association.

Filler, L. (Ed.). (1965). *Horace Mann on the crisis in education.* Yellow Springs, OH: The Antioch Press.

Fishkin, J.S. (1984). *Beyond subjective morality.* New Haven, CT: Yale University Press.

Ford, P.L. (1962). Introduction. In P.L. Ford (Ed.), *The New-England Primer.* New York: Teachers College Press.

Fraser, J.W. (Ed.). (2001). *The school in the United States: A documentary history.* New York: McGraw-Hill.

Fraser, W.J. (1971, July). William Henry Ruffner and the establishment of Virginia's public school system. *The Virginia Magazine of History and Biography, 89.*

Fraser, Jr., W.J. (1970). *William Henry Ruffner: A liberal in the old and new south.* Unpublished Ph.D. dissertation, University of Tennessee.

Fullerton, H.S. (1936). Preface. In H.C. Minnich (Ed.), *Old favorites from the McGuffey Readers.* New York: American Book Company.

Gailbraith, R.E., & Jones, T.M. (1975). Teaching strategies for moral dilemmas: An application of Kohlberg's theory of moral development to the social studies classroom. *Social Education, 39,* 16-22.

Garnett, J.M. (1909, January). James Mercer. *William and Mary Quarterly, N.S. XVII*(3), 220.

Gibbs, J.C. (1991). Toward an integration of Kohlberg's and Hoffman's theories of morality. In W.M. Kurtines & J.L. Gewirtz (Eds.), *Handbook of moral behavior and development, Vol. 1: Theory.* Hillsdale, NJ: L. Erlbaum.

Gilligan, C. (1982). *In a different voice: Psychological theory and women's development.* Cambridge, MA: Harvard University Press.

Glenn, C. (1988). *The myth of the common school.* Amherst: The University of Massachusetts Press.

Goble, F., & Brooks, D. (1983). *The case for character education.* New York: Green Hill.

Goldman, L. (1996). Mind, character, and the deferral of gratification. *Educational Forum, 60.*

Griffin, W.E. (1889, April). The public schools and religion. *The Andover Review, XI.*

Guilday, P. (1932). *A History of the Councils of Baltimore* (1791-1884). New York: The Macmillan Company.

Guilday, P. (Ed.). (1954). *The national pastorals of the American Catholic hierarchy 1792-1919.* Westminster, MD: The Newman Press.

Gutek, G.L. (1986). *Education in the United States: An historical perspective.* Englewood Cliffs, NJ: Prentice-Hall.

Harper, C.A. (1939). *A century of public teacher education.* Washington, DC: National Education Association.

Harris, W.T. (1889, June). Religious instruction in the public schools. *The Andover Review, XI.*

Havighurst, W. (1957, August). Primer from a green world. *American Heritage, viii*(5).

Helmreich, E.C. (Ed.). (1964). *A free church in a free state?* Boston: D. C. Heath and Co.

Hicks, C.S. (1912). The influence of faculty supervision on the moral effects of athletics in high schools and colleges. *Journal of Proceedings and Addresses of the National Education Association of the United States 1912.* Ann Arbor, MI: The Association.

Hinspale, B.A. (1911). *Horace Mann and the common school revival in the United States.* New York: Charles Scribner's Sons.

Hoard, W.D. (1889). Governor's message. In *Governor's message and accompanying documents of the State of Wisconsin, 1889.* I. Madison: Democrat Printing Company.

Hoffman, M.L. (1987). The contribution of empathy to justice and moral judgment. In N. Eisenberg & J. Strayer (Eds.), *Empathy and its development.* New York: Cambridge University Press.

Hoffman, M.L. (1991). Empathy, social cognition, and moral action. In W.M. Kurtines & J.L. Gewirtz (Eds.), *Handbook of moral behavior and development* (pp. 275-301). Hillsdale, NJ: L. Erlbaum.

Houston, P.D. (1998, May). The centrality of character education. *School Administrator, 55*(5).

Huitt, W.G. (1994). Problem solving and decision making: Consideration of individual differences using the Myers-Briggs type indicator. *Journal of Psychological Type, 24*, 33-44.

Hunt, T.C., & Wagoner, Jr., J.L. (1988, Spring). Race, religion, and redemption: William Henry Ruffner and the moral foundations of education in Virginia, *American Presbyterians: Journal of Presbyterian History, 66*(1).

Jefferson, T. (1961a). To Peter Carr, with enclosure. In G.C. Lee (Ed.), *Crusade against ignorance: Thomas Jefferson on education.* New York: Teachers College Press.

Jefferson, T. (1961b). Report of the commissioners appointed to fix the site of the University of Virginia. G.C. Lee (Ed.), *Crusade against ignorance: Thomas Jefferson on education.* New York: Teachers College Press.

Jefferson, T. (1961c). Notes on the State of Virginia,. G.C. Lee (Ed.), *Crusade against ignorance: Thomas Jefferson on education.* New York: Teachers College Press.

Jenkins, T.J. (1886). *The judges of faith: Christian versus godless schools.* Baltimore: John Murphy and Co.

Jernegan, M.W. (1931). *Laboring and dependent classes in colonial America, 1607-1783.* New York: Frederick Unger Publishing Co.

Johnson, A.W. (1934). *The legal status of church-state relationships in the United States.* Minneapolis: The University of Minnesota Press.

Johnson, C. (1904). *Old-time schools and school-books.* New York: The Macmillan Company.

Kaestle, C.F. (1973). Introduction. In C.F. Kaestle (Ed.), *Joseph Lancaster and the monitorial school movement: A documentary history.* New York: Teachers College Press.

Kaestle, C.F. (1982). *Pillars of the republic: Common schools and American society, 1780-1860*. New York: Hill and Wang.

Katz, M.B. (1968). *The irony of early school reform: Educational innovation in mid-nineteenth century Massachusetts*. Boston: Beacon Press.

Katz, M.B. (1971). *Class, bureaucracy & schools: The illusion of educational change in America*. New York: Praeger Books.

Kendrick, J.R. (1889, September). Romanizing the public schools. *Forum, VIII*.

Kennedy, W.B. (1966). *The shaping of Protestant education*. New York: Association Press.

Kinney, Rev. M.P. (1859, September). Religious instruction in common schools—Method of imparting it. *Wisconsin Journal of Education, IV(3)*.

Kliebard. H.M. (Ed.). (1969). *Religion and education in America: A documentary history*. Scranton, PA: International Textbook Company.

Kohlberg, L. (1979). Moral stages and moralization: The cognitive-developmental approach. In T. Lickona (Ed.), *Moral development and behavior: Theory, research and social issues*. New York: Holt Rinehart and Winston.

Kohlberg, L., & Candee, D. (1984). The relation of moral judgment to moral action. In W.M. Kurtines & J.L Gewirtz (Eds.), *Morality, moral behavior, and moral development*. New York: Wiley.

Kohlberg, L., & Mayer, R. (1972). Development as the aim of education. *Harvard Educational Review, 42*, 449-496.

Kohn, A. (1990). *The brighter side of human nature: Altruism and empathy in everyday life*. New York: Basic Books.

Kohn, A. (1991, March), Caring kids: The role of the schools. *Phi Delta Kappan*, pp. 496-506.

Krug, E.A. (Ed.). (1966). *Salient dates in American education, 1635-1964*. New York: Harper and Row.

Krug, E.A. (1969). *The shaping of the American high school, 1880-1920*. Madison: The University of Wisconsin Press.

Lancaster, J. (1973). Improvements in education as it reflects the industrious classes of the community. In C.F. Kaestle (Ed.), *Joseph Lancaster and the monitorial school movement: A documentary history*. New York: Teachers College Press.

Larkin, E.P. (1859, October). Moral instruction in schools. *Wisconsin Journal of Education, IV(4)*.

Lee, G.C. (1961). Introduction. In G.C. Lee (Ed.), *Crusade against ignorance: Thomas Jefferson on education*. New York: Teachers College Press.

Leming, J.S. (1993, November). Synthesis of research: In search of effective character education. *Educational Leadership, 51(3)*, 63-71.

Lewis, C.S. (1947). *The abolition of man*. New York: Macmillan.

Lewis, C.S. (1984). *Mere Christianity*. New York: Macmillan.

Lickona, T. (1991). *Educating for character*. New York: Bantam Books.

Lickona, T. (1993). The return of character education. *Educational Leadership, 51(3)*, 6-11.

Lickona, T. (2004). *Character matters: How to help our children develop good judgment, integrity, and other essential virtues*. New York: Touchstone, Simon & Schuster.

Mann, H. (1838a). *First annual report covering the year 1837*. Boston: Dutton and Wentworth State Printers.

Mann, H. (1838b). *First annual report of the Board of Education together with the sixth annual report of the Secretary of the Board, covering the year 1837.* Boston: Dutton and Wentworth, State Printers.

Mann, H. (1841a). *Fourth annual report covering the year 1840.* Boston: Dutton and Wentworth, State Printer.

Mann, H. (1841b). *Fourth annual report of the Board of Education together with the sixth annual report of the Secretary of the Board, covering the year 1840.* Boston: Dutton and Wentworth, State Printers.

Mann, H. (1842a). *Fifth annual report covering the year 1841.* Boston: Dutton and Wentworth, State Printers.

Mann, H. (1842b). *Fifth annual report of the Board of Education together with the sixth annual report of the Secretary of the Board, covering the year 1841.* Boston: Dutton and Wentworth, State Printers.

Mann, H. (1843). *Sixth annual report of the Board of Education together with the sixth annual report of the Secretary of the Board, covering the year 1842.* Boston: Dutton and Wentworth, State Printers.

Mann, H. (1845). *Eighth annual report covering the year 1844.* Boston: Dutton and Wentworth, State Printers.

Mann, H. (1846a). *Ninth annual report covering the year 1845.* Boston: Dutton and Wentworth State Printers.

Mann, H. (1846b). *Ninth annual report of the Board of Education, together with the ninth annual report of the Secretary of the Board, covering the year 1845.* Boston: Dutton and Wentworth, State Printers.

Mann, H. (1848). *Eleventh annual report covering the year 1847.* Boston: Dutton and Wentworth, State Printers.

Mann, H. (1849a). *Twelfth annual report covering the year 1848.* Boston: Wentworth and Dutton, State Printers.

Mann, H. (1849b). *Twelfth annual report of the Board of Education, together with the annual report of the Secretary of the Board of Education, covering the year 1848.* Boston: Dutton and Wentworth, State Printers.

Mann, H. (1855a). Means and objects of common school citation (1837). In H. Mann (Ed.), *Lectures on education.* Boston: Ide and Dutton.

Mann, H. (1855b). Special preparation: A prerequisite to teaching (1838). In H. Mann (Ed.), *Lectures on education.* Boston: Ide and Dutton.

Mann, H. (1855c). The necessity of education in a republican government (1839). In H. Mann (Ed.), *Lectures on education.* Boston: Ide and Dutton.

Mann, H. (1855d). What God does, and what he leaves for man to do in the work of education. In H. Mann (Ed.), *Lectures on education.* Boston: Ide and Dutton.

Mann, H. (1855e). An historical view of education: Showing its dignity and its degradation (1841). In H. Mann (Ed.), *Lectures on education.* Boston: Ide and Dutton.

Mann, H. (1969). Special preparation: A prerequisite to teaching, In H. Mann (Ed.), *Lectures in education.* New York: Amo Press and *The New York Times.*

Mann, H. (1974b). The perspective of the common school journal (1838). In S. Cohen (Ed.), *Education in the United States: A documentary history* (Vol. 2). New York: Random House.

Maxwell, W. (1826, September 28). *An oration on the improvement of the people.* Delivered at the Literary and Philosophical Society of Hampden-Sydney College, at the Third Anniversary Meeting, Thursday, September 28, 1826. Norfolk, VA: Thomas G. Broughton [n.d.].

McAtee, Rev. W.A. (1891). The Bible in the public schools. In the *Minutes of the Synod of Wisconsin of the Presbyterian Church 1891.* Madison: Tracy, Gibbs and Co.

McAtee, Rev. W.A. (1890a, April 2). Letter to the editor. *Wisconsin State Journal.*

McAtee, Rev. W.A. (1890b). Must the Bible go? Madison, WI: Tracy, Gibbs and Co.

McAvoy, T.T. (1957). *The great crises in American Catholic history, 1895-1900.* Chicago: Henry Regnery Company.

McClellan, B.E. (1992). *Schools and the shaping of character: Moral education in America, 1607-present.* Bloomington, IN: ERIC Clearinghouse for Social Studies/ Social Science Education and the Social Studies Development Center, Indiana University.

McClellan, B.E. (1999). *Moral education in America: Schools and the shaping of character from colonial times to the present.* New York: Teachers College Press.

McCluskey, N.G. (1958). *Public schools and moral education.* Westport, CT: Greenwood Publishers.

McCluskey, N.G. (Ed.), (1964). *Catholic education in America.* New York: Teachers College Press.

McSweeney, P.F. (1888, January). Heartless, headless and godless. *Catholic World, XLVI*(274).

McQuaid, B.J. (1889, December). Religious teaching in the schools. *Forum, VIII.*

Mercer, C.F. (1826). *A discourse on popular education.* Princeton, NJ: Princeton University Press.

Meriwether, C. (1907). *Our colonial curriculum 1607-1776.* Washington, DC: Capital Publishing Co.

Merrell, E.H. (1890, April 20). The Bible outlawed from the public schools. *Our Church Work, IX*(7).

Messerli, J. (1972). *Horace Mann: A biography.* New York: Alfred A. Knopf.

Michaelsen, R.S. (1970). *Piety in the public school.* New York: The Macmillan Company.

Minnich, H.C. (1936). *William Holmes McGuffey and his Readers.* New York: American Book Company.

Morgan, E.S. (1966). *The Puritan family.* New York: Harper and Row.

Morgan, J.W. (1936). *Horace Mann: His ideas and ideals.* Washington, DC: National Home Library Foundation.

Mosier, R.D. (1947). *Making the American mind: Social and moral ideas in the McGuffey Readers.* New York: King's Crown Press.

Muller, M.J. (1872). *Public school education.* New York: D. J. Sadlier and Co.

Neumann,H. (1913). Moral values in pupil self-government. *Addresses and Proceedings of the National Education Association of the United States 1913.* Ann Arbor, MI: The Association.

Nord, W.A. (1995). *Religion & American education: Rethinking a national dilemma.* Chapel Hill: The University of North Carolina Press.

O'Leary, K.L. (1950). *Cyrus Peirce: Educator of the nineteenth century.* Unpublished Master's thesis, University of Massachusetts.

Ortenzio, P.J. (1977). *The problem of purpose in American education: The rise and fall of the educational policies commission.* Unpublished doctoral dissertation, Rutgers University, New Brunswick, NJ.

Orton, Justice H.S. (1890). *Opinion, decision of the Supreme Court of the State of Wisconsin relating to the reading of the Bible in public schools.* Madison: Democrat Printing Company.

Overy, D.H. (1967). *Robert Lewis Dabney: Apostle of the old south.* Unpublished Ph.D. dissertation, University of Wisconsin.

Page, L. (1995, September 8). A conservative Christian view on values. *School Administrator, 52.*

Perkinson, H.J. (1991). *The imperfect panacea: American faith in education 1865-1990* (3rd ed.). New York: McGraw-Hill.

Peters, R.S. (1981). *Moral development and moral education.* London: George Allen & Unwin.

Piaget, J. (1965). *The moral judgment of the child.* (C.M. Gabain, trans.), New York: Free Press.

Piaget, J. (1981). *Intelligence and affectivity: Their relationship during child development.* (Terrance A. Brown & C. E. Kaegi, trans.), Palo Alto, CA: Annual Reviews.

Pierce, J. (1974). Report of the Superintendent of Public Instruction of the State of Michigan (1837). In S. Cohen (Ed.), *Education in the United States: A documentary history* (Vol. 2). New York: Random House.

Pipher, M. (1994). *Reviving Ophelia—Saving the souls of adolescent girls.* New York: Ballantine Books.

Pringle, H.F., & Pringle, K. (1955, January 22). He scared the devil out of grandpa. *The Saturday Evening Post, 227*(30).

Purpel, D.E. (1991). Moral education: An idea whose time has gone." *The Clearing House, 64.*

Quaife, M.M. (Ed.). (1919). *The convention of 1846.* Madison: Wisconsin Historical Society.

Quaife, M.M. (Ed.). (1928). *The attainment of statehood.* Madison: State Historical Society of Wisconsin.

Rachels, J. (1989). Some basic points about arguments. In J. Rachels (Ed.), *The right thing to do: Basic readings in moral philosophy.* New York: Random House.

Rankin, G.W. (1925). *William Dempster Hoard.* Fort Atkinson, WI: W. D. Hoard and Sons.

Raths, L.E., Harmin, M., & Simon, S. (1966). *Values and teaching.* Columbus, OH: Charles E. Merrill.

Raths, L.E., Harmin, M., & Simon, S. (1978). *Values and teaching: Working with values in the classroom* (2nd ed.) Columbus, OH: Charles E. Merrill.

Ravitch, D. (1974). *The great school wars: New York City, 1805-1972.* New York: Basic Books.

Rawls, J. (1971). *A theory of justice.* Cambridge, MA: Harvard University Press.

Rest, J.R. (1979). *Development in judging moral Issues.* Minneapolis: University of Minnesota Press.

Ruffner, H. (1840, June 23). Address to the Agricultural Society of Rockbridge, at its Annual Fair, at Fancy Hill, October 17, 1839. *The Lexington Gazette.*

Ruffner, W.H. (1852). *Africa's redemption: A discourse on African colonization in its missionary aspects, and in its relation to slavery and abolition.* Philadelphia: William S. Martien.

Ruffner, W.H. (1871a, February). Colored and white schools. *The Educational Journal of Virginia, II*(4), 154-155.

Ruffner, W.H. (1871b). *First annual report of the Superintendent of Public Instruction of Virginia for the year ending August 31, 1871.* Richmond, VA.

Ruffner, W.H. (1871c). Some remarks on moral training. *First Annual Report of the Superintendent of Public Instruction of Virginia for the Year Ending August 31, 1871.*

Ruffner, W.H. (1874, May). The co-education of the white and colored races. *Scribner's Monthly, 8.*

Ruffner, W.H. (1876a, May 26). Education and crime. In *Virginia School Doctrines* (Vol. I. 2nd Series). Ruffner Papers, Historical Foundation, Montreat.

Ruffner, W.H. (1876b, May 8). *Virginia school doctrines* (Vol. I. 2nd Series). Ruffner Papers, Historical Foundation, Montreat.

Ruffner, W.H. (1878a). *Eighth annual report of the Superintendent of Public Instruction of Virginia for the Year ending August 31, 1878.* Richmond, VA.

Ruffner, W.H. (1878b). The moral tendency. *Eighth Annual Report of the Superintendent of Public Instruction of Virginia for the Year Ending August 31, 1878.*

Ruffner, W.H. (1878c). The religious tendency. *Eighth Annual Report of the Superintendent of Public Instruction of Virginia for the Year Ending August 31, 1878.*

Ruffner, W.H. (1878d). Education and government. *Eighth Annual Report of the Superintendent of Public Instruction of Virginia for the Year Ending August 31, 1878.*

Ruffner, W.H. (1880, March). Congress and the education of the people. *The Educational Journal of Virginia, XI*(5).

Ruffner, H. (1901). Proposed plan for the organization and support of common schools in Virginia. In *Report of the Commissioner of Education for the Year 1899-1900* (Vol. I). Washington, DC: Government Printing Office.

Ruffner, W.H. (1904). *History of Washington College, 1830-1848.* In Washington and Lee University Historical Papers, No. 6. Lynchburg, VA: J. P. Bell Company Printers.

Ruggles, A.M. (1936). *The story of the McGuffeys.* New York: American Book Company.

Rush, B. (1965/1786). Plan for the establishment of public schools. In F. Rudolph (Ed.), *Essays on education in the early republic.* Cambridge, MA: Harvard University Press.

Sears, B. (1868). *Education: An address delivered to the Constitutional Convention, State of Virginia, Thursday, January 23, 1868.* Richmond, VA: Office of the New Nation.

Shea, J.G. (1888a, October). Wanted—A new text book. *The American Catholic Quarterly Review, XIII*(52).

Shea, J.G. (1888b, April). Federal schemes to aid common schools in the southern states. *The American Catholic Quarterly Review, XIII*(50).

Smith, B.M. (1839). *The Prussian primary school system*. A Report Submitted to the Governor of Virginia on January 15, 1839. Reprinted from House Document 26, Virginia.

Simon, S., Howe, L., & Kirschenbaum, H. (1972). *Values clarification: A handbook of practical strategies for teachers and students*. New York: Hart.

Simon, S., & Kirschenbaum, H. (Eds.). (1972). *Readings in values clarifications*. Minneapolis, MN: Winston.

Simon, S.B., & Wendkos-Olds, S. (1976). *Helping your child learn right from wrong: A guide to values clarification*. New York: Simon and Schuster.

Solomon, D., Schaps, E., Watson, M., & Battistich, V. (1992). Creating caring school and classroom communities for all students. In R.A. Villa, J.S. Thousand, W. Stainback, & S. Stainback (Eds.), *Restructuring for caring and effective education: An administrative guide to creating heterogeneous schools*. Baltimore, MD: Paul H. Brookes Publishing Co.

Spring, J. (1986). *The American school 1642-1985*. New York: Longman.

Spring, J. (1997). *The American school, 1642-1996*. New York: McGraw-Hill.

Steiner, B.C. (1919). *Life of Henry Barnard*. Washington, DC: Government Printing Office.

Stevens, T. (1974b). General education—Remarks of Mr. Stevens (1835). In S. Cohen (Ed.), *Education in the United States: A documentary history* (Vol. 2). New York: Random House.

Sullivan, M (1932). *Our times: America finding herself*. New York: Charles Scribner's Sons.

Superka, D.P. (1976) *Values education sourcebook*, Boulder, CO: Social Science Education Consortium.

Thayer, J.B. (1890). Discussion. *National Education Association Journal of Proceedings and Addresses*. Session of the Year 1890, held at St. Paul, Minnesota. Topeka: Kansas Publishing House.

Thursfield, R.E. (1945). *Henry Barnard's American Journal of Education*. Baltimore: The Johns Hopkins Press.

Troen, S.K. (1975). *Shaping the St. Louis System, 1838-1920*. Columbia: University of Missouri Press.

Tyack, D.B. (1967). *Turning points in American educational history*. Waltham, MA: Blaisdell Publishing Company.

Tyack, D.B. (1970). Religion in the American common school. In P. Nash (Ed.), *History and education*. New York: Random House.

Tyack, D., & Hansot, E. (1982). *Managers of virtue: Public school leadership in America, 1820-1980*. New York: Basic Books.

Urban, W.J., & Wagoner, Jr., J.L. (2000). *American education: A history* (2nd ed.). New York: McGraw-Hill.

Vail, H.H. (1911). *A history of the McGuffey Readers*. Cleveland, OH: The Burrows Brothers Co.

Wayland, F. (1963). *The elements of moral science*. Edited by J.L. Blau. Cambridge, MA: Harvard University Press.

Webster, N. (1831). *The American spelling book, containing the rudiments of the English language for the use of schools in the United States*. Middletown, CT: William H. Niles.

Webster, N. (1965). On the education of youth in America. In F. Rudolph (Ed.), *Essays on education in the early republic.* Cambridge, MA: Harvard University Press.

Welter, R. (1962). *Popular education and democratic thought in America.* New York: Columbia University Press.

Westerhoff, J.H. (1978). *McGuffey and his Readers.* Nashville, TN: Abingdon.

Whitford, H.C. (1869). Early history of education in Wisconsin. *Reports and Collection of the State Historical Society of Wisconsin* (Vol. V, Part Ill). Madison, WI: Atwood and Rublee.

Williams, E.I.F. (1937). *Horace Mann: Educational statesman.* New York: Macmillan.

Wilson, C.R. (1981, January). Robert Lewis Dabney: Religion and the southern holocaust. *The Virginia Magazine of History and Biography, 89,* 77-89.

Wolff, G.D. (1886, October). The public school and Protestantism. *The American Catholic Quarterly Review, XI*(44).

Wynne, E. (1989). Transmitting traditional values in contemporary schools. in L. Nucci (Ed.), *Moral development and character education: A dialogue* (pp. 19-36). Berkeley, CA: McCutchan.

Younker, D.L. (1963, November). The moral philosophy of William Holmes McGuffey. *The Educational Forum, xxvii*(1).

GAYLORD S

Printed in the United States
30593LVS00002B/240